FIGHT, FLIGHT, OR CHILL

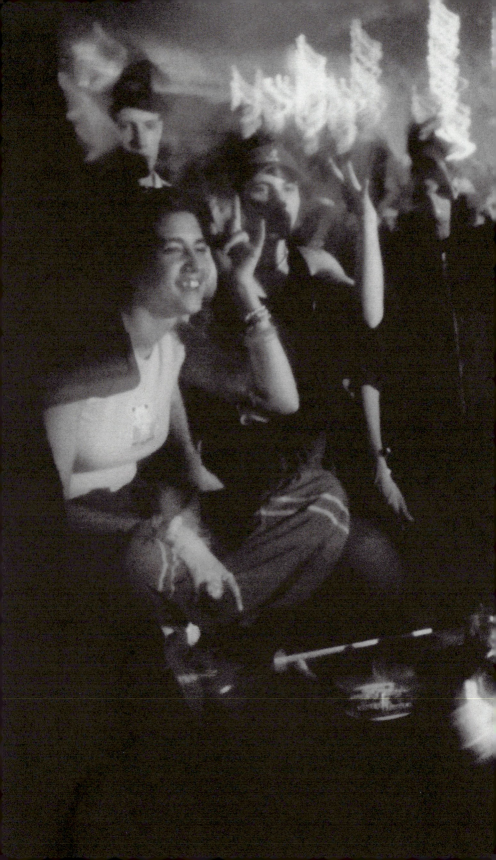

FIGHT

FLIGHT

OR CHILL

Subcultures, Youth, and Rave into the Twenty-First Century

Brian Wilson

McGILL-QUEEN'S UNIVERSITY PRESS

Montreal & Kingston · London · Ithaca

© McGill-Queen's University Press 2006

ISBN 0-7735-3013-4 cloth
ISBN 0-7735-3061-4 pbk

Legal deposit second quarter 2006
Bibliothèque nationale du Québec

Printed in Canada on acid-free paper that is 100% ancient forest free
(100% post-consumer recycled), processed chlorine free

This book has been published with the help of a grant from the Canadian
Federation for the Humanitites and Social Sciences, through the Aid
to Scholarly Publications Programme, using funds provided by the
Social Sciences and Humanitites Research Council of Canada.

McGill-Queen's University Press acknowledges the support of the
Canada Council for the Arts for our publishing program. We also
acknowledge the financial support of the Government of Canada
through the Book Publishing Industry Development Program (BPIDP)
for our publishing activities.

Library and Archives Canada Cataloguing in Publication

Wilson, Brian, 1969–
Fight, flight, or chill : subcultures, youth and rave into the
twenty-first century / Brian Wilson.

Includes bibliographical references and index.
ISBN 0-7735-3013-4
1. Rave culture—Ontario. 2. Youth—Recreation—Ontario.
3. Youth—Ontario. 4. Rave culture—Case studies. 5. Youth—Ontario—
Case studies. I. Title.

HQ799.2.R38W54 2006   305.235   C2005-906514-1

This book was designed and typeset by studio oneonone in Meta 10.5/13

Contents

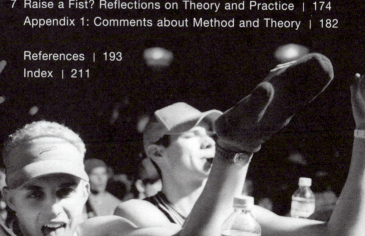

Acknowledgments

This book emerged from a dissertation project that was funded through a doctoral fellowship from the Social Sciences and Humanities Research Council of Canada. Parts of chapters three and five of this manuscript are drawn from an article I published in 2002 in the *Canadian Journal of Sociology* (27, no. 3: 373–412) entitled "The Canadian Rave Scene and Five Theses on Youth Resistance."

This book represents research and writing completed during my time in graduate school in the sociology department at McMaster University, during my postdoctoral work in the School of Communication at Simon Fraser University, and in my current position at the University of British Columbia in the School of Human Kinetics. Much gratitude is owed to my dissertation committee of Graham Knight (my supervisor), Peter Donnelly, Billy Shaffir, and Phil White. They supported me often and challenged me when necessary – and in doing so contributed to an exceptionally positive graduate school experience. I am also most appreciative for the editorial comments offered by David Schwinghamer and for the help offered by Aurèle Parisien, Joan McGilvray, and others at McGill-Queen's University Press. I would similarly like to thank those who made editorial suggestions on earlier versions of the book, especially Siobhan McMenemy, Chris Bucci, and the two anonymous reviewers for the Aid to Scholarly Publishing Programme.

Thanks also to many others who offered suggestions and ideas over the course of the work. This includes the external examiner on my doctoral dissertation, Charles Acland, as well as my graduate school friends and colleagues Michael Atkinson, Peter Berry,

James Gillett, Laura Hurd Clarke, and Jennifer Smith Maguire. I similarly recognize the contributions made by my "old" friend Chris Hawke, who first introduced me to rave parties and remained interested in the project and research from beginning to end. Thanks to Gerry Veenstra, my colleague at the University of British Columbia, for reading and commenting on an earlier draft of the manuscript and for offering encouragement throughout the process. In particular, I'd like to thank Dan Lauckner (www.vidman.ca), (DJ) Marty McFly (www.mcfly.ca), and Andrew McCallum (www.mentalfloss.ca) who made rave-related photographs available for the project. Thanks are owed also to Jim McKay and Bob Sparks for their ongoing support through my time in graduate school and beyond, and their advice about all matters to do with academia.

I am most indebted, though, to the ravers who so generously offered their time and insight. I am extemely grateful to Desirée Sattler for inspiring thinking about how this and other books might be useful for practitioners working in youth-related fields, and for bringing attention to the roles young people can and already do play in community development. Without the support and interest of ravers like Dan, Marty, and Andrew, this book could not have been produced.

FIGHT, FLIGHT, OR CHILL

INTRODUCTION

1
Youth Culture, Complexity, and Rave

Images of Youth

Self-Destructive
They rove city streets in the early hours, groups of teenagers and twentysomethings in sparkly bell-bottoms and lime-green platforms, their faces pale and tranquil-looking. They've probably just emerged from a warehouse basement downtown and a significant number will probably have popped the recreational pill called ecstasy. The drug has become increasingly popular over the last decade, especially among revellers seeking the energy to dance hour after hour at all-night "rave" parties ... [However], scientists at the respected Johns Hopkins University in Baltimore, Maryland, have just found that users of the drug ... risk inducing brain damage that may be irreversible. (Steven Edwards, *National Post*, 1998)

Misdirected
A generation after a great rethinking of gender roles and the forces that classify children by sex, the results are in: girls are behaving more like boys and it isn't always a pretty picture ... they are now smoking, drinking and using drugs as often as boys their age. And though they're not nearly as violent as boys, girls are increasingly more likely to find their way into trouble with the law. (Barbara Vobejda and Linda Perlstein, *Toronto Star*, 1998)

Criminal

Youth crime is on the rise and something has to be done about it. At least that's the perception of Scarborough MPP Jim Brown, a member of the Ontario Crime Control Commission and one of the authors of the commission's Preliminary Report on Youth Crime. Brown believes the justice system has to begin getting tough on young offenders because the present "slap on the wrist" sentences allow young people to feel they are above the law. (Richelle Forsey, *Toronto Star*, 1998)

Impressionable

For 15 year old Michael Eugene Thomas, it definitely was the shoes ... Thomas was found strangled on May 2, 1989. Charged with first degree-murder was James David Martin, a basketball buddy who allegedly took Thomas's two-week-old Air Jordan basketball shoes and left Thomas's barefooted body in the woods near school. Thomas loved Michael Jordan, as well as the shoes Jordan endorses, and he cleaned his own pair each evening. He kept the cardboard shoe box with Jordan's silhouette on it in a place of honor in his room. Inside the box was the sales ticket for the shoes. It showed he paid $115.50, the price of a product touched by deity. (Rick Telander, *Sports Illustrated*, 1990, 37)

Apathetic

We live small lives on the periphery; we are marginalized and there's a great deal in which we choose not to participate. (Douglas Coupland, *Generation X*, 1991, 11)

Victimized/Labelled

Lost in the media coverage and in the sea of pop-culture images is the fact that there is little evidence that the kids today are any worse than kids five or twenty-five years ago ... If the question is what's wrong with kids today, the answer might be "you." (Katrina Onstad, *Saturday Night*, 1997, 48)

Determined

If you sometimes despair that today's youth show little interest or connection to global issues their generation will face, one Toronto teenager's activities reaffirms faith in the determination, ingenuity, and power of young people. Tanya Roberts-Davis is petite and featherweight, just 15. Yet she has already traveled to Third World countries speaking out against child labour. She can move veteran social activists to tears with her heartfelt descriptions of children chained to rug looms nine hours a day. She has personally talked to some of those children whom she has met, now attending factory schools established because of the work of human rights fighters whose ranks she has joined (Ellie Teshler, *Toronto Star*, 1998)

Cool

Fashion plates show up donned in bikini tops with short skirts or ballerina's tutus. Brightly coloured huge plastic belts are all the rage, and hair that is anything but its natural hue is worn in baby clips or pig tails. Ravers often carry glow sticks ... and wear skin glitter, glow-in-the-dark rings, bracelets and headbands. They dance for hours to the sounds of deejays spinning vinyl records and flawlessly mixing tracks of techno, trance, house and other kinds of electronic records. (Elisa Landale, *Toronto Star*, 1998).

Cutting Edge

One of the most valuable new members was a Stanford robotics grad who called himself Pig. The day he moved in he began wiring up the entire [warehouse] with phone lines he diverted from a juncture box on a pole across the street ... He had worked on a few award-winning computer games, and gave talks at places like MIT about how to control machines over the Internet. He had a big scar on his forehead that he'd earned while working with guys at Survival Research Laboratories building robots that fired lasers and blew up things ... The easiest way to win him over was to approach him looking for an elegant solution to a problem rather than just a quick fix. Pig was well connected in the hacker underground, too, and enlisted his cohorts to help him make a telephone junction box and to

> divert the ISDN lines to each of our rooms. (Douglas
> Rushkoff, *Ecstasy Club*, 1997, 39)

Complexity and Youth Culture

> knowledge of reality, and therefore, for practical purposes, reality
> itself, is intertextual: it exists only in the interrelations between all that
> a culture has written, spoken, visualized about it. (Fiske, 1987, 115)

> We are in a universe where there is more and more information and
> less and less meaning. (Baudrillard 1983b, 95)

> The study of subcultural style, which seem[s] at the outset to draw us
> back to the real world, to reunite us with "the people," ends by merely
> confirming the distance between the reader and the "text," between
> everyday life and the "mythologist" whom it surrounds, fascinates and
> finally excludes. (Hebdige 1979, 140)

Youth appear to be, among other things, criminal, self-destructive, misdirected, impressionable, apathetic, victimized, determined, cool, and cutting edge. Evidence supporting any particular interpretation of youth and their cultures provides limited clarification or insight. The statistical measurements of youth criminal activity that are often cited in mass media and academic reports fail to show the number of youth who never commit crime, or the number that do not get caught. In many cases, a false link is created between youth crime, youth deviance, and youth culture. Recent reviews of scholarly research have confirmed that there is an overall lack of in-depth qualitative research on youth culture, especially in Canada. Specifically, there is relatively little known about the meanings that youth give to their cultural activities (Young and Craig 1997; O'Bireck 1996; Tanner 1996). And of course, mass media producers offer an excess of images that influence, exaggerate, and only possibly reflect "the realities" of contemporary youth culture (Acland 1995).

    Despite this fragmented picture, the tendency in both the media and academe is to talk about "today's youth" in simple terms. Frequent attempts are made to "tell it like it is" about a problem generation, and to make no-nonsense recommendations about how to deal with the difficulties youth present to society – how to deal with "troubling" youth – and the difficulties youth experience in their everyday lives – how to deal with "troubled" youth. An example of this approach to the "youth problem" is the implementation of supposedly rehabilitative boot camps in Ontario to assertively deal with "undisciplined" delinquent youth – an approach that emphasizes solutions at the level of the individual while being inherently insensitive to the structural problems that lead certain youth to be incarcerated.* For the commentators who share these views, and for others who more responsibly acknowledge the difficulty of depicting youth culture in a cohesive manner, complexity and contradiction are considered barriers to understanding.

What is seldom considered, however, is the possibility that these complexities and contradictions should be examined, studied, and described for what they are, rather than avoided or "resolved." Justin Lewis (1991) articulated this position: "The problem with a society that nurtures and guides its citizens towards common meanings is its tendency to suppress not only the ambiguity of things, but the very *idea* of ambiguity. We behave as if the meanings of things were natural and inevitable. The failure to come up with the socially agreed meaning is often interpreted as stupid or troublesome … Herein lies the resistance to cultural diversity" (55).

In youth cultural studies, some critics have recognized the need to avoid oversimplifying the complexity of youth-related phenomena, either through their critiques of existing research (e.g., Young and Craig 1997), through the assembly of edited collections of studies about diverse youth groups (Bennett and Kahn-Harris 2004; Epstein 1998; Skelton and Valentine 1998), or through study of the evolution of youth culture in an increasingly mediated world (Hebdige 1988; McRobbie 1994). However, even those authors who have taken on this issue seldom consider both the complex social circumstances in which we live (e.g., how mass media and the Internet might impact the the nature of subcultural affiliations), and the complexity of subcultural life itself (e.g., the various reasons youth get involved in subcultures and the varying levels of commitment youth have to subcultural groups).

*See Jaffe and Baker 1999 and Tyyska 2001 for discussions about the problems with these forms of rehabilitation.

The need to study complexity in social life has been recognized in various contexts outside of youth cultural studies. Post-
modernists have theorized the fragmentation of cultures (e.g.,
Baudrillard 1983a, 1988), feminists have theorized diversity in marginalized groups (e.g., A. Hall 1996; Wheaton and Tomlinson 1998),
communications theorists have examined the ambiguity of media
messages (e.g., Barthes 1973) and audience interpretations (e.g.,
Lewis 1991), and Marxist theorists have speculated about complexity in "postmodern times" while continuing to explain social life using
concepts like ideology and hegemony (e.g., S. Hall 1986; Laclau and
Mouffe 1985).

Commentators working within these disciplines have identified important questions about the nature of complexity and our
ability to study it. Related concerns have been raised about the
extent to which "real world" issues are reasonably addressed within
apparently abstract theoretical models. The most common target of
these critiques has been "postmodern" theories that describe the
frightening pervasiveness of mass mediated culture and the dis-
solution of conventional forms of identity, such as those based on
social class (Eagleton 1991, 1996). Critics have argued that postmodern approaches to complexity do not adequately account for the
meanings that people give to their daily activities and the ways people actively interpret, negotiate, and resist on an everyday basis
(Prus 1996a). Debates have also raged about the extent to which
postmodernism can be usefully integrated with classical sociological
perspectives – a critique that has come from interpretive and critical
sociologists alike.* Underlying these assertions are related disputes
about what "postmodernism" actually means. For example, the term
has historically referred to, among other things, an artistic style and
architectural form; an epoch (social life in the late capitalist, globalized 1990s and twenty-first century); a research method (e.g., a sub-
jectivist, multitextual, critical method); and, more generally, to a
social theory (Rail 1998). Postmodern social theory, which is pertinent to many discussions that appear throughout this book, is especially problematic because of its association with a range of authors,

*See Maines (1996), Plummer (1990), and Prus (1996a) for symbolic interaction-
ist critiques, and Jameson (1984), Harvey (1989), and Witheford and Gruneau
(1993) for neo-Marxist ones.

including Jean Baudrillard, Michel Foucault, Jacques Derrida, and Jean François Lyotard, and a diversity of perspectives. Some postmodern theorists attempt to explain the domination of global information technologies and the related blurring of conventional boundaries such as race, gender, politics and nationalism (McRobbie 1994). Others have argued that mass mediated symbols and images have become "better than reality," what Baudrillard (1983b) has termed "hyper-reality." Denzin (1990, drawing on Althusser 1971) argued that in this postmodern world, individuals can never "measure up" to these mass-mediated images. As he states: "in the postmodern system, human beings constantly confront pressures to become ideological constructions, or subjects who have particular needs, desires, feelings and beliefs which conform to the new conservative political ideologies concerning health, the body and its desires" (146).

Emerging from these broader debates about and depictions of contemporary social life is a series of important questions for those interested in studying youth culture into the twenty-first century. They include the following: How can a fragmented youth culture that is, according to some, so complex it defies any kind of traditional analysis be studied and theorized in an understandable and progressive way? Is it feasible to integrate traditional theoretical and methodological approaches to youth culture, such as symbolic interactionism, neo-Marxism, and critical ethnography, with theories that emphasize ambiguity and complexity in social life – such as those often associated with postmodernism? Can such a model simultaneously account for the meanings that youth give to their cultural activities, the structural constraints that frame these meanings, and the supposedly postmodern circumstances that envelop this shifting relationship? Can such an approach be pragmatically adopted for empirical studies of youth culture(s)?

The Goals and Topics of this Book

This book is motivated by and engages these issues and questions. In doing so, two broad contributions are sought, the first theoretical and the second empirical and substantive. Theoretically, I have developed and rationalized an approach to studying youth cultural behaviour that allows for balanced, succinct, and "honest" analyses of complexity and contradiction in the social worlds of young people (honest in the sense that the unavoidable complexities of youth culture are grappled with openly). Working toward this goal, I critically examine existing theories of youth subcultures over the course of this text, while introducing what Douglas Kellner has called the "multiperspectival approach" (Kellner 1995, drawing on Nietzsche 1968, 1986) to studying cultural activity. In this context, the variety of interpretations of youth cultural activity are considered for their positioning on a conceptual continuum, with perspectives that emphasize the ways that youth are passive "cultural dupes" on one end of the continuum, and approaches that highlight the active and creative aspects of youth behaviour and culture on the other end. As will be described in chapter five, this method for organizing theories of youth culture will provide readers with a clear framework from which to envision and consider the extent to which youth are (or are not) given credit for their ability to be critical and creative in their thinking and actions. These perspectives are also examined for how well they apply to a millennium culture that is rife with ever faster developments in technology and media.

Various explanations of youth cultural activity are further explored in this book through a case study of a notorious millennium youth subculture – *rave*. Rave is a middle-class culture of youth that is renowned for drug use, an interest in computer-generated music known as "techno," and attendance at all-night "rave" dance parties. Two underlying thematic questions are explored in the context of rave: (1) to what extent are raver youths' experiences constrained within or determined by our contemporary high-tech, mass-mediated culture and; (2) to what extent do raver youth creatively and proactively subvert these constraints and interpret their experiences in novel and empowering ways?

These questions are pursued in chapters two through six, where the history of rave abroad and in Canada is presented and research findings are reported – findings from interviews with ravers, rave DJs, and rave promoters, from observation sessions at raves in Toronto, from media and Web site analysis, and from ongoing involvements with various rave-related Internet newsgroups. These chapters also explore the relevance of study findings to existing theories of youth culture. In the conclusion to this book, the study of rave acts as a departure point for commentary about the relationship between "theory and practice" and about (over)reactions to the "youth problem."

With this background, the remainder of this introductory chapter includes a historical discussion of the ways that youth have been understood in society, a specific rationale for studying youth culture in Canada and abroad, a brief history of youth cultural studies, and a justification for the choice of rave as an empirical case study.

Youth, Teenager, and Adolescent: Context and Definitions

The term "youth" has taken on numerous meanings that have emerged from, among other influences, news coverage, advertising, and academic research. For example, Hebdige (1988) explained how the term "teenager" emerged in the 1950s, a period of relative afflu-ence, as a label for a generation of youth that had become a crucial market segment for businesses selling leisure items and services, such as records, magazines, clothing, and dances. Hall and Jefferson (1976) defined youth as a "metaphor for social change," referring to the capacity for working-class young people to respond creatively to the oppressive social conditions that they faced in post-war Britain.

In more social-psychological work, the youth-derived term "adolescence" has been used to describe a life stage characterized by increased concerns with roles and role changes as part of iden-tity formation. As Coleman (1992) explained, "there can be little doubt that adolescence, from this point of view, is seen as being dominated by stresses and tensions, not so much because of emo-tional instability, but as a result of conflicting pressures from the outside" (15–16).* As will be discussed later in this chapter, this tense process of identity formation, and the related "alienation" that some youth experience during this life stage, play a major part in the development of youth cliques and subcultures. This under-standing of the social process of adolescence is consistent with understandings of subcultural development offered by cultural theorists, although less focused on external social determinants, such as social class, gender, and race.

*See also Côté and Allahar 1994.

As noted above, these definitions are historically-derived. Work on pre-industrial societies has shown that there were no clear distinctions between youth and adult, and that the term "youth" did not hold the same stigmatized meaning as it does today. As Tanner (1996, drawing on Aries 1962) explained:

[In pre-industrial Europe] terms such as youth and adolescence were in currency but corresponded more closely to contemporary notions of young adulthood than to an intermediary phase in the life cycle. Similarly, in classic antiquity (Greece and Rome) the term "youth" was employed to describe healthy, productive persons rather than a category of individuals no longer children but not yet adults. In Europe, before the eighteenth century, children entered the world of work and leisure at a considerably earlier age than they do in our own time; moreover, the different age groups were more closely integrated than they are today. Medieval French children, for instance, worked alongside adults from the age of 7 onwards ... Children, in effect were treated as little adults – indicated by their dress, games and legal status. (19)

Building on Musgrove (1964), Tanner argued that the transition toward viewing youth as being troubled and delinquent can be traced to the industrial revolution, a time when there was both a scarcity of jobs and a movement toward humanitarian reforms that opposed exploitative work conditions for young people. What this led to was the creation of a class of street youth that were in some cases forced to "steal to survive." In this way a new societal problem known as "juvenile delinquency" appeared (Bernard 1992; Gillis 1974; Tanner 1996). From these early journalist- and reformer-led moral panics emerged the Juvenile Delinquent Act of 1908, the official origin of juvenile delinquency in Canada (Best 1989; Tanner 1996).

More important for this book was the development of discourses surrounding youth during World War II and in the post-war period. During the war, a time when male and female teenagers were either working within industry – which in itself meant that many youth were leaving school at an early age – or were being left relatively unsupervised at home, concerns were being raised about the inevitability of a "delinquent outcome" for young people who were independent economically and lacking in parental supervision. In the post-war period, this panic was focused in part on the "crisis of motherhood," where working women were either urged or forced to leave the workplace and take care of their children who, without proper supervision, were believed to be at risk for delinquent behavior (Adams 1997; Pierson 1986).

In this same period, perceptions of the "youth problem" were reinvigorated in ways that are centrally relevant today. This is largely attributable to the emergence of a "teen culture" that was reinforced and fueled by a commercial industry driven by adults (Hebdige 1988). In contrast to the pre-1950s, when teenage styles and fads were generally created and maintained by teens themselves, the adult-created commercial culture was now encouraging youth, and particularly middle-class youth – a group that now had more disposable income and leisure time – to buy into the popular culture of the time. In this sense, and as noted earlier, the youth or "teen" had become a target group for the marketing of magazines, rock and roll, movies, and clothing. In essence, the "modern teenager" was discovered, and although "middle-class and working-class young people had unequal access to the products of this market, and would ascribe different meanings to its products, they were all affected by it" (Adams 1997, 42).

Out of this history of youth emerged the contemporary framing of youth as "troubled and troubling." Teenagers, now considered to be a distinct age group, had become a source of public concern because of their links with the evils of popular cultural consumption and other day-to-day trappings that lead youth – the most impressionable of unsupervised groups – toward a delinquent life. As Adams (1997) noted in her study of post-war youth and the social construction of heterosexuality, the National Film Board of Canada and other film houses produced educational movies to help explain youth behaviour to adults, while academics and journalists alike began to develop theories to explain youth behaviour and youth culture. However, and as I have articulated throughout this chapter, the development of theories about youth was seldom accompanied or complemented by research that explored the meanings that youth assign to their cultural experiences – a trend that has continued to the present day.

Studying Youth Culture: Media, Methods, and Gaps

Downtown Toronto was engulfed by a mob of young marauders who stormed along Yonge St. last night in an orgy of looting, vandalism and violence ... As hundreds of rioters – of all colours – surged north on Yonge, police were pelted with rocks and eggs, hundreds of windows smashed and stores looted. (Duffy et. al. 1992)

In developing a rationale for studying youth cultural activity, I begin with a discussion of what has been considered the most compelling and visible example of youth frustration and rage in recent Canadian history. The above noted uprising, coined the "Yonge Street Riots" of 1992, emanated both from an organized, peaceful protest of the acquittal of four Los Angeles police officers in the trial of the Rodney King case (the trial surrounding the savage beating of African-American motorist Rodney King that was caught on videotape and later broadcasted to America) and from a death by shooting of a black man at the hands of Metro Toronto police. Many police sources, journalists, and sociologists of youth suggested that the incident was not only connected to racial issues, but also to restlessness and anger among youth of all races. More than a mass-mediated moral panic, the Yonge Street Riots were widely interpreted as symptomatic of broader perceptions that, for many young Canadians, life at the millennium is a struggle.*

This landmark incident and apparent statement about Canadian youth reinforced an always-lingering, mass-mediated public concern about "today's youth." However, and as many social commentators and media critics suggest, there is good reason to be sceptical of mainstream, hard-news, journalistic accounts that fuel periodic moral panics, particularly when statistical research is cited as proof that youth crime is growing. Hall et al. (1978) explain why: "Statistics – whether crime rates or opinion polls – have an ideological function: they appear to *ground* free floating and controversial impressions in the hard, incontrovertible soil of numbers. Both the media and the public have enormous respect for 'the facts' – *hard facts*. And there is no fact so hard as the number – unless it is the percentage difference between two numbers" (9). Glenday (1996)

*See Mathews (1993) for a more detailed discussion of concerns about youth that emerged following the Yonge Street Riots.

similarly described how statistics used in Canadian scholarly work on youth can provide a basis for misleading claims about, for example, the behaviours of "lower class" youth: "exclusive reliance on school and home samples [in research on youth in Canada] has diverted attention from less protected settings, like the street ... [The] link between class and crime is only weakly (if at all) reflected in self-report analyses based on individual adolescents attending school and this has lead some to call for the complete abandonment of research to link class and crime" (152).

Furthermore, official statistics that sometimes show increases in youth crime do not inherently mean that today's youth have a heightened propensity for deviant activity compared to youth of the past. These statistics more likely reflect an increased willingness by police officers to lay more charges for minor incidents in a time of social and political concern about youth deviance, and, similarly, they likely also reflect the public's increased sensitivity to the problem of youth violence, which in turn affects citizens' willingness to report incidents that might have been ignored in the past (Schissel 1993; Sprott 1996; Tanner 1996). For example, while statistics on youth crime in 1992–93 taken from the Canadian Centre for Justice Statistics showed a 9 percent increase in violent crime over the previous year, careful scrutiny shows that two-thirds of this increase in crimes "was due to greater reporting of minor assaults, such as fights and scuffles" (Visano 1996, 152). Furthermore, changes in the law over time make direct comparisons difficult because what is legal at one point might be illegal at another.*

Moreover, these statistics only provide a measurement of youth crime rates, rendering little to no insight into the culture of youth delinquents (including those that do not "get caught"), or into the culture of "deviant" youth groups that are not law-breakers. On this basis, I argue in this book that ethnography – specifically, in-depth interviewing and participant observation – is the method best-suited for gaining intimate familiarity with cultures and social settings (see Appendix 1). Lull (1985) encapsulated the common sense argument for this methodological preference when studying youth activity:

*See Bibby (2001) and Carrington (1999) for a more detailed discussion of this point.

imagine asking punk rockers outside the concert hall how they feel about "slam dancing," for instance, by requiring them to respond to items on a semantic differential. How would they react to a set of Likert type scale indices? ... In the administration of the questionnaire the researcher might suddenly become an involuntary partner in his or her first slam dance. This hypothetical turn of events is presented here to illustrate the enormous gap that exists between some of the most interesting things that take place in various cultures and the ability of quantitative methods of analysis to reflect their nature adequately. (219)

Overall, evidence supporting claims of escalating youth violence in Canada is ambiguous and largely anecdotal (Mathews 1993, 9–10).* The "new" trend toward a deviant youth culture is challenged both by research showing that mediated panics about youth recur in intervals over time and by research demonstrating that recent articles about "today's problem youth" versus the "tame" youth of years past are unfounded, and contradictory (Tanner 1996; Vaughan 1992).

Despite this haziness, there have been frequent demands to revamp the Young Offenders Act in Canada in order to better "crack down" on youth crime, demands that are based largely on the general perception that youth crime is on the rise. For example, in 1994 Canada's justice minister, Allan Rock, tabled Bill C-37 to amend the Young Offenders Act to lower the age limit for those who face adult punishment for committing "serious criminal acts" (first-degree murder, manslaughter, kidnapping, armed robbery, rape, and aggravated assault) from eighteen to sixteen years old. This change would mean, among other things, that sixteen and seventeen year olds charged with murder would now be tried in adult court rather than youth court, where the penalty is life imprisonment instead of ten years (Visano 1996, 77). Ultimately, in March 1999, the replacement of the Young Offenders Act with a tougher Youth Criminal Justice Act was approved. There is little doubt that this change was motivated, in part, by public opinion polls, such as a 1991 *Maclean's* magazine poll where 45 per cent of Canadian adults indicated that "the behaviour of young people in the community where they live"

*See also Schissel (1997).

has become worse, while 14 per cent thought it was better and 38 per cent thought it was the same (Bibby and Posterski 1992, 303).

Similarly, the claim that youth are more troubled than in years past, while contentious, is rationalized by commentators who describe the millennium as a time characterized by a fragmentation of youth culture, such as the breakdown of traditional class and gender markers and alliances (Furlong and Cartmel 1997). The crucial point for these authors is that the feelings of community that were hallmarks of class-based (sub)cultures of years past are less easily attained in a contemporary culture where young people's identities are more individualistic and driven by media-created desires. In other words, youths' increased exposure to a variety of choices about how to dress, what music to listen to, which Web sites to visit, and which identities to embrace has resulted in fewer stable relationships with any social group. This perspective has been adopted by those who argue that youth feel more alienated, insecure, anxious, and unfulfilled now than at any other time in history, and for this reason are more "at-risk" for dangerous, escapist, and thrill-seeking behaviours.* Authors like Carrigan (1998), who identified a recent increase in reports of female-related violence and gang-related violence, similarly argued that a destabilization of the family unit in recent years might have led to a culture of youth who are angrier and more disdainful of authority than in years past. As above, however, the complexities of these claims – claims that might be disputed by authors like Kelly (1998), Akers et al. (1998), Tyyskä (2001), and Galloway and Hudson (1996), all of whom continue to study and describe powerful race, class, and gender-related dynamics in youth peer groups – are only beginning to be examined empirically.

Current Research on Canadian Youth (Sub)cultures

Although youth cultural activity has received research attention over the years in countries like Britain and the United States (as outlined later in this chapter), to date there have been relatively few studies on the topic in the Canadian context. Some commentators attribute

*See Cieslik and Pollock (2002) and Furlong and Cartmel (1997) for more detailed discussions about risk and contemporary youth.

this lack of attention to the social conditions in Canada, conditions that, until recently, were considered unfavourable for the development of oppositional youth subcultures and therefore did not attract attention from the public or research community. These conditions were believed to include a strong economy that did not segregate classes in ways that allowed resistant "working class" subcultures to evolve and flourish; a relatively sparse population that prevented the emergence of centralized subcultures, such as the visually spectacular youth groups that appeared in Britain and the ethnically developed subcultures in America; and long and severe winters that localized youth cultures to shopping malls in the cities, where "collective gatherings are easy to control" (Brake 1985, 145).

In reaction to this disparity of research, some scholars have tried to explain why Canadian youth subcultural deviance and delinquency have, in fact, emerged in recent years. Brake (1985) argued that with Canada's economic decline in the 1980s, youth who lacked the cultural resources to achieve through work and school were marginalized and turned to "unconventional" (i.e., subcultural) and sometimes deviant leisure pursuits.* Others argued that the postmodern developments in social life at the turn of the century – such as the mass development and distribution of media information and technologies and the related increase in awareness about many physical, social, and political dangers (drugs, cigarettes, alcohol, unprotected sex, violence, ecological disasters) – led youth from a variety of social and economic backgrounds to seek cultures of avoidance and abandonment (as McRobbie 1993 argued about British youth). Still others have proffered that because of the increasing globalization of youth culture through television, film, music, and the Internet, and because of the relatively "late" emergence of visible youth cultures in Canada, Canadian youth borrowed subcultural styles and resources from other countries, and, as a result, Canadian youth culture was less authentic and less resistant than British and American youth culture (Brake 1985, 145). Of course, what these theorists failed to acknowledge is that "all subcultures, including British articulations, tend in some way to borrow from the cultural expressions of other groups" (Young and Craig 1997, 177).

The problem with many of the above claims is that they are upheld, at best, by limited research produced by few scholars, and

*See also Baron (1989a, 1989b) and Tanner (1996).

at worst, are based on sensationalized journalistic accounts of atyp-ical (but headline-worthy) youth behaviour. Currently, there is a growing body of ethnographic research on youth culture in Canada that could be drawn upon to support some of these ideas, although the literature is quite recent and focuses primarily on the controver-sial Young Offenders Act. For this reason, authors have emphasized the continued need for this kind of research on Canadian youth cul-tures. Some of the studies in this broad area include O'Bireck's 1996 compilation of ethnographic research on youth crime, deviance, and subcultures; Baron's 1997, 1989a, and 1989b work on the punk rock subculture and skinheads; Young and Craig's 1997 research on skin-heads; Young's 1988 work on rituals of deviance surrounding varsity rugby; Solomon's 1992 research on experiences of race in a Toronto high school; Tanner's 1978 research on youth culture in an Edmonton high school; Frieson's 1990 work on heavy metal music listeners; Hagan and McCarthy's 1992 study of street youth; Atkinson's 2003a and Wood's 2001 work on the Straightedge punk subculture; Atkin-son's 2003b study of tattooing culture and youth resistance; Currie's 1999 study of young female readers of adolescent magazines; Math-ews's 1993 and Gordon's 1995 research on youth gangs; Kelly's 1998 and Wilson and Sparks's 1996 and 1999 work on adolescence, race, and youth culture; Van Roosmalen and Krahn's 1996 work on alco-hol, drugs, and delinquency in street-based youth cultures; Smith's 1997 work on youth shopping mall culture and the social production of space; and Wilson and White's 2001 and Wilson et al.'s 2001 research on youth culture in recreation and drop-in centres. One of the only works on rave culture was conducted by Weber (1999b), a study referred to later in this book.

In sum, while "moral entrepreneurs" (Becker 1963; Blumer 1971) in the media and politics make commonsense assumptions about the problems with and best ways to deal with today's youth, there is a lack of evidence-based knowledge about youth cultural activity. Clearly, the myths and realities of youth deviance and youth culture in Canada require closer examination.

A Brief History of (Sub)cultural Studies

As noted earlier, outside of Canada, especially in Britain and to a cer-tain extent in the US, youth subcultures have been a central topic of

concern. In these contexts, scholars have offered a variety of perspectives on and explanations of youth cultural activity. These sociological interpretations of youth cultural activity can be organized
along a conceptual continuum, with perspectives that emphasize
the ways in which youth are passive, uncritical, and impressionable
on one end of the continuum, and approaches that highlight the
active and creative aspects of youth behaviour on the other. Underlying most classical approaches to understanding youth is the
somewhat optimistic view that youth tend to "find solutions" to
problems such as alienation and marginalization – solutions that
range from "subtle to spectacular" and "symbolic to real."

Researchers working within the American Delinquency
tradition that emerged out of the University of Chicago in the 1920s
tended to argue that youth from lower socio-economic backgrounds
respond to their inability to achieve the dominant middle-class standards by finding a community of similarly positioned peers and, in
turn, creating a new value system. Youth within this new "subcultural" value system give positive meanings to and feel empowered
by activities that are considered to be subversive by middle-class
authority figures.* As Albert Cohen (1997, originally published in
1955) explained:

Status problems are problems of achieving respect in the eyes of one's
fellows. Our ability to achieve status depends upon the criterion of status applied by our fellows, that is, the standards or norms they go by in
evaluating people. These criteria are an aspect of their cultural frames of
reference. If we lack the characteristics or capacities which give status in
terms of these criteria, we are beset with the most typical and yet dis-
tressing of human problems of adjustment. One solution is for individuals
who share such problems to gravitate towards one another and jointly to
establish new norms, new criteria of status which define as meritorious
the characteristics they *do* possess, the kinds of conduct of which they
are capable. It is clearly necessary for each participant, if the innovation
is to solve his status problem, that these new criteria be shared with others, that the solution be a group and not a private solution ... Such new

*Arguments resembling this one are embedded in the classical works of
Cloward and Ohlin (1960), A. Cohen (1955), Merton (1957), and Sutherland
(1937).

status criteria would represent new subcultural values different from or even antithetical to those of the larger social system. (51)

Other American authors, such as Matza (1964), brought nuance to this base model, arguing that "chance" encounters and "bad timing" were also important factors in understanding how some young people tend to "drift" into a delinquent lifestyle.

British subcultural theorists at the University of Birmingham's Centre for Contemporary Cultural Studies (cccs) in the 1970s took the "reactive" model of youth resistance proposed by Cohen a step further, suggesting that the styles and cultural activities of youth were intentional, creative, and proactive responses to their marginalized social positioning (usually working-class positioning), and that the outrageous, shocking personas that some youth adopt – for example as a punk rocker or skinhead – were symbolically anti-establishment and meant to express feelings of dissatisfaction (Hall and Jefferson 1976; Hebdige 1979). Of particular significance was the cccs's use of "culture," "subculture," "homology," and "bricolage" as concepts to explain practices and patterns of youth consumption and behaviour. In this context, the term "culture" encompassed more than the "peculiar and distinctive 'way of life' of the group or class" (Hall and Jefferson 1976, 10) – a classic definition drawn from a long tradition of sociological and anthropological research.* For these theorists, culture and cultural expression – shared language, symbols, and activities – are the arsenal used in the struggle between the dominant culture/class and marginalized groups. Although the focus of the cccs's work was largely on the resistive capacities of youth cultural groups, their arguments continue to inform understandings of social struggle more generally. The following definition of culture offered by McRobbie (1991) incorporates this more encompassing view of the term: "Culture is about the pre-structured but essentially expressive capacities of the group in question. The forms which this expressivity takes are 'maps of meaning' which summarize and encapsulate ... social and material life experiences. But these cultural artifacts or configurations, are not created out of nothing. Individuals are born into what are already constructed sets of social meanings which can then be worked on,

*See also Williams (1977).

developed and even transformed ... the cultural is always a site of struggle and conflict. Here hegemony may be lost or won; it is an arena for class struggle" (36).

Extending this view of culture, Hall and Jefferson (1976) defined "subcultures" as "sub-sets – smaller, more localized and differentiated structures" within the larger cultural class configuration noted above (13). These authors went on to explain that youth subcultures are "focussed around certain activities, values, certain uses of material artefacts, territorial spaces etc. which significantly differentiate them from the wider culture" (Hall and Jefferson 1976, 14). Youth subcultures were also thought to be characterized by their "double articulation" – that is, their relationship to their "parent" culture (e.g., a working-class youth's relationship to working-class culture) and to the dominant culture. In this way, the researchers and theorists at the cccs were interested in both the internal configuration of subcultures and the relationship between subcultures and such broader societal structures as mass media, school authorities, and police.

A key concept for subcultures theorists interested in describing subcultural expressions through style is "homology." Homology refers to the way the structure and meaning of cultural items that are incorporated by youth subcultures "parallel and reflect the structure, style and typical concerns, attitudes, and feelings of the social group" (Willis 1978, 191). For example, Willis described how the motorcycle in "biker" culture was a symbol of freedom, power, and risk – values consistent with or homologous with the central perspectives of bikers. Clarke (1976, drawing on the classical work of Claude Levi-Strauss) defined a related and similarly important concept, bricolage, as "the reordering and recontextualisation of objects to communicate fresh meaning" (177), or, in other words, using everyday objects in often "unintended" ways. Hebdige (1979) adopted the concept in his analysis of the punk rock subculture to show how "unremarkable and inappropriate items – a pin, a plastic clothes peg, a television component, a razor blade, a tampon – could be brought within the province of punk (un)fashion" (107). So, for these spectacular youth cultures, discontent and disenchantment were expressed through stylistic attempts to appall and offend "the mainstream." While not all of the research at the cccs was focused on spectacular youth or outlandish forms of opposition per se,* the centre is most well-known in youth studies for its theoretical treatment of these kinds of overt stylistic displays of resistance.

Hegemony, Ethnography, and Semiology

A central goal for theorists at the cccs was to explain the relation-ship between more powerful groups, such as the ruling classes and corporate elite, and less powerful groups, especially working-class youth. In this context, the centre's work attempted not only to ex-plain the meanings of young people's symbolic expressions, but also to better understand how and why these expressions are tolerated by the more powerful groups. Just as pertinently, researchers as the centre considered the extent to which youth-driven social resistance actually impacts and alters the structures that systemically margin-alize the less powerful.

To help conceptualize these processes of social struggle, members of the cccs drew on the classical works of early twentieth-century Italian revolutionary Antonio Gramsci, adopting the Grams-cian, neo-Marxist notion of "hegemony." Hegemony can be defined as domination that is consented to by subordinate groups, or as Joll (1977) suggested, it is when the dominant class has "succeeded in persuading the other classes of society to accept its moral, political and cultural values" such that the ruling class does not have to rely on coercive force to maintain power (99). A preferred method used by the dominant group for securing consent and maintaining this hegemonic relationship is to control the distribution of ideas, which might be achieved, for example, by controlling what is taught in schools and how it is taught, and by influencing the content and framing of mass media reports and images. When discourses are assembled and articulated in ways that make the subordinate group's status appear "natural," the subordinate group will often consent to and contribute to the continuation of existing social

*The works of Willis (1977), McRobbie (1977), and Corrigan (1979) were notable exceptions to this trend of research and writing focused on spectacu-lar youth. The work of Phil Cohen (1972; 1999) was also significant in this context. Cohen explored the strategies used by mods and skinheads to sym-bolically "solve" the dilemmas associated with their marginalized working class position through leisure and style.

conditions. This is especially relevant in research that has demon-strated how popular cultural forms such as television work symboli-cally to establish dominant ideological meanings that reinforce the oppression of subordinate groups. For example, a study by Robert Sparks and myself that focused on adolescent male understandings of media images of African-American athletes revealed how exclu-sionary attitudes towards minority groups tend to be reinforced when these groups are depicted in certain ways (Wilson and Sparks, 1999).

Gramsci (1971) also recognized that there is an emotional component to hegemony, what he called "feeling-passion." When "feeling-passion" can be generated, according to Gramsci, the affec-tive allegiance of subordinate groups to dominant systems and structures is more easily obtained. An example of this is the mobi-lization of emotions around spectator sports events. It is common practice for media producers to use nostalgic images of memorable sports events or moments (e.g., Paul Henderson's still-revered, last-second goal in Canada's hockey triumph over the Soviet Union in the 1972 Summit Series) to help generate powerful memories of and uncritical support for one's nation – while at the same time reinforc-ing the capitalist interests (e.g., those that underlie professional sport). In order to maintain such emotional support, many aspects of sports like hockey must go largely unnoticed or uncriticized by spectators. These include that professional hockey is played mostly by white men; that the pro-game is at its core a business; and that the sport has many known links with drug and alcohol abuse, vio-lence towards women, and child molestation (Nauright and White 1996; Robinson 1998).

Sociologist Graham Knight (1998) discussed how feeling-passion is similarly generated among audiences through "bad news" newspaper stories about such topics as juvenile delinquency. Ac-cording to Knight, these stories generate anger and distress about something that happened (e.g., a school shooting) and create fear or anxiety about what may happen next (another school shooting). This then results in a "breach" or gap between ideal normative condi-tions (a safe school) and what is apparently happening "out there," and creates an opportunity for a group seeking hegemony to offer a solution (120–1). The solution, to the extent that it is consistent with the group's ideological position and is accepted by the audience, then secures hegemony for the group. One example of such a solu-

tion for a "constructed social problem" would be the neo-conserva-
tive "boot camp rehabilitation solution" to youth crime mentioned
earlier. Later in this book, the marketing of nostalgia by rave party
promoters is considered through this lens of creating hegemony
through feeling-passion.

In addition to these elaborate mechanisms for maintaining
the status quo, Gramsci described how dominant groups make concessions to subordinate groups – concessions that are meant to
make the subordinate groups "feel better" about their situation
without fundamentally altering or threatening the status of the dominant group. As he explained: "The fact of hegemony presupposes
that account be taken of the interests and the tendencies of the
groups over which hegemony is to be exercised, and that a certain
compromise equilibrium should be formed – in other words, that the
leading group should make sacrifices" (1971, 161). Unclear in this
account, as Gramsci recognized, was the extent to which these concessions are "given by" the dominant groups, and the extent to which
subordinate groups "take from" the dominant group. Hall and Jefferson (1976) described this dubious hegemonic relationship:

Hegemony, then, is not universal and "given" to the continuing rule of a
particular class. It has to be won, reproduced and sustained. Hegemony
is, as Gramsci said, a "moving equilibrium," containing "relations of
forces favourable to this or that tendency." It is a matter of the nature
of the balance struck between contending classes: the compromises
to sustain it; the relations of force; the solutions adopted. Its character
and content can only be established by looking at concrete situations,
at concrete historical moments. The idea of "permanent class hegemony," or of "permanent incorporation" must be ditched. (40–1)

It is this imperfect hegemonic relationship, in the form of youth subcultural struggle, that was the conceptual foundation for the work
done at the cccs and is a key departure point throughout this book
for understanding power relations and youth culture.

Out of this understanding and adoption of the hegemony
concept emerged two strands of research and theory at the cccs
that were embodied in the works of two of the Centre's most prominent theorists, Paul Willis and Dick Hebdige. For his part, Willis tried
to understand young people's everyday experiences in relation to

the political and economic backdrop of 1970s post-war Britain. To do this, he conducted an interview and participant observation-based study of twelve working-class youths' day-to-day lives at school – a micro-sociological approach to research that was the basis of part one of his book *Learning to Labour: How Working Class Kids Get Working Class Jobs*. Significantly, Willis drew on this qualitative, ethnographic data to argue that the group's masculinist attitudes and activities (e.g., sexist humour, vandalism, horseplay) were fatalistic attempts to resist oppressive social conditions that, in the end, reinforced class hegemony. It was this critical, neo-Marxist analysis that became the foundation of part two of his book.

Although the ethnographic methodology endorsed by Willis is generally considered to be the most applicable tool for understanding human experience,* it was on this issue that Hebdige's work departed from that of Willis. Hebdige (1979, 1987) used "semiology" – a method for studying signs (symbols) and sign associations – in his research on youth culture and style.† Semiologists separate the "sign" into two components: the "signifier" and the "signified." The "material vehicle" of meaning (such as the word *rose*) is the signifier; the signified is the intended meaning (*rose* might be intended to mean or be interpreted as meaning "romantic"). When "decoding" youth style, the semiologist attempts to link the cultural object (such as the black T-shirt that says "Cause Stone Cold Says So" on it) to the cultural knowledge of the youth using the object (many youth would be aware that "Stone Cold" is the nickname of professional wrestler Steve Austin, a man renowned in his wrestler role for "not taking crap from anybody"). Signs, then, can have different meanings for different people depending on one's acquired knowledge and cultural experiences. That is to say, the meanings intended by culture producers – people, for example, who construct television commercials aimed at a youth audience – do not always match the meanings given to media messages by audiences, although there is believed to be a

*See the works of Blumer (1969) and Prus (1996a) for more elaborate discussions on the applicability of ethnography for the study of human lived experience. See also appendix one for a commentary about and description of ethnographic research as it was used in the study of rave reported in this book.
†For classical work focused around semiology, see Barthes (1973) and De Saussure (1966).

"preferred" or dominant interpretation that most people will have (Hall 1980). In a classic essay on the topic, renowned cultural and media theorist Stuart Hall proposed the "encoding-decoding model" that underlies this view of relationships between media audiences, media messages, and media producers. In his essay, Hall acknowledged the possibility for "oppositional" and "negotiated" readings/ decodings of media texts, by which is meant readings that either contradict or are only partially aligned with the meanings intended by those who "encode" these texts.

In this way, decoding requires more than looking at individual cultural objects – it requires an understanding of the ways these objects work together to create a message and the way these messages might be integrated into individuals' lives (e.g., the appeal of the T-shirt to the youth's peer group). So, instead of studying youth culture in an ethnographic sense, as Willis did, Hebdige drew from various sources – interviews in popular music magazines, mass media reports, record albums, and music lyrics – piecing together cultural artifacts from various relevant genres and times to produce "readings" of style and culture. While Hebdige's adaptation of the classic resistance thesis was aligned with a Marxist, hegemony-influenced position, his play with youth-related signifiers (e.g., those in music and in clothing styles) was aligned with some of the postmodernist sensibilities described earlier. McGuigan (1992) supported this position in his review of Hebdige's 1987 book *Cut 'n' Mix*: "The title ... *Cut 'n' Mix* ... captures the sense of cultures combining and recombining, of bits and pieces plucked from various sources and then put together in novel combinations, such a typical feature of black music from the time of slavery to rap and hip-hop, and which is emblematic of the postmodern supersession of cultural 'purity" the blurring of boundaries between different forms and styles" (101–2). The divergence of Willis's and Hebdige's theoretical and methodological work was magnified in the 1980s and beyond, with Willis (1990) continuing to emphasize the importance of ideology and everyday experience in *Common Culture* and Hebdige (1988) engaging and incorporating postmodern thought into his analyses of the multiple and shallow meanings of cultural artifacts in youth culture in *Hiding in the Light*.

Classical approaches to understanding subcultural activity, and especially those out of the cccs, have been subject to major criticisms. Commentators have argued, for example, that symbolic forms of resistance or response in no way alter existing conditions of oppression or challenge those in power and, moreover, that many youth do not actually give resistive meanings to their subcultural activities (see Brymer 1991; Davies 1994; Tanner 1996). Others suggested that "soft subversions" (Guattari, 1996) from the dominant order are consented to by a hegemonic power bloc that is all too happy to make concessions to groups who do not present any real challenge to their relatively secure authority position. Authors such as Young and Craig (1997), Beal (1995), and Willis (1977) similarly point out that some subcultural activities and values ironically reinforce mainstream values that support exclusion and marginalization – for example, racism in skinhead culture, sexism in skateboarding, and working-class youths' rejection of middle-class schooling. Others have critiqued theory and research that glorifies extremely subtle forms of resistance, suggesting that "pro-resistance" work tends to misrepresent the actual oppositional potential of subcultural acts and forms, and in doing so dilutes the explanatory power of the resistance concept (see Gruneau, 1988; McGuigan, 1992). Still others (Atkinson and Wilson 2002; Stanley 1997) have argued that "subcultural resistance" is now a tired concept because cultural symbols or activities intended to shock and outrage have become mundane and common in a millennium culture. Consider, for example, the wide acceptance of previously "shocking" tattoos and body piercings.

In reaction to these criticisms, and as a response to the increasingly distinct social conditions of the 1980s, 1990s, and the present, a body of largely British "post-cccs" work emerged that attempted to explain the meaning of youth cultural activity in these apparently "new times." Among the first of these post-cccs treatises was Steve Redhead's 1990 book *End of the Century Party: Youth and Pop Toward 2000*, which described a "late century" youth and music culture that was more superficial and more cynical than previous work. Especially pertinent was Redhead's suggestion that the optimistic view of a proactive youth cultural resistance offered by Hall and Jefferson and others was out of date. The primary impetus for the release of Redhead's volume and subsequent books was the emergence of the rave subculture in the late 1980s in Britain, a subculture considered to be distinct from previous generations of subcultures, and one that embodied the apolitical, escapist, and hedonistic attributes of the times. While the diverse and sometimes contradictory interpretations of rave offered in these books continue to inspire theoretical work on rave and post-rave culture in Britain (e.g., Bennett and Khan-Harris 2004), there remains an almost complete absence of research on the meaning of rave in Canada. In the same way, there is a scarcity of work that reflects on the ways that manifestations of rave in Canada can inform both classical and contemporary theories of youth cultural activity.

Studying Ravers

With the goal of contributing to existing empirical and theoretical work on youth culture in Canada, this book presents a case study of rave, a group considered by many to be the prototypical "twenty-first century," "postmodern," "millennium" youth subculture. This case is noteworthy for several reasons beyond the broad theoretical ones noted above. First, there are widespread concerns about social problems associated with raving, particularly the apparent centrality of amphetamine drug use to the culture's all-night rave dance parties. This concern is evident both in popular media and in government-related health reports. For example, countrywide warnings from Health Canada about the potentially fatal effects of some forms of the most well known of the rave-related drugs, "ecstasy" (MDMA or methylenedioxy-methamphetamine), have been widely disseminated through popular media (Blanchfield 1996). The cover story of an issue of *Maclean's* newsmagazine included the title caption "Rave Fever: Kids Love These Parties, But the Drugs Can Kill" (Oh 2000), while a cover story of *Time* magazine's Canadian edition was entitled "What Ecstasy Does to Your Brain" (Cloud 2000). The CBC's *National News* commonly contains segments on "drugs and rave," including reports outlining an inquest into drug-related rave deaths. In 1997, the ABC show *20/20* included a piece on the drug-related dangers of the rave scene in Southern Florida and alluded to the widespread appeal of this "problem activity" across America. A British movie entitled *Loved Up* – shown on Canada's Showcase Network – followed the life of a fictional young woman who became captivated by the rave scene and addicted to the drug ecstasy. Episodes of popular television shows, such as *Beverly Hills 90210* and *New York Undercover,* have also focused on the use of drugs at raves.

Conversely, there is an increasing tendency for various media to emphasize the neo-hippie views upheld by the ravers. This glamorization of the rave scene is most evident in the wave of late 1990s popular fiction books that include rave and ecstasy-related story lines. The most notorious examples are the now cult-classic books by Irving Welsh *The Acid House*, *Trainspotting,* and *Ecstasy: Three Tales of Chemical Romance.* Another book, *Ecstasy Club,* by renowned popular culture commentator and writer Douglas Rushkoff, depicted a San Francisco warehouse commune that subscribed to pseudo-rave ideals and threw weekly rave parties. Other recently-released compilations of fictional short stories reflect rave's positioning in a futuristic, twenty-first century culture. For example, Sarah Champion's edited books *Disco 2000* and *Disco Biscuits*, which include chapters by Rushkoff, Welsh, and acclaimed Canadian writer Douglas Copeland (who wrote the celebrated book *Generation X* about disillusioned youth) include vivid depictions of usually rave-related, twenty-first century excesses and experiences. As well, less critical/panicked articles in newspapers and magazines have tended to depict rave as an appealing, romantic, "new age" youth subculture.*

The problem is that these depictions of rave as either a societal concern or glamorous and sensational are usually overly simplistic and/or based on speculation. Seldom do these writings include any discussion about, for example, how raver youth are differentiated according to their roles and experiences in the rave scene, or how ravers might have diverse opinions about and perspectives on raving. The research presented in this book attempts to account for this diversity. For example, the perspectives of the often jaded veteran ravers, who tend to dwell on the "fall of the scene" and irresponsible drug use, are counterpoised against the vibrant optimism of neophyte ravers, who tend to view the rave party as an "urban sanctuary." Similarly, the business-oriented, profit-focused motives of some disc jockeys and promoters are counterpoised against

---

*Newspaper articles written by Bradley (1994), Landale (1998), and McLaren (1998) portray rave in this way.

the more altruistic views expressed by others in the scene. At the same time, the ethical dilemmas faced by DJs and promoters who struggle with the pro-rave versus pro-business issue are acknowledged. In a more general way, the research is attentive to topics such as the evolution of rave culture over time, the evolution of ravers' perspectives on and involvements in their scene, and the ways that globalization processes might be linked with the rise and development of the rave scene abroad and in Canada.

Rave and Youth Cultural Studies

More specific features of rave that are uniquely relevant to conceptual issues in youth cultural studies also inspired some of the explorations in this book. Four of these are outlined below.

First, ravers exist in urban and virtual social spaces – warehouses, dance clubs, fields, basements, chat rooms, and newsgroups, to name but a few. A concern in this book is the extent to which ravers are active and creative in these locations, and the extent to which they are constrained, controlled, monitored, and manipulated by adults, media-created images, and each other.

Second, ravers are simultaneously resistant to dominant cultural expectations and subject to group conventions and the impacts of mass mediated culture. In the rave culture, mass media panics about drug use, nightclub norms of intimidation and "attitude," and the marketing of trendy music and clothes are often subverted – although the group's movement away from underground status toward mainstream has threatened this resistance. The different ways that the youth group "resists," and, more importantly, the different meanings that resistance can take for various rave-related groups – and for the researcher who interprets youth activity – are considered here. For example, resistance can be viewed as activism, subversion, indifference, disobedience, deviance, and transgression. The extent to which practices of resistance actually "make a difference" (i.e., the extent to which they are effective forms of social opposition) and the extent to which ravers are actually and intentionally resisting at all are also of interest.

Third, an understanding of the ways that raver youth use the rave and rave activities as part of negotiating their identities provides a crucial departure point for studying stylistic expression, lifestyle preference, and youth culture. The rave culture is a spectacular culture, akin to the British youth subcultures of the 1970s, such as the punk rockers, skinheads, and Rastafarians. Ravers are characterized by their distinct musical preferences, clothing styles, dancing techniques, and by their tendency to use amphetamine drugs as a part of intense weekend party-escapes. This is a conspicuous group that has gained notoriety in the mass media.

However, not all ravers participate equally in the various rave-related activities (e.g., drug use), nor do they all adopt the same raver-look (e.g., not all youth carry a whistle and/or have a pacifier in their mouths – two of the more celebrated rave-style props). Similarly important then, although less attention-getting and media-worthy, are the unspectacular aspects of rave culture. A key question in this context is whether raving could be "replaced" by another seemingly rebellious activity for a young person seeking to establish an anti-establishment cultural identity. Put another way, are outlandish rave-related subcultural displays akin to more "common" forms of identity-formation, such as playing sports or joining the school band?

Authors like Tanner (1996) emphasize these concerns in identifying the propensity for both scholarly research and journalistic work on youth to focus on high profile youth cultures, suggesting that this overemphasis on spectacular youth deflect attention away from "the fact that most adolescent deviance is not of this attention-grabbing type" (83). For Willis (1990), the "idea of spectacular subculture is strictly impossible because all style and taste cultures, to some degree or another, express something of a general trend to find and make identity outside the realm of work" (16). Although Willis's work (likely because of its timing) failed to acknowledge the potential historical importance of rave culture's positioning as a technology-based counter-culture, or the implications of its visible but subtle subcultural transgressions, his point lends support to this book's contention that the spectacular and unspectacular aspects of youth cultural groups must be studied together if a balanced understanding of youth culture is to be attained. In this context, it is crucial to consider how various symbolic expressions are interpreted by (rave) subcultural participants and, on this basis, discuss whether the intensity or level of a group's visual transgression from mainstream style can be reasonably linked to the group's overall alignment with or against mainstream culture.

Fourth, and as noted earlier, it is also pertinent that rave culture exists in somewhat unique social and cultural circumstances, what some refer to as "postmodern" times. That is to say, rave exists in a culture and time period arguably defined by a fragmentation and blurring of conventional social categories – one where class, race, and gender distinctions are increasingly less pronounced – and a highly dispersed and developed media. In this culture and period, youth have been exposed to, among other media-related influences, a proliferation of youth-focused advertising and such technological developments as the Internet. The rave subculture has been called the first postmodern subculture by authors like McGuigan (1992, 101) because of the group's interest in "hyper-real" (i.e., better than real) computer-generated music that cannot be produced by conventional instruments, its tendency to de-emphasize race and gender difference, and its focus on fun, escape, and excessive consumption, rather than the more edgy and overtly rebellious counter-cultural styles and lifestyles that are hallmarks of punks and skinheads.

However, not all youth – ravers or otherwise – live equally in a postmodern world, and moreover, conventional forms of difference and oppression are in no way absent from rave culture, despite the postmodern hype. The "real" distinctions between and within youth cultures require consideration within more grounded theories of social difference (e.g., neo-Marxism) and interpretation (symbolic interactionism). This is especially crucial considering the continued need for work that engages the intricacies of middle-class youth culture (Atkinson 2003a). Brake's early work on bohemian counter and youth cultures, where he identified some of the resistant and non-resistant activities and dispositions of groups like the "beatniks" and the "hippies," is among the few sophisticated analyses of middle-class youth subcultures (1980, 86–114).

On these bases, a study of rave culture provides a departure point from which to explore how class, race, and gender are still pertinent in millennium youth culture and to consider the tensions between the various existing and emerging explanations of youth cultural activity. The next chapter begins this process.

PART 1

Rave Culture, History, and Social Experience

2
From New York to Ibiza to Britain to Toronto
Rave Histories, Contexts, and Panics

The optimistic ...
The venue was spacious and well ventilated. The music was the usual
Techno, although not as harsh as some, and I tried to follow a friend's
advice to move with the bass and ignore the rest. I got into dancing
in my usual self-conscious way, keeping an eye on what other people
were doing and well aware that I am older than most. Then, impercepti-
bly, I gradually relaxed and melted into the ambience, and knew I was
part of it all ... I experienced a feeling of belonging to the group, a kind
of uplifting religious experience of unity ... It was as though I was
surrounded by fellow members of an exclusive tribe, bonded by some
shared understanding, yet full membership was mine for the $15.00
ticket and $22.50 tablet.
(Nicholas Saunders, *Ecstasy: Dance, Trance and Transformation*,
1996, 3)

This whole scene – now over a decade old – has helped bring together
so many different kinds of people who would otherwise have nothing
in common. The creativity and constant growth of the scene amongst
people worldwide who are now as passionate about clubs and music
as I was aged sixteen, surely make this the first youth culture to go
truly global.
(DJ Billy Nasty, in M. Harrison's edited *High Society: The Real Voices
of Club Cultures*, 1998, xi)

When I go to raves and use Ecstasy it breaks down barriers. It breaks
down preconceptions, it makes it easier to meet people ... you think
about how it changes you and how you feel while you're on it as

opposed to how you feel when you're not and you try and take the
feeling that you get when you're high and relate it to your own life.
Do you really need social barriers, do we really need the defenses
that we have and would life be better off if we didn't have some of the
defenses that we have? Would it be easier to meet people, easier to
communicate? It all comes down to communication because there is
a lack of communication obviously in our society.
(interview, male raver, Toronto 1995)

The pessimistic ...
When the rave scene first started here there was only one promotion
company called *Chemistry*. They were great. It was cheap. They had
parties with swimming pools, soap suds, crazy stuff. Once the scene
got publicized, they had one last great party and then got out. They
were great parties. People weren't getting baked and running around
like madmen. When *Chemistry* folded, I think it was the beginning
of the end for the rave scene. As for the future of the rave scene, if it
keeps going the way it's going, the scene is gonna be sickly. Black-
eyed 14 year olds sniffing powders and going home to the wrong
address under the guise that they're having a good time.
(interview, male raver and jungle and trip hop DJ, Toronto 1995)

Rave is dead, or so the pundits say. Yet there's a sense in which it's bigger than ever. Not only is the spectrum of nineties culture dominated
by the ever widening delta of post-rave scenes ... but it also seems
obvious that more people are involved in the weekender/ecstasy
lifestyle than ever, as veteran ravers hang on in there, while each year
produces a wave of new recruits. But as for the rave myth, the ideal
of love, peace, unity, positivity – well, that's been smelling funny for
quite a while.
(Simon Reynolds,from Redhead's *The Clubcultures Reader*, 1997, 102)

and the ambivalent ...
labour market conditions have also been used to explain the (brief)
flowering of less predatory youth cults such as the "rave" culture ...
From small beginnings, rave culture has attracted the more Bohemian
members of "Generation X" ... While rave seems to be a more ephemer-
al and less desperate kind of subculture than those associated with
delinquency, those who participate in it see it as an outlet for disaffili-
ated youth ... As with other subcultural solutions, there is an emphasis

upon the search for community ... [However] youth cults like the rave culture have been primarily the subject of media reports and specula-tion rather than actual research.
(Julian Tanner, *Teenage Troubles: Youth and Deviance in Canada*, 1996, 144–5)

Ravers, it's not hard to notice, like to play with toys. Their cultural aes-thetic is one of playful innocence, and yet one out of every three ravers I met claimed to be an ecstasy dealer. This underlines the central para-dox of rave culture: the tension between innocence and experience.
(L. McLaren, *Globe and Mail*, 1998)

The remarkable disparity of views on the state, the significance, and the future of the rave scene are akin to the complex and contradic-tory images of youth presented in chapter one. Not surprisingly, the emerging problem and question about research on youth culture parallels that expressed here about rave. That is, *(how) can the com-plexity of the rave cultural phenomenon be "captured" through empirical study and theoretical discussion?* Endeavouring to speak more directly about this issue/question and about the diversity of views on rave offered above, I introduce this chapter with two broad theoretical convictions that guided the study presented in this book.

The first point, which draws on W.I. Thomas's adage that "if men [and women] define situations as real, they are real in their consequences" (1923, 81), is that the various interpretations noted above are the realities of the rave scene – a scene that is simulta-neously threatening, dangerous, excessive, enlightening, beautiful, resistant, and so on. From this perspective, the complexities of rave exist in the diverse ways that people understand the scene, and the goal of research should be to arrange these views, interpretations, and experiences for audiences and readers, without privileging any one view over another. Collin's view (1997) of rave culture embodies this perspective: "The story of Ecstasy culture [i.e., rave culture or acid house culture] is itself a remix – a collage of facts, opinions and experiences. Differing outlooks and vested interests combine to deny the possibility of a history that everyone can agree as truth; some things are forgotten, others are exaggerated; stories are embellished, even invented, and the past is polished to suit the necessities of the present. Behind one narrative are hundreds of thousands of unwritten ones, and who is to say that any one of them is not equally important" (8)? In the context of rave cultural studies, Collin's social constructionist argument requires serious consideration because of its explicit respect for the realities of and interpretations made by those who are part of a diverse and highly complex culture.

The second point is that research which is focused exclusively on the meanings that people give to their rave activities does not adequately address questions surrounding the broader social significance of a group that many consider to be *the* major youth culture at the millennium along with rap and hip hop. With this in mind, it would seem that trivializing the historical significance of rave in favour of a non-partisan, relativist evaluation is not adequately sensitive to (or critical of) the various ways that power and culture are structured in everyday life. Following this argument – an argument that is akin to the classical one made by Willis in his two-part study *Learning to Labour* – it makes sense to consider, along with the meanings that ravers give to their activities, which we will see in chapters three and four, the temporal location of rave at the millennium, the geographical location of the scene both globally (spreading from its origins in Britain and New York) and in offspring locales such as Canada, and the extant power relations in these contexts.

Rave History: Globally and in Canada

The roots of the rave scene can be traced back to four related movements: (1) the New York City dance scene of the 1970s, a predominantly gay, black, and Puerto Rican scene; (2) the Chicago "house" music scene as it existed in the late 1970s to early 1980s; (3) the Detroit "techno" music scene of the early 1980s; and (4) the British "acid house" scene of the mid to late 1980s that grew out of dance clubs in the holiday-sun location Ibiza, Spain. Underlying these developments is the evolution of the "ecstasy" drug culture and its movement into the world of dance music.

Pre-Disco, New York City, and Underground Gay and Black Club Culture
As noted above, the New York City dance scene emerged and evolved from a series of early alternative clubs and a related tradition of DJS

who founded and refined an innovative version of technologized "soul" music, now known as "house." Key to these developments was the 1970 opening of Salvation in the Hell's Kitchen district of the city, one of New York's first "flamboyantly out" gay dance clubs. From Goldman's (1978) and Collin's (1997) descriptions, it appears that Salvation was a significant precursor to the rave scene in both the content and form of the club's culture – a spectacular culture of defiance and escape. The club's cultural significance is further accentuated when considered for its emblematic links with a historic clash that took place a year earlier at an after-hours gay bar in Greenwich Village called the Stonewall Inn, what came to be known as the "Stonewall Riots." The incident, a zealous retaliation by customers to a routine harassment raid by eight plainclothes police officers, came to be viewed as the symbolic beginning of the gay liberation, power, and pride movement (Collin 1997; Garratt 1998; Young 1995). It was in spaces such as Salvation that this movement was embodied and solidified through the development of the underground dance scene.

The post-Stonewall emergence of the gay club movement was widely interpreted as a reaction to and escape from mainstream straight-white society (Collin 1997; Garratt 1998). Collin (1997) powerfully encapsulated the marginalized positioning of those attending the clubs at the time, and the importance of the clubs as spaces for expression and unity:

The almost devotional intensity of the atmosphere in the black gay clubs of New York created an ideological template that has been employed, knowingly or not, in dance cultures ever since. It was euphoria born out of necessity: as black people, they were excluded from the economic and social benefits of mainstream America; as homosexuals, they were excluded from its moral universe; as black homosexuals, they were even prevented from expressing their identity within their own communities. This contributed to the powerful, pent-up frustration which found its release in the clubs, the only place they could truly be themselves and play out their desires without fear or inhibition. The explosion of energy, therefore, was enormous; the bonding too ... You can hear it in the music: disco [which closely followed this movement] and house both mix the secular, the invocations of orgy and sexual abandon, with the spiritual, the wistful utopian yearnings for a "better day" when "we will all be free." (17)

The movement's message of resistance through escape, consumption, excess, decadence, and community cannot be separated from the spectacular forms of the movement – the ways, that is, that the gay-dance philosophy was articulated symbolically and homologously. For example, Salvation was constructed as a template for this indulgent community, with drinks being sold from chalices and pews, and a decor that included a "huge painted devil flanked by a host of angels, genitals exposed and locked in sexual communion" (Collin 1997, 11).

Moreover, the culture that developed in these early clubs had long-standing influences on music making and music performance that extend to the contemporary rave music and DJ scene. For example, pioneer DJ Francis Grasso invented what was known as "slip-cueing," where one musical track would be mixed with another track without stopping the songs and while maintaining a continuous beat. As Goldman (1978) wrote, Grasso's *"tour de force* was playing two records simultaneously for as long as two minutes at a stretch. He would super the drum beat of Chicago's 'I'm the man' over the orgasmic moans of Led Zeppelin's 'Whole Lotta Love' to make a powerfully erotic mix" (quoted in Garratt 1998, 9). This style of playing, and the celebrity status that DJ Grasso received in this context, foreshadowed the culture and positioning of the contemporary rave DJ and the varieties of mixing and beat-matching that appear in performances at raves.

Although peoples' experiences in these clubs were clearly enhanced by amphetamines ("uppers") and Quaaludes ("downers"), this early connection between drugs and dance was not considered to be of the same magnitude as it was in the early rave scene, a culture that for many, and particularly the mass media, was defined by drug use (Reynolds 1998; Thornton 1994). This is not to say that drugs were not central to the emerging disco scene – they absolutely were according to Collin, Garratt, Goldman, and others – but they were viewed as only part of a somewhat balanced homological relationship between dance, music, style, attitude, and emotion.

Saturday Night Fever, Disco, and the Commercialization of the Scene
The evolution of the underground dance scene into a mainstream phenomenon has been linked to the appearance of synthesizer-produced dance music tracks in the US Top 40 charts and to the open-

ing of dance clubs like New York's Infinity – clubs that were increasingly attended by a straight crowd attracted by the spectacle of "intoxicating music and flashing lights" (Garratt 1998, 10). The transition to mainstream status was completed with the release of the 1977 movie *Saturday Night Fever*. The film portrayed working-class youth whose identities were defined by their weekend excesses (dancing, drinking, and drugs) at a disco nightclub. The film symbolically articulated the transition from the 1960s hippie era to the realities of the 1970s recession – that is, "kids could no longer run away from home, drop acid and drop out … instead they worked hard to support their families, escaping into the fantasy world of the disco on Saturday nights" (20).

The film had other far-reaching consequences. As Collin (1997) suggested, it caricatured and effectively "flattened" a dance scene previously defined by its depth (i.e., its symbolic-resistive meaning) and complexity (e.g., its gay, black, and Puerto Rican context). Perhaps most importantly, it transformed the underground dance scene from a social movement into a mainstream, commercialized fad, as Garratt (1998) explained in her discussion of disco's demise:

Codified, commercialized, disco began to stagnate. Middle-of-the-road-crooner Andy Williams made a disco record. Middle-aged America hummed along to a tune like the Salsoul Orchestra's "You're Just the Right Size" without dreaming what it implied, and the US Navy almost adopted the Village People's "In the Navy" for a recruitment campaign until its camp subtext was explained. Reduced to a formula and severed from its black soul roots, the music was considered production line fodder, mechanical and soulless … By 1980 … bored of the formula, mainstream America had retreated from the dancefloor too. Disco was considered over, a finished fad, and many of the major labels closed down their disco departments or modified them into more general dance departments. (21)

The underground music and dance scene continued to creatively develop in other directions after the "death of disco" in the early 1980s. "Garage" music (a combination of gospel voice and uptempo dance music) and other mixed genre audio innovations were being played at Paradise Garage, a former truck garage in Soho, New York

City, where one of the most well-known and celebrated of the early dance music DJs, Larry Levan, worked the turntables on weekends from 1975 to the club's closing in 1987. It was in the Paradise Garage that the combination of music and drug use was being further explored as part of an ongoing "sensual experiment":

Levan was a scientist who mixed as if he was trying to work the drugs that were percolating through the dancers' brains – trying to play their body chemistry – creating a homology between sonic texture and the chemically elevated cortex ... At the Garage, the drugs that raised the spirit were Ecstasy, mescaline, cocaine and LSD; although drug taking was far less open than it would become at the British clubs, an astounding pharmacoepia of substances was being consumed in the name of pleasure ... the club buzzed with energies of all kinds: sexual, spiritual, musical, chemical. (Collin 1997, 16)

Paradise Garage remained an alternative to the mainstream post-disco dance movement. The clientele were still predominantly gay, black, and Puerto Rican and the music was "more hedonistic ... more underground than the playlists of other New York clubs" (Kempster 1996, 14). Moreover, according to Kempster (1996), with its particular focus on musical experimentation, Paradise Garage contrasted the renowned Studio 54, which had become a Mecca for high-profile socializing, with the music being a relative afterthought.*

Chicago and the Two Strands of House
Underground scenes were also developing in other cities in the post-disco era. A friend of Larry Levan's, fellow DJ Frankie Knuckles, is most well known for his elevation of the Chicago house music scene – a scene to which he introduced the "electronic soul music" at a club called The Warehouse. In fact, it is from The Warehouse that the term "house music," one of the original genre names within the electronic dance music scene, was derived.

A key development in Chicago's house music culture – a development which reflects a current trend in the Toronto rave scene, as I explain in later chapters – was the emergence of two distinct

*See Haden-Guest (1997) for a more detailed discussion and analysis of Studio 54.

music consumption communities. While Frankie Knuckles attracted a usually older crowd that was interested in more cleanly mixed and soulful dance music, those interested in "less sophisticated," raw, energetic music attended nights at a rival club called The Music Box, where DJ Ron Hardy played. Kempster (1996) explained this dichotomy: "By 1983, Knuckles had moved from the Warehouse to a new venue, The Power Plant. But on Chicago's south-side another club, The Music Box, opened with Ron Hardy ... behind the decks. Hardy was a mercurial talent, addicted to heroine and a heavy user of a varied selection of hard drugs. While The Power Plant offered a polished, orderly experience, Hardy unleashed a repetitive onslaught of rhythms and grooves, dropping hot records like Blue Magic's 'Welcome to the Club' ... into a Dionysian frenzy of Philly soul and Euro-disco" (14–15).

A distinction could be drawn here between the types of house music played by these DJs – the variation sometimes called "deep house" played by Knuckles, and the more upbeat, purposefully unpolished house played by Hardy. Even the drugs used by the respective audiences reflected these music-based variations – again foreshadowing later developments in the rave scene. The "sophisticated" crowd who followed Knuckles were for the most part taking relatively more expensive experiential and sensual drugs, such as acid and MDA – a compound similar to but less effective or ecstatic than ecstasy/MDMA – to enhance their time. In The Music Box, where the usually younger crowd went to see Hardy, the drugs were less expensive and intended to induce a state of hyperactivity, an effect which allowed users to keep up with (and stay up all night for) the rampant music sets that Hardy played. Although the Chicago scene continued to evolve into the late 1980s, it was these music and drug cultures associated with Knuckles and Hardy that are the most notable developments for the purposes of the current study.

Detroit "Techno" Music

House [music] still has its heart in 1970's disco ... [The techno music that we produce] is strictly future music. We have a much greater aptitude for experiment. (Detroit techno music innovator Derek May, quoted in Kempster 1996, 19)

[Techno music is] a complete mistake. It's like George Clinton [a musical innovator renowned for combining Rhythm and Blues with hard rock to create "funk" music] and Kraftwerk [computer-music innovators from Germany] stuck in an elevator with only a sequencer to keep them company. (ibid.)

While Chicago house DJs were creating updated genres of disco, three young musicians in Detroit – Derek May, Juan Atkins, and Derek Saunderson – were developing an electronic and futuristic sound that was less influenced by the New York and Chicago black and gay scenes (although Hardy's raw, high speed, "electric disco" did have a notable impact) and more influenced by New Wave electronic music that was coming out of Europe, including the alternative, synthesizer-driven music of Kraftwerk, the Human League, Gary Numan, and Devo. Considered sociologically, these artists produced music that, for them, was a reaction to the existing social conditions of their home city Detroit. In the early 1980s, Detroit was in recession and had become both an industrial wasteland and the murder capital of the world. "Detroit techno," as it came to be known, both embodied this urban decay, as the predominantly technological music reflected the obsolescence of modern forms of industry and increasingly *techno*logized approaches to manufacturing, and looked beyond it, being science-fiction inspired, computer-generated, and "futuristic-sounding." As Trask (1996) and Collin (1997) noted, these musicians, who were influenced by video games and futuristic movies like Ridley Scott's *Blade Runner*, saw the "other worldly" character of the future to be a better alternative to the racisms and ghetto life of present and past.

These early developments are the basis for many of the themes underlying the contemporary rave scene, although the symbolic relevance of Detroit techno was at least partially lost in its appropriation. For example, in Toronto and elsewhere, the names of record labels and rave parties often integrate terms and slogans that were originally developed in Detroit as part of marketing the scene, music, or event in question – although Detroit and Toronto share little social or musical history. Moreover, and importantly, through their musical experiments these Detroit techno-pioneers demonstrated to aspiring DJs how music-making is accessible to almost anyone through technology. In this sense, these DJs were at least partially responsible for the democratization of this artistic form.

Aside – Kraftwerk and German Techno: The Melding of Humanity and Technology

Although the technological advancements made by the DJ innovators in New York City and Detroit were key, some commentators argue that the German band Kraftwerk, with its early experimental synthesizer productions, most succinctly predicted and influenced the future of modern electronic music. According to Sinker (1996), Reynolds (1998), and Collin (1997), the band's vision of a synthesis between human and machine was extremely influential for black American dance music, leading American artists to rework some of Kraftwerk's original electronic music by adding "rapped" lyrics – thus creating a new genre of dance music called "electro." Although this fusion of soul music and electronic music is the basis for contemporary genres of rave music, some commentators suggest that Kraftwerk's influence can also be viewed as a reflection of broader social and artistic trends. Sinker (1996) offered two contradictory perspectives on Kraftwerk's melding of humanity and technology in music production. These interpretations are especially relevant in the context of the 1990s and millennium, a time when electronic music has become a dominant musical form and integral to debates about the positive and negative impacts of technology on music-related cultural life:

The first [theory] suggests that their [Kraftwerk's] genius lies in their ability to edit the soul out of modern music. By stripping the emotion from it (and any subtexts which that might carry) they have created pure music from their machines. Music which demands to be listened to on its own terms, with its own internal reference points and logic. Modernist music taken to its ultimate conclusion. The second, and almost diametrically opposed theory is that the music which Kraftwerk makes is, in fact, pure electronic soul. The brilliance is located in an uncanny ability to invest those same machines with emotion and feeling. Their music is not modernist but post-modernist. What they do, in fact, is to drag the Beach Boys and Karlheinz Stockhausen and the Velvet Underground, kicking and screaming through micro-chip filters and circuit boards in an alchemical flurry of eclecticism. They polish it up and make it all new again for our late 20th century tastes. (Sinker 1996, 94)

These views of Kraftwerk as either high-modern or postmodern reflect contemporary understandings not only of technological music forms, but also of methods of music production. For example, there are debates in the Toronto rave scene about the "(sub)cultural ethics" of using pre-programmed laptops when DJing live at parties, instead of "live" mixing of records on turntables, a social practice and artistic form that is in some respects threatened by these pro-technology developments.*

Ibiza and Britain

Although the culture that resembles what is now thought of as "rave" came to fruition in Britain, the roots of the movement can be traced back to Ibiza, Spain – an inexpensive holiday-sun location for bohemian British working-class youth in the early 1980s (Collin 1997; Eisner 1994; Garratt 1998; Reynolds 1998). The influx of tourism to Ibiza at this time coincided with the import of house music to the island's night clubs from America and the increasing availability of the drug ecstasy – LSD, mescaline, and cocaine were the stimulants of choice until this time – thus creating a stage for a radical adaptation of the American dance club.

The original pre-rave parties were held at an Ibiza club named Amnesia, where DJ Alfredo Fiorello, "a former journalist who'd fled the fascist rigors of his native Argentina for the laid-back bohemian idyll," began to spin and mix imported house music from New York City and Chicago (Reynolds 1998, 58). DJ Fiorello gained a loyal audience of British youth whose background and activities were described by Collin (1997) as follows:

Most of them originated from the southern fringes of the capital, the stretch of London where inner city and suburbs meet ... This area – completely unremarkable to the eye – had continually been influential in nurturing cultural movements through the seventies and eighties.

*These sorts of discussions about music, technology, authenticity, and ethics are explored by Gilbert and Pearson (1999) in their book *Discographies: Dance Music, Culture and the Politics of Sound.*

The bohemian milieu that spawned David Bowie was centred around Beckenham; the original punks and the first followers of the Sex Pistols were the Bromley Contingent ... [In Ibiza, on holiday, groups of these youth] would meet at bars ... head out ... to Amnesia where they would take Ecstasy and carouse until sun-up ... The summer became an extended vacation in an alternate reality. (51)

This following of young British youth included Paul Oaken-fold, a British DJ who had been to Larry Levan's Paradise Garage in New York, and had unsuccessfully attempted to open an Amnesia-style club in Britain in 1985. In hindsight, according to Oakenfold, the missing element in the 1985 attempt was the drug ecstasy. After his first ecstasy experience in 1987, Oakenfold and his business partner Ian St. Paul opened up an after-hours club called the Project where "Ibiza veterans" would come sporting an "Ibiza look and atti-tude" that was a "weird mix of Mediterranean beach bum, hippie, and soccer hooligan – baggy trousers and T-shirts, paisley bandan-nas, dungarees, ponchos, Converse All-Stars sneakers – loose fitting because the Ecstasy and non-stop trance dancing made you sweat buckets" (Reynolds 1998, 58–9). Following the Project's opening, a series of house-music nights emerged at other locations – particu-larly in a club named Shoom – and an exclusive pre-rave scene had come into existence. Reynolds (1998) explained the irony of these origins, an irony that foreshadowed recent developments in the Canadian rave scene: "The Shoom ethos was love, peace and unity, universal tolerance, and we-are-all-the-same. It was supposed to be the death knell of clubland's [conventional dance clubs or bars] snobbish exclusivity, but there was an essential contradiction in the way that the Shoom experience was restricted to the original clique and their guests, plus a few minor celebrities" (61).

Despite its origins as a privileged "in" party-crowd, rave culture – known at this time as the "acid house" culture – soon began to spread, as did importing of the drug ecstasy into Britain. Other acid house nights began taking place and the scene was becoming almost too popular for the previously "alternative" Ibiza originals. However, for the broader British youth population, the dis-covery of acid house/rave music and community, along with the drug ecstasy, led the rave movement to its peak in the summer of 1988 – what has been called the second "summer of love."

This climaxing music-dance-drug movement was characterized by the integration of different classes, races, and sexual preferences at the same parties. Perhaps most notably, these raves – as they were now known – appeared to transcend the well-established city territories that were previously defined by soccer team loyalties. Reynolds (1998) described this surprising scene: "Almost overnight, the box cutter-wielding troublemaker was metamorphosed into the 'love thug,' or as Brit rapper Gary Clail later put it, 'the emotional hooligan.' 'Football firms' (warring gangs who supported rival teams) were going to the same clubs, but to everyone's surprise, there was never any trouble. They were so loved up on E [ecstasy] they spend the night hugging each other rather than fighting" (64). Social commentators like Redhead (1997; Redhead et al. 1997), Reynolds (1998), and others have drawn parallels between British football (soccer) and the rave movement, arguing that in 1980s Thatcherism, the "soccer match and the warehouse party offered rare opportunities for the working class to experience a sense of collective identity" (Reynolds 1998, 64). Of course, like many subcultural movements, rave's incubation period was rather short, and as Reynolds noted, soon after the summer of love, the "love thugs" turned back to "their old, tried and true techniques of getting a rush" (64).

The Aftermath and the Present: Moral Panics and Club Culture
According to most commentators, the end of the summer of love was as abrupt as the beginning. People were becoming immune to ecstasy's effects, and, of course, what is "too popular" (e.g., disco) tends to become passé very quickly. As Redhead (1997) argued, "the summer of 1988 was over when, on 1 October, the *Sun* signalled the dawn of acid house as 'cool and groovy'" (57). Moreover, an "antirave law" was passed – the infamous Criminal Justice Act of 1994 – and other mainstream media were generating "moral panics" about rave, sensationalizing, for example, high profile ecstasy-related deaths (Thornton, 1994, 1995). Redhead (1997) memorialized the summer of 1988 in the following way: "The 'summer of love 1988,' itself a reworking of another mythical summer – the summer of love 1967 – looks set to take its place in the hallowed halls of pop legends. While the 1960s once slipped lazily into the early 1970s, pop time has now accelerated with a vengeance – as if reclaiming borrowed time –

according the public phenomenon of acid house little more than a long weekend" (56).

What evolved, according to many, is what Sarah Thornton called "clubculture." This is a culture governed less by peace, love, and togetherness and more by a subcultural class system – akin to the "hierarchy of hipness" described in Howard Becker's 1963 study of the jazz musician community. Thornton found that for clubbers it matters what you wear, how you dance, and how you talk. Although this evolved rave was similar in some respects to the scene in the summer of 1988 – dance, electronic music, and drugs still being present – it was apparent that people's interpretations of rave-related activities in 1988 were radically different from views on the post-rave scene, with "be free" in 1988 having given way to "be cool" in the mid and late 1990s and beyond.

A History of Toronto's Rave Scene: Incubation, Fluctuation, Commercialization, and Fragmentation

The origins and early development of the rave scene in Toronto are reminiscent of the scene's history generally, although the timing and character of the Toronto movement is distinct. With this in mind, I have summarized the development of the Toronto rave scene into five stages. Although parts of this historical development are well known by some veteran ravers and others, it has not been well documented to date. For this reason, the data for this section is drawn from a combination of local, underground dance music magazines and webzines (particularly the column "Bricklayers" in the webzine *Klublife*), from reputable Web sites (that is, Web sites put together by established individuals in the Toronto rave party, dance, and music scene), from interviews with some individuals who have been associated with the scene at various times over its development, and from a chapter in Silcott's 1999 book *Rave America: New School Dancescapes* that offers a version of Toronto's rave history.

Stage 1: Early Dance Club Scene

In 1983, I was standing in line with my future partner at the Diamond Club, the first New York style nightclub in Toronto. It was the first time I experienced something different in Toronto, notorious at the time for using lots of brass and mirrors in their venues. I liked what I saw, it was exciting. We were into it so much we made plans right away to open our own place right away. (underground club innovator Charles Khabouth, quoted in webzine *Klublife*, no. 8, www.klublife.com)

Club Z, a venue owned by renowned Toronto club owner Charles Khabouth, was one of the first Toronto clubs to feature house music. In a magazine interview, Khabouth described how Club Z was a safe place for a diverse crowd which included "a lot of oriental, black, white and gay and other ethnic backgrounds" (*Klublife*, no. 8). Club Z was followed by other after-hours clubs, as well as periodic warehouse parties, that featured house music tracks, including Stilife (also owned by Khabouth), Twilight Zone, and Klub Max (ibid.). This style of dance club still exists today, although the emergence of the rave scene in Toronto led to at least a partial split between those who continued to attend the often gay clubs, and those who became part of the rave movement.

Stage 2: Chris Shepperd, Dance Radio, and the Imported Rave Scene

After the "Summer of Love" in 1988, Richard [Norris] and I wanted to create that vibe in Toronto. It was October 1988 that we threw our first party trying to create the "love one another ... be free carnival vibe" that was so apparent in this scene. (radio DJ and music producer Chris Shepperd, quoted in *Klublife*, no. 6)

Chris Shepperd, known under his rave DJ name as "Dogwhistle," has long been one of Canada's premier personalities in the alternative music scene. Responsible on 23 October 1988 for Canada's first rave party, he continued to import ideas derived from various trips to New York City and England into the Toronto and Canadian dance music scene. Shepperd and a Toronto entrepreneur known in rave circles as "Happy Dog" opened the first "rave club" – akin to the acid house/rave clubs of Britain. The club, called 23 Hop, took its name from the date of Shepperd's first Canadian rave performance. The impact of 23 Hop on the rave scene was acknowledged by interviewees in the current study and was described as follows on Shepperd's Web site "Pirate-Sounds 2000": "From its inception the original '23 Hop' was widely acknowledged as the birthplace of rave culture in Canada and the launching pad for the country's first two rave companies, *Exodus* and *Chemistry*. Although Dogwhistle [Shepperd's DJ name when working raves] wasn't the only DJ to spin at the new club, he was without question the most influential, especially after returning from his many trips abroad" (http://piratesounds.com/index.html).

It was during this early period that Shepperd was introducing acid house/rave music to Toronto on CFNY radio, then on Energy 108 (Toronto's first all-dance music station), and eventually on his nationally syndicated "Pirate Radio" show. His exalted on-air persona included "Shepisms" such as calling Toronto "the city of love," referring to his listeners as "brothers and sisters," and describing his show as "often imitated, never duplicated." It is worth noting that as Chris Shepperd became better known to mainstream dance crowds, and especially since he began producing mainstream dance music CDs, his stock in the underground rave community dropped dramatically with those who perceived him to be a "sell out" – although his early contributions to the scene are still generally recognized. Another innovator in the Toronto scene, Don Burns (rave DJ name Dr. Trance) made a similarly successful transition from alternative music on CFNY to spinning "rave music" on Toronto-based stations and through the Internet on the "Global Groove Network."

Stage 3: Promotion Companies, Competition, and Growth
Following Shepperd's first rave in 1988 and the opening of 23 Hop, rave promotion companies emerged in the Toronto rave scene. According to rave lore, these companies were responsible for organizing the initial rave warehouse parties, considered the classic rave event along with, perhaps, outdoor raves. In the late 1980s and early 1990s, raves were infrequent but much anticipated, occurring approximately once a month, not counting the semi-regular events at 23 Hop. According to interviewees who attended early parties, promoters of these raves – such as the Exodus and Chemistry promotion companies – were most concerned with providing a good show and a good time, and less with making money. Alex Clive, a notorious promoter for the company Chemistry, is an icon for altruistic rave promotion:

An admitted "production obsessive," Clive was interested in creating total rave environments. He spent days spray-painting seascapes and attaching dangling fish cutouts to a warehouse ceiling for a Chemistry rave called 20,000 Leagues under the Sea. He ordered hundreds of beach balls for one summer rave. He hired red double-decker buses as shuttles and covered up the windows so no one could identify the secret location of a rave called Magical Mystery Trip ... At one point, Clive decided that he wanted to serve alcohol at an event ... He found a disused factory building, rented it three weeks in advance, and then beavered away with tools and plywood, building a second set of walls to line the immense room; the space between his plywood and the original walls was used to accommodate secret bars, which could be concealed behind sliding shutters [in case police invaded the party looking for unlicensed activity]. (Silcott 1999, 82)

As the popularity of this still underground culture began to rise, other rave companies, such as Nitrous, Pleasure Force, Atlantis, and Better Days formed. Although rave parties were still taking place in warehouses, old clubs, and outdoor locations, interviewees who were part of the scene during its inaugural years suggested that promoters were increasingly "in it for the money," unlike the earlier times when it was more about the music and the party. These tensions continue to the present. Of course, this key difference between the "good old days of rave" and the present might be, at least in part, attributable to the selective memory of those who remain nostalgic for times past – as discussed in chapter five.

Stage 4: The Rise, Fall, and Transformation

In the years from 1992 to 1996, the rave scene in Toronto became increasingly "above-ground" and popular, particularly with younger teens, and the parties were becoming easier to find and larger. There were regular locations and nights for some raves. The Destiny promotion company, for example, held weekly events called "Destiny Fridays" just off of Yonge Street in Toronto at an old club location called Club Generation. According to interviewed ravers, an increasing number of people attended raves because "it was cool" and because of the drugs, not because of the community aspect of rave culture. The scene appeared to be getting dark and dangerous, with only some promoters throwing "safe" parties that were intended to promote the music and the positive "vibe." Stories emerged about some promoters turning off water in the washrooms so that dehydrated ravers would be required to buy overpriced bottled water. Some ravers talked about a new element of people, usually referring to males, who attended the parties with the intention of "picking up" or "getting high" rather than enjoying the music and dancing. A female tattoo artist and raver who was interviewed labelled these individuals "toxic ravers." In this context, Silcott described how the emergence of the promotion company Pleasure Force in 1993 signified a low point in the scene:

With Pleasure Force at the helm, Toronto's rave scene changed dramatically: as it had in the UK, rave went rough and dark, not only in terms of sound but also structure and vibe. The Pleasure Force raves would regularly lure over five thousand people, a big jump from Alex Clive's crowds of fifteen hundred only a couple of years before. The Pleasure Force crowd was notoriously young. Cocaine and strong speed like metamphetamine had worked their way into their circle. Ravers would stack meth over their Ecstasy and would often use other drugs like valium to come down at the end of the night. (1999, 90–2)

Counterpoised against this view of rave's downfall were the perspectives of those who revered rave companies that retained a focus on creating and maintaining a "positive vibe" by, for example, using their flyer-advertisements and Web sites to educate ravers about the rave philosophy and responsible drug use. Non-profit raves that were periodically promoted are evidence of this movement to maintain or save the scene. For example, former all-female promotion company Transcendence was commonly praised for its positive vibe parties.

Stage 5: Mainstreaming and Fragmentation
Compared to what happened in Britain, for example, the Toronto scene's movement toward mass-promoted and mass-attended raves – regularly over 1,000 people – and the commercialization of its rave culture followed a relatively long incubation period, arguably from the late 1980s until about 1996. Regardless of the exact timing, the mainstreaming of the rave scene in 1996 and beyond was characterized by the emergence of several "rave nights" and locations, such as Destiny Fridays, as well as after-hours clubs featuring known DJS

from the Toronto area. The rave product was now available virtually every night of the week. This mainstreaming coincided with the increasing fragmentation of rave music genres. Although different types of rave music always existed in the Toronto scene and abroad, distinct camps of ravers who preferred one type of music over another were becoming increasingly segregated with the variety of club options – a separation that changed the nature of the rave subculture from one mid-sized community to a series of mid-sized communities, essentially a larger, more fragmented scene. Having said this, there was still significant interaction between these scenes since ravers seldom limit themselves to just one genre of electronic music.

The ages of those attending various parties were also becoming notably differentiated. On one hand, more traditional rave parties that were committed to a non-alcoholic policy, high energy techno music, and a distinctly rave decor and etiquette often attracted a younger crowd of roughly fifteen to twenty-one year olds. On the other hand, more dance-club oriented venues catered to older ravers aged roughly nineteen to thirty who preferred to drink and listen to more soulful dance and house music. For example, until recently, Toronto had a renowned rave club called Industry Nightclub that sold alcohol at a bar in the club until the legal serving hours ended, in accordance with Ontario law. For the rest of the night, Industry was an after-hours club. The club consistently featured internationally recognized DJS – again, often house music DJS for the older crowd. This dichotomy is reminiscent of the early Chicago house music scenes where the older "more sophisticated crowd" attended Frankie Knuckles's nights at The Warehouse (and later The Powerplant) for his more soulful mixes of house music, while the younger crowd attended Ron Hardy's more frantic, fast-paced house music parties. In the same way, the less expensive drug "crystal," considered to be a more dangerous version of ecstasy, has often been associated with the "younger parties" in Toronto, and ecstasy with the older.

Both types of parties have become extremely well-publicized. The tradition for rave locations to be undisclosed except for those "in the know," a practice which existed in the early 1990s and to a certain extent in the mid-1990s, had all but disappeared. Still, some locations are kept under wraps until just before the party as part of keeping an artificial mystique around the rave – the tradition of taking a bus with covered windows to an unknown rave-location is now rarely practiced. This is, in part, because most of the raves are now held in legal venues because unlawful party locations put promoters who might have significant amounts of money invested in bringing high profile DJs in from Europe or the US at risk to take a devastating loss if the party is shut down by police. Having said this, it is worth noting that Toronto police are notoriously tolerant of the rave scene, according to interviewed promoters who have worked in Buffalo in the US and in Canada. Silcott's 1999 history of the early Toronto rave scene includes the story of a meeting between former Chemistry promoter Alex Clive and Toronto police, where it became apparent that local authorities knew about the parties, but "took a nonreactionary stance, seeing the benefits of parties that could keep kids off the streets" (Silcott 1999, 83). Still, most promoters who I spoke with indicated that they had learned at least a few "hard lessons" about the financial risks of promoting parties, and relayed stories about monetary loss resulting from poor marketing and planning. Moreover, more recent mediated panics surrounding raves and drugs and the related threat by Toronto Mayor Mel Lastman to outlaw raves have contributed to this tendency for promoters to take fewer risks, knowing that a major incident could put the scene in jeopardy.

As a general reaction to the mainstreaming of the formerly "underground" culture, some ravers have continued to throw smaller raves with only word-of-mouth invitation lists. This return to more intimate parties can be interpreted in either of two ways or both. It may be viewed as a resistance or reaction to the commercialization of the rave, with this resistance expressed through a move back to "the original vibe" of the early parties that were attended only by those who supported the rave values of community, peace, and love. This "return" may also be seen as the creation of an exclusive, contradictory subculture that attempts to maintain the original values of the rave at the expense of one of its central values – inclusiveness. Of course, examining the meanings that the ravers give to these word-of-mouth parties is a crucial step in attaining an informed understanding of these historical developments.

Contemporary Perspectives on Youth (and Rave)

As noted in chapter one, the emergence of rave and subsequent rave-related developments inspired a series of largely British, post-cccs writings on youth subcultures of the 1990s and post-millennium. It is in the works of British scholar Angela McRobbie (and those influenced by her), Sarah Thornton (who conducted one of the first empirical studies of club and rave culture in Britain), and Steve Redhead and his now former affiliates from the Manchester Institute of Popular Culture (MIPC) that the study of rave as a contemporary youth cultural phenomenon emerged most prominently. McRobbie's work, which is quite distinct from Redhead's and the MIPC's, is characterized by optimistic descriptions of the ways that contemporary youth seek and use "pleasure" as a symbolic escape from the social tensions of their times. McRobbie views these pleasure-seeking and pleasurable behaviours as up-to-date versions of subcultural resistance, and argues that if "we deconstruct the notion of resistance by removing its metapolitical status ... [and] reinsert it at a more mundane, micrological level of everyday practices ... then it becomes possible to see the sustaining, publicizing and extending of the subcultural enterprise" (1994, 162). Resistance in this sense lacks the "in your face" rejections of mainstream culture that is associated with some manifestations of youth rebellion.

Influenced by McRobbie, Maria Pini (1997) contended that "the rave dance floor ... is one of the few spaces which afford – and indeed, encourage – open displays of physical pleasure," and that these pleasures "do not clearly 'fit' standard, patriarchal definitions of sexuality, and eroticism" (167). Similarly, Ben Malbon (1998, 1999) emphasized the temporary, fleeting, and apolitical character of the rave scene, arguing that rave's "resistance is found through losing yourself [e.g., in the music, in the dance, in the social and physical surroundings], paradoxically to find yourself" (1998, 281).

Unlike McRobbie, Pini, and Malbon, who saw empowerment and social resistance to be an intregral and assumed part of the escapist and pleasurable activities of young people, Thornton (1995) suggested that youth are largely concerned with attaining status – or what Thornton calls subcultural capital – by becoming successfully integrated into the exclusive, underground club/rave culture. Being a "high status" clubculture member, in the context of

Thornton's research, meant demonstrating knowledge of "hard-to-find" dance parties and music collections, and showing skill on the dancefloor.* Thornton went on to argue that this view of youth could be adopted as part of a broader critique of past work on subcultures. As she explained:

Youthful interest in distinction is not new. One could easily reinterpret the history of post-war youth cultures in terms of subcultural capital. In a contemporary context, however, dynamics of distinction are perhaps more obvious for at least two reasons. First, unlike the liberalizing sixties and seventies, the eighties were radical in their conservatism ... unlike Young's hippies [i.e., the hippies described by researcher Jock Young] and Hebdige's punks, then, the youth of my research were, to cite the cliché, "Thatcher's children." Well versed in the virtues of competition, their cultural heroes came in the form of radical young entrepreneurs, starting up clubs and record labels, rather than politicians and poets of yesteryear. (Thornton 1995, 166)

Thornton's point is that youth in the 60s and 70s celebrated difference through politically motivated, though often symbolically expressed, social movements, while the distinctions sought by youth in today's finely graded social structure are ambiguous, and *not* progressive or resistant, whether symbolically or politically. Thornton argued that the negative media responses actually confirm the hierarchical, "hip" (sub)cultural status of the club culture by creating a "thrill of censorship" for those associated with the culture, and by (publicly) verifying the transgressive identities of these "clubber" youth. Thornton's focus on the influence of the media and her understanding of the hierarchies of hipness and subcultural capital effectively reversed previous subcultural analyses that were overly focused on the sovereign, resistant youth consumer.

In a departure from the optimistic portrayals of youth that characterize McRobbie, Malbon, and Pini's work, and the ambivalent view of youth espoused by Thornton, the more pessimistic Steve Redhead and MIPC theorized an increasingly "postmodern, post-punk" 1990s and millennium youth culture characterized by a loss of mean-

*Thornton's "subcultural capital" concept is an adaptation of Pierre Bourdieu's (1984) notion "cultural capital."

ing, where underground cultural forms have become indistinguish-able from mainstream forms; an inability to transmit shocking mes-sages through style, because "shock" is now mundane, redundant, and unoriginal; and nostalgia, a return, for example, to clothing styles of the past. It was these trends that inspired Redhead (1990) to pro-claim "the end of youth culture" – the end, that is, of the "subcultural resistance" model – and to argue for a movement from classic con-ceptions of "subculture" (as articulated by Hall and Jefferson 1976 and Hebdige 1979) to a radically updated notion of "clubculture" or "post-subculture" (Redhead 1997; Redhead et al. 1997).

In this context, Redhead (1997, xi) depicted the phase of post-war society in Britain from the mid-1980s to the present as one of "hedonistic individualism," while Stanley (1997, 43), supporting Redhead's view, described how "hedonism and desire" are mani-fested through the "nomadic, disruptive, disordered, [and] deregu-lated" uses of social space in computer hacking, joyriding, and raving. According to Stanley, these activities are played in the "wild zone" or "postmodern wilderness" – a deregulated, alternative space of consumption. In this sense, Stanley identifies and celebrates the moments of disruption that some youth create within monitored and controlled social spaces. Stanley goes on to suggest that these mo-ments take place against an ominous social backdrop of (over)-regulation – the "tame zone" of mainstream space. To illustrate this, Stanley describes and interprets an allegorical album cover by the band Prodigy, a band linked with the techno music of the rave move-ment. The final statement in Stanley's interpretation, "Not drowning but waving," is a purposeful adaptation and inversion of a Stevie Smith poem entitled "Not Waving But Drowning": on the album cover "a rope bridge crosses a ravine: on one side stand an angry police force against a background of industrial pollution and urban decay [the tame zone]; on the other side, complete with gigantic sound systems, are ravers [the wild zone]. One of the ravers is cut-ting the rope bridge while 'giving the finger' to the police. The terri-tory of the ravers is sunlit and green: not drowning but waving" (1997, 36–7).

On these bases, Stanley and some of his MIPC colleagues depicted a social world defined less by conventional forms of youth resistance and more often by (problematic) escapist activities. Rey-nolds (1997), for example, while acknowledging the pleasures of

rave culture's "desiring machine" *when it's running smoothly* (drawing on Deleuze and Guattari 1987), affirmed this more cynical perspective in his argument that "rave culture has never really been
about altering reality, merely exempting yourself from it for a while"
through a weekend party escape (109).

Rave and Community
While the resistance concept has received the bulk of attention in
youth cultural studies, related work has explored the notion of community, asking such questions as, Do subcultures actually provide
young people with a "sense of community"? and, To what extent are
subcultures actually cohesive entities? Akin to the continuum of optimistic, ambivalent, and pessimistic views on "youth and resistance"
noted above, there are a variety of perspectives, ranging from upbeat
to cynical, that describe the relationship between rave and community.

On the optimistic side, theorists like Pini (1997), Tagg (1994),
and Tomlinson (1998) celebrate rave's tendency to value "connect-
edness and acceptance" and its ability to transcend gender, race,
class, and age barriers in raver gatherings and attitudes. These authors
described how raves are idyllic spaces for communal experiences,
spaces where people share feelings that are music, drug, and dance
induced. In this instance, rave spaces are counterpoised against
conventional dance clubs and bars that tend to be associated with
masculinist, intimidation-based norms of interaction. On this basis,
Pini (1997) portrayed rave as a "text of sameness" and "accessible
to everyone," rationalizing that the "'unisex' clothes [of the early
British rave scene] and the whole 'dress to sweat' emphasis of the
scene are important factors in the perceived erosion of [for example],
sexual differences ... Although this perceived erosion of social differences is related to the empathetic effects of 'ε' [the drug ecstasy],
many enjoy raving without this. For this reason it becomes implausi-
ble to attribute the emergence of this theme solely to the drug – the
drug is just one part of the ensemble" (161). Similarly, Tomlinson
(1998, drawing on Tagg 1994) suggested that rave music itself, with
its emphasis on background sounds and de-emphasis on melody,
symbolically prioritizes the group over the individual.

These optimistic interpretations were again contradicted by
Thornton (1995), who emphasized the subcultural distinctions within
the rave and club culture, where the cool "in" crowd is distinguished

from those who are outside of the scene (the "out-group") within a social hierarchy.* It is crucial to emphasize, though, that Pini's work was focused more on the early British rave scene of the late 80s and early 90s, where parties were held in illegal warehouse and field locations, whereas Thornton's work focused more on the club-based youth culture of the early-mid 90s. Furthermore, and as Pini (1997, 2001) herself has argued, despite its tendency toward social integration, openness, and acceptance, the rave is still a gendered space, evident from the preponderance of males in the primary rave-occupations of DJ and promoter.

In a departure from Pini's view of a united rave and Thornton's divided one, Malbon (1998, 1999) argued that in contemporary club culture (i.e., post-rave culture), it is preferable to focus on the ways that youth use the social *space* of the club. That is to say, and according to Malbon, studies of lasting friendship and subcultural groups are less appropriate now because youth tend to drop in and out of different groups more frequently than ever before, and are often part of several subcultures at once. For this reason, studying the spaces that these multiple- or fluid-identity youth inhabit is a more suitable way to attain insight into the fragmented nature of contemporary subcultures. As he explains: "relatively diverse elements (groups) and individual identities are subsumed within the wider and much more fragile identification present within that space. Uniformity and unity are still apparent in certain strands of clubbing. But unity of identity, and in particular an identification with a specific sub-cultural grouping, appear to be far less significant" (Malbon 1998, 277–8). On this basis, Malbon adopted the notion of "neo-tribes" or "transitory tribes" (building on Maffesoli 1991, 1995) to theorize and emphasize the ways that youth move between groups or communities – with the critical aspect of these tribal identifications being, as noted above, the "spaces of identification" (Malbon 1998, 280). This is an innovative reaction to more traditional ways of understanding the complexities of subcultural membership. In essence, Malbon replaced the standard notion of "unity" – a term linked with classical and more deterministic descriptors of communities, such as class, race, and gender – with *unicity*, described as "a much more open and heterogeneous condition" (284).*

*Simon Frith (1987) made a similar argument in his earlier work on popular music.

This position is akin to Straw's (1991, 1997) distinction be-tween "music communities" and "music scenes" in the Canadian context, with Straw's scene resembling Malbon's tribal community. Straw (1997) differentiates between community and scene as follows:

One may posit a musical scene as distinct, in significant ways, from older notions of a musical community. The latter presumes a population group whose population is rather stable – according to a wide range of sociological variables ... A musical scene, in contrast, is that cultural space where a range of musical practices coexist, interacting with each other within a variety of processes of differentiation, and according to widely varying trajectories of change and cross-fertilization ... At one level, this distinction simply concretizes two countervailing pressures within spaces of musical activity: one towards the stabilization of local historical communities, and another which works to disrupt such conti-nuities, to cosmopolitanize and relativize them ... the point is not that of designating particular cultural spaces as one or the other, but of exam-ining the ways in which particular musical practices "work" to produce a sense of community within the conditions of metropolitan music scenes. (494–5, drawn from Straw 1991)

For Straw (1997) then, the unity of the dance music scene in the Canadian context is "grounded more fundamentally in the way in which ... spaces of musical activity have come to establish a distinc-tive relationship to historical time and geographical location" (497).

In an intriguing combination of Pini's united rave, Malbon's neo-tribal rave, and Thornton's hierarchical club/rave, Simon Rey-nolds (1997) pessimistically portrayed rave as a scene that has evolved and fragmented into a number of scenes that are still loose-ly defined by class, race, region, and taste, arguing that the "rave myth of transracial, cross-class unity remains in tatters" (104). Draw-ing on a historical analysis of music scenes and related drug scenes in various countries, Reynolds (1997) observed:

Just as the Woodstock convergence gave way to the fragmentation of seventies rock, just as punk split into factions based on disagreements about what punk was about and what was the way forward, so too has

*See also Gore (1997) and Bennett (1999, 2000) for a similar application of Maffesoli's notion of tribalism in the context of rave-related dance culture.

rave E-sponsored unity inevitably fractured ... Each post-rave fragment
seems to have preserved one aspect of rave culture at the expense of
the others. House music, in its more song-ful, hands-in-the-air, handbag
form, has reverted to mere disco ... Progressive house and garage is
just your pre-rave metropolitan clubland coked-out elitism back in full
effect. Techno, ambient and electronica strip rave of its, well, raveyness,
to fit a white student sensibility ... Jungle ... [is] the post-rave offshoot
that has most thoroughly severed itself from rave's premises. You could
call it "gangsta rave," in so far as jungle has taken on hip-hop and
regga's ethos of masked self-containment and controlled dance moves,
and shed rave's abandonment and demonstrativeness. (103)

This portrayal of a fractured post-rave scene is at least tentatively
endorsed by writers who have offered historical or evolutionary
depictions of dance music culture – for instance, Kempster's 1996
and Rietveld's 1998 work on house music – and more so by those
that have focused on the development of more specific sub-genres
of house, such as James's 1997 work on jungle music, a.k.a., drum
and bass – a rave related music form that combines elements of
electronic techno music and reggae.

    In some respects, it is reasonable to argue that the more
contemporary perspectives on youth offered by McRobbie, Redhead,
and others effectively filled some of the gaps left by those who were
inadequately sensitive, understandably, to the late century developments in youth culture. They did this by offering explanations of
resistance that were sensitive to the potential for youth to be, on
one hand, apathetic and passive in their cultural activities, and on
the other, optimistic and creative in utilizing alternative methods of
empowerment and resistance (e.g. dance) – characterizations that
hardly resemble the spectacular views of resistance that typified
classical interpretations of punks and skinheads. Having said this, a
closer look at previous work shows that some classical research in
fact provides a more useful departure point for explaining rave than
is generally acknowledged. For example, Westhues's argument (1972)
that hippie youth's behaviour could be interpreted as (a) sometimes
non-resistant; (b) pleasure affirming; and (c) countercultural, rather
than overtly political, is surprisingly similar to the arguments made
by the post-subculturalists about rave. The parallels between the
middle-class ravers and the working-class "mods" of 1960s and

1970s Britain (the group popularized in the cult film about post-war British youth, *Quadrophenia*) are also worth considering in this context – the mods being a group that was renowned for their tendency to use amphetamine drugs as part of weekend dance party escapes from otherwise mundane existences working at tedious office jobs or going to school (Hebdige 1979).

Another concern about the range of views on rave culture is that they are seldom understood as a range – with some authors offering simplistic representations of rave as a "culture of pleasure seekers" or of "escaping youth," without considering the diversity of perspectives on the group. A related issue, especially in mid and late 1990s writings on the topic, is that there has been little dialogue between these authors or their positions except for those embedded in Reynolds insightful, theoretical ponderings of the works of authors like Deleuze, Guatarri, and Adorno. More recent texts and articles by Muggleton (2000) and Bennett (1999, 2000; Bennett and Khan-Harris 2004) are more effective in this regard.

Approaching the Canadian Rave Scene

I have a theory that there is an inverse relationship between the vitality of a pop genre and the number of books written about it. Compared with the thousands of biographies, essay collections, and critical overviews that clog up rock's arteries, only a handful of tomes (academic efforts included) have addressed the dance-and-drug culture – despite the fact that it has been the dominant form of pop music in Europe for nearly a decade. I guess this theory makes my own effort here one of the first nails in the coffin. (Reynolds 1998, 390)

The apparent lack of research on rave culture in Europe – a disparity that is dissipating with the wave of books on the topic in recent years – pales in comparison to the dearth of work on the phenomenon in Canada. Only recently has rave been taken seriously as a Canadian youth subcultural movement, although most writing on the group is still confined to magazines and newspaper articles. To date, little academic work exists that examines the group with both empirical and theoretical rigour. That is to say, although there are studies on rave in Canada that document activities of ravers, especially drug use, seldom are research findings considered in a way that offers insight into, on the one hand, relationships between the broader social structures and circumstances that frame youth involvements in rave, and on the other, the meanings that youth give to their rave experiences. Even Tanner's comprehensive 1996 book on youth and deviance in Canada had only mass media reports to inform a cursory discussion of ravers, a group that still exists in the subcultural shadows of punks and skinheads in Canadian youth culture literature. More striking is a relatively recent discussion of rave in Canada by Vappu Tyyskä (2001) in her book *Long and Winding Road: Adolescents and Youth in Canada Today* – a discussion based almost exclusively on media portrayals. My goal in identifying these shortcomings is not to critique attempts to describe the rave scene (these authors were simply drawing on available evidence) but instead to imply that there remains a startling lack of empirical work for commentators of youth to bring into play. Of course, this lack of research attention might be perceived as a sign that this group has effectively maintained its underground status, as Reynolds noted above. This appears to be a dubious rationale, though, considering the mass media attention the group has garnered and the culture's now-recognized status as a major player in Toronto's youth entertainment scene. It is more plausible to suggest that a major youth cultural phenomenon has been overlooked in Canadian research circles – or at least by those concerned with linking cultural phenomena such as rave with the broader characteristics of Western societies into the twenty-first century. That said, the following section critically examines the limited existing work on rave in Canada.

Existing Research

One of the few rigorous studies of a Canadian rave culture was conducted by Tim Weber, when he was working with the Addiction Research Foundation (ARF) of Toronto, now called the Centre for Addiction and Mental Health (CAMH). In a preliminary report and subsequent journal article (Addiction Research Foundation 1998; Weber 1999a, 1999b), Weber (1999a) identified important background characteristics of the Toronto rave scene:

• The majority of those who attend raves are Caucasian, middle-class, and from fifteen to twenty-five years old.
• People attend raves because they like the non-judgmental atmosphere,

compared to clubs or parties, and they enjoy dancing and music.

- The most frequent drug used was cannabis, although several others are available and being used, including cocaine, crystal, ecstasy, GHB (commonly known as the "date rape" drug), ketamine, LSD, marijuana, and psilocybin.
- Most drugs were considered acceptable to use – the exceptions being crack cocaine and intravenous drugs – and it was generally agreed that alcohol does not belong at raves.
- Trends over time include that the average age of ravers has decreased; raves are now larger and more commercial; raves are attracting a more diverse following; and more people are looking to buy drugs.

Based on his research findings, Weber suggested that youth attendance at raves acted largely as a temporary challenge to authority – usually that of parents – in that most respondents were adopting a weekend identity while conforming to work and school related norms the rest of the week. Weber also identified how rave culture in Toronto was characterized by its tendency to contest traditional notions of gender, with females being less often treated as objects at raves than in other contexts.

Other work in the Canadian context by authors like Dubey (1996, 2000) and Luciano (1999) has similarly dealt with drug-related cultural activities in the rave scene, focusing in particular on the links between rave culture and drug use and abuse, the dangers of tainted (impure) ecstasy at raves, and the increased use of other types of potentially dangerous drugs such as ketamine, a.k.a. "Special K." A recently released technical report assembled by the Alberta Alcohol and Drug Abuse Commission (AADAC) is a particularly impressive Canadian study that was intended to inform harm reduction initiatives around youth drug use, but in doing so offered a comprehensive examination of the Alberta rave scene and culture (AADAC 2004). The information gathered over the course of the AADAC's research – information attained through interviews, observation sessions, and the use of a survey – enabled the authors of the report to describe the meanings youth give to the scene and to present demographic information about ravers.*

*Comprehensive work on drug-related aspects of raves has also been done outside of Canada by researchers like Saunders (1996) and Cohen (1998).

Other work, by Fritz (1999), Takahashi and Olaveson (2003), and McCall (2001), includes references to and discussions of rave in Canada as part of a more global discussion of the culture. McCall's work, which is especially noteworthy in this context because she engaged some of the key British theories on rave, acts as a departure point for my discussion of rave and politics in chapter five.

The Canadian Media and Rave Culture

In recent years, the Canadian rave phenomenon has gained notoriety through an influx of journalistic reports and commentaries. The nature of media coverage of rave, a topic pursued by Thornton in the British context (Thornton 1994, 1995) and Hier (2002) in Canada, is intriguing, with accounts tending to be aligned with one of two contradictory perspectives. On one hand, articles emphasized the "deadly" use of drugs at raves, moral issues surrounding a culture of youth that attends all-night dance parties each weekend to escape from reality, and concerns about the noise problems that rave parties create in residential areas. Consider the following panic-feeding headlines:

"Death and Crystal Meth" – cover of Hamilton, Ontario's *View* magazine, vol. 4, no. 50 , 23 December 1999

"Drug Called Ecstasy Remains Pillar of 'Rave' Dance Scene" – *The Record* (Kitchener/Waterloo), 9 March 1996, D4

"Rave Drug GHB Doesn't Mix Well: T.O. Club Goers Increasingly End Up in Hospital" – *National Post*, 9 March 1999, B4

"Richmond Turns Down Volume on Raves: Complaints from Vancouver Residents Led Councillors to Draft Tough New Regulations" – *Vancouver Sun*, 17 September 1998, B4

"UBC [University of British Columbia] Calls an End to All-Night Rave Parties: A Party on the Weekend Ended with Four Overdoses and a Home Invasion" – *Vancouver Sun*, 2 June 1998, B3

"Drug Chic Hits the Mall: The Buzz at Eatons – Ravers and Marijuana Aficionados Are Reading a Lot of Nudge, Nudge, Wink, Wink into

the Latest Advertising Campaigns Such As Eaton's, Roots, and
The Body Shop. The Companies Say It's A Non-Issue. Whatever" –
National Post, 29 December 1998, B5

"Study Says Ravers Risk Memory Loss and Other Brain Damage
If They Take Ecstasy" – *National Post*, 2 November 1998, D3

These messages/panics were reinforced by coverage in other print
and electronic media, such as *Maclean's* and *Time* news magazines,
and in reports on *20/20* and the CBC, as noted in chapter one.

    On the other hand, mass and niche media also tended to
revere the neo-hippie attitudes of the subculture, depicting rave as
an appealing, romantic, new age youth subculture (e.g., Bradley
1994; Landale 1998; McLaren 1998). Some commentators described
how rave music, dance, and atmosphere help one achieve a meditative state where social barriers disappear and a connection is made
"with a larger community" (Lehmann-Haupt 1995, 78). The drug ecstasy was described as "a capsule of Zen, promoting a state of open-
minded receptivity" (Reynolds 1994, 56). Headlines in this context
highlighted the "hip" and inviting aspects of the rave, while others
emphasized the positive contributions and aspects of this often stigmatized group:

"And the Beat Goes On, and On, and On: 'Sharing!' 'Hugging!' 'Back
Rubs!' 'Fun!'" – *The Globe and Mail*, 6 June 1998, D1

"Rave New World" – *High Times Magazine*, West, R. and S. Hager,
vol. 17, 1992, 8

"Raves Are All the Rage" – *Winnipeg Free Press*, 18 July 1994, 5

"Rave Culture All the Rage to 'Connect': Raves a Convergence of
Love and Music" – *The Toronto Star*, 14 July 1998, F1

"Raving: Techno-Hippies Preach Peace and Love amid Clandestine
Party Scene in Warehouses and Farm Fields" – *The Toronto Star*,
27 March 1993, K1

"Sacred Raves – These All Night Dance Marathons Look Like

Hedonistic Escape, But Raves May Just Be The Defining Spiritual Expression of a New Generation" – Lehmann-Haupt, R., *Yoga Journal*, May/June 1995, 76–81

These trends are consistent with work that describes the propensity for media to waver between commercializing and glorifying youth subcultures and stigmatizing them.* Researchers have also demonstrated how subcultural groups counter and challenge these mass-mediated labels and ideologies through alternative media forms. The existence of this resistance-media movement highlights the need to rethink conventional ways of understanding relationships between youth and the media. As McRobbie and Thornton (1995) argue: "every stage in the process of constructing a moral panic [as outlined by media scholars], as well as the social relations that support it, should be revised ... We argue that 'folk devils' [e.g., deviant youth subcultures] are less marginalized than they once were; they not only find themselves vociferously and articulately supported in the same mass media which castigates them, but their interests are also defended by their own niche and micro-media" (559).

In a general way, then, the often-contradictory journalistic portrayals of rave are only part of a mass mediated, intertextual story of rave – the story told in fictional and non-fictional books, movies, and television shows. In the next chapter, I present research findings from a study that was conducted to inform and amend these portrayals.

---

*For similar evidence in the British context, see Redhead (1997), Saunders (1996), and Thornton (1994).

At the rave party "Bittersweet" in Toronto, 2002
(from Dan Lauckner's photo collection)

Below: At the party "Bring it On," in Kitchener, Ontario, 2001
(from Dan Lauckner's photo collection)

Glowing "alien heads" on display as a vendor sells fruit, candy, chips, glowsticks, bracelets, and other rave-related paraphernalia at the "Slammin Sounds" rave in Toronto, 2001 (from Dan Lauckner's photo collection)

Top: The morning after the main party at the World Electronic Music Festival, in an old airplane hangar in Dunville, Ontario, 2001 (from Dan Lauckner's photo collection)

Middle: The morning after the main party at the World Electronic Music Festival in Sauble Beach, Ontario, 1999 (from Dan Lauckner's photo collection)

Bottom: The "idance" protest against a proposed anti-rave law in Toronto in 2000 (from Andrew McCallum's photo collection)

DJ Mistress Barbara at the World Electronic Music Festival in Dunville, Ontario, 2000 (from Dan Lauckner's photo collection)

Left: DJ Marty McFly in the zone, at the party "ha ha" in Buffalo, New York, on April Fool's Day, 2000 (from DJ Marty McFly's photo collection)

DJ Spock from Holland spinning at the "Slammin Sounds" party in Toronto, 2001 (from Dan Lauckner's photo collection)

Right: New Years Rave in Guelph, 1999–2000 (from Dan Lauckner's photo collection)

Left and below: The music, the DJs, and the times – schedules for all-night music at the "Foundation" rave party in Waterloo, Ontario, and at "Solid" in Guelph, Ontario, both in 1999 (from Dan Lauckner's photo collection)

This page: Dancing at the "Slammin Sounds" party in Toronto, 2001 (from Dan Lauckner's photo collection)

Left: Dancing in the streets, the morning
following a Hullabaloo "Happy Hardcore"
party in Toronto, 1999
(from Dan Lauckner's photo collection)

Above: At the party "Spectrum" in Guelph,
Ontario, 2001
(from Dan Lauckner's photo collection)

Right: Sticker sponsored by the Toronto rave magazine *Tribe* protesting the threatened ban on rave parties in Toronto in 2000. The protest, called "idance," was organized by the Dance Safe Committee and the PartyPeopleProject (from Dan Lauckner's photo collection)

Bottom: At the World Electronic Music Festival in Sauble Beach, Ontario, 1999 (from Dan Lauckner's photo collection)

At the "Silent Storm" rave
party in Guelph, Ontario, 1999
(from Dan Lauckner's
photo collection)

3
Doctrines, Disappointments, and Dance
Perspectives and Activities in the Rave Scene

To be modern is to find ourselves in an environment that promises us adventure, power, joy, growth, transformation of ourselves and the world – and, at the same time that threatens to destroy everything we have, everything we know, everything we are. Modern environments and experiences cut across all boundaries of geography and ethnicity, of class and nationality, of religion and ideology: in this sense, modernity can be said to unite all mankind. But it is a paradoxical unity, a unity of disunity: it pours us all into a maelstrom of ... struggle and contradiction, of ambiguity and anguish. To be modern is to be part of a universe in which, as Marx said, "all that is solid melts into air."
(Marshall Berman, *All That Is Solid Melts into Air*, 1988, 15)

Our most creative constructions and achievements are bound to turn into prisons and whited sepulchers that we ... will have to escape or transform if life is to go on.
(Marshall Berman, *All That Is Solid Melts into Air*, 1988, 6)

In his book *All That Is Solid Melts into Air*, Marshall Berman powerfully articulated how the interaction between individuals and structures in contemporary culture is both ambiguous and patterned – a "unity of disunity." This is a particularly compelling observation in light of the theoretical arguments made in this book; it reminds us to be attentive to the predictable ways that youth come to be involved in subcultures and use them for negotiating and confirming their identities – while at the same time requiring us to be sensitive to the various and often unforeseen features of youth involvements within a dynamic and evolving near-millenium culture. Paying particular attention to these patterns and ambiguities, in this chapter I present findings from the case study of rave in the Toronto area and am guided by two broad and intricately related goals. The first is to illustrate how rave was defined by its wide range of forms and characteristics – a range that existed simultaneously across the subculture (e.g., the various sub-communities who were affiliated with different genres of rave music), across the careers of individual ravers (e.g., the waning of idealism over time), and across the life of the Canadian rave scene (e.g., the scene's evolution from underground to mainstream to fragmented). The second is to "bring life" to rave by describing the culture from within, with particular attention to the perspectives, activities, identities, relationships, and commitments of the youth associated with it.

Setting the Stage: A Depiction of a Rave Party, a Study of Rave Culture

In many respects, a rave party is akin to a large nightclub or dance bar. There is a dance floor full of people; there is loud music with a heavy beat; there are flashing lights; there is a place to get refreshments; there is a DJ; there is a cover charge to get in; and it is nighttime. However, a closer look reveals notable differences that are fundamental to the unique character of the rave setting. The people at a rave are often males and females ranging for the most part from fourteen to twenty-five years old, which is much younger than at a typical club. The people are dancing, but unlike at most nightclubs, where people face one another dancing in social circles, ravers tend to face the DJ and make sure that each person has their own space to dance in. The music at a rave is much louder than at a typical club, so loud that talking to the person standing beside you if you are anywhere near the speakers is difficult. In the rave, there are usually two rooms with different kinds of music. In one room, the music has a beat that is much faster than the kinds of music played in typical clubs. "Techno," as this music is called, is entirely electronic and played at a frenetic pace of up to 200 plus beats per minute. In the other room, the music is typically slower than in the techno room, and is characterized by a meandering, meditative sound, and few lyrics. This music is known as "ambient." These two musical genres are both unique and quite different from popular club music, which typically has a medium and sometimes fast beat and significant lyrical content.

The flashing lights of clubs are often complemented at a rave by additional spectacular props, such as a mini Ferris wheel or rows of television screens showing colourful computer generated forms. Instead of alcohol, the refreshments served at raves are "smart drinks." These energy drinks are made in blenders at the "bar" and are full of high calorie ingredients, such as sugars and fruits (although in recent years the blurring between conventional nightclubs and raves has meant that alcohol has become increasingly part of the scene). The DJ at a rave usually manipulates two records that are played simultaneously, thus producing a unique musical mix. At most clubs, the role of the DJ is to play compact discs, adjust sound levels, and introduce songs. The cover charge at a rave is as high as fifty dollars and rarely less than ten dollars, much more expensive than the average bar. The rave party is usually just "starting to roll" – that is, reaching its peak attendance and beginning performances from the headline DJs – at about 3:00 AM and ends as late as 12:00 PM, not including the "after-party" that sometimes continues into the following evening at another location. A nightclub, on the other hand, usually begins to fill with people at about 10:00 PM and is rarely open past 3:00 AM. Also, the nightclub is a stable location, whereas the rave space changes each week. Common rave locations include abandoned warehouses, former nightclub locations, and secluded fields. As noted above, however, over the course of the research for this book, from 1995 to 1999, the distinctions between raves and night or dance clubs became increasingly hazy. Rave locations have become more predictable and clubs have taken on many characteristics of raves, especially their increasing play of alternative techno music.

Data collection for this study of rave culture took place over a three and a half year period, starting September 1995 and continuing up to March 1999. The research was conducted in several southern Ontario locales, including Hamilton, St. Catherines, Kitchener, and Guelph, and with Toronto as the focal point. Various collection strategies were used in the research, following what Willis (1978, 196) called a "cluster" of methods. These are outlined below.

Participant observation, the primary means of data collection, was undertaken during two research phases. Phase one was from September to December of 1995, at which time I attended seven raves, and phase two from December 1997 to April 1998, when I attended six raves. All participant observation sessions took place in Toronto, the centre of the southern Ontario rave world. I also spent time at rave record stores in Toronto, sat in on "rave radio" sessions at two campus radio stations, and attended a community meeting in Toronto that was focused on drug issues related to rave culture. The meeting was attended by health-care professionals, police, parents, educators, and a few members of the rave community.

Over the course of the research, I conducted in-depth, open-ended, semi-formal interviews with various members of the rave scene (n=37, 10 females and 27 males). The interviews derived from (1) a series of networks that were established with groups of ravers in Toronto and some outlying areas, and (2) contacts with individuals who were part of the scene or were previously part of the scene. This diverse sample allowed for an analysis of the rave "scene," rather than an analysis of a relatively closed raver group within the scene. The interviewed ravers were individuals who either currently or previously were "regular rave goers" (as opposed to subcultural interlopers). Most of those interviewed had occupations outside the rave scene. These included students (several from colleges and universities, and some from high schools), tattoo artists, a journalist, a graphic designer, a nurse, coffee shop workers, record store workers, and a bank worker. The amount of background information I attained from the interviewees varied according to the type of agreement that was reached prior to the interview. For the most part, those interviewed grew up in middle-class families, were attending, attended or planned to attend post-secondary institutions, were "white" (one black male, one Asian female, and one Asian male were also part of the sample) and were between the ages of eighteen and thirty-five (most interviewees were in their early twenties). The interviews varied in length from forty-five minutes to four hours. Several follow-up interviews and discussions also took place. Ongoing e-mail discussions about rave-related topics continued with several of the respondents. Interviews were held in various locations, including coffee shops, respondents' work places, university cafeterias, campus radio stations, respondents' homes, and rave-related functions. Other comments from ravers were drawn from two of the Internet newsgroups where I recruited several ravers for interviews.*

I emphasize that this sample is not meant to be "representative" in the traditional positivist sense since the purpose of the research was to study the various *forms* of raving, the types of involvements, and to assess generic concepts (following the work of Corbin and Strauss 1990). This argument for studying forms and processes is not intended to preclude being attentive to the demographic characteristics of ravers. Rather, the suggestion is that for research focused on gaining insight into rave *culture*, attending to some aspects of the characteristics and histories of the individuals involved, while relevant, is not as central as the study of the forms and processes – i.e., the what, where, how, and when of culture (Prus 1987, 1996a, 1996b).

"Underground" magazines (hard copies and Internet-based), flyers advertising rave events (which often included statements about the rave promoter's philosophy and the theme of the upcoming rave party), Toronto "rave radio" shows (usually campus radio), and independently-produced "live" recordings of raves (these tapes usually included comments by the DJ) were also considered in the analysis.

The Life World of Rave: PLUR, Pro-Technology, and Pleasure: Rave Perspectives, Doctrines, and Ideals

The philosophies and ideals that were espoused and sometimes practiced in the rave scene can be grouped into three broad and interconnected categories of intention: (1) to support and uphold values related to "peace, love, unity, and respect," known as the PLUR ideal; (2) to support the use of high technology as a means to gain pleasure and empowerment; and (3) to seek and experience pleasure as an end in itself. Although ravers in this study did not all sub-

*For more details on the methodological issues underlying work on on-line cultures and on the on-line component of the research, refer to a forthcoming *Canadian Journal of Education* article I wrote on the topic: "Ethnography, the Internet and Youth Culture: Examining Social Resistance and 'Online-Offline' Relationships."

scribe equally to the rave doctrine, and although ravers' interpretations of rave doctrine also tended to change over time, this doctrine
at least tentatively guided the actions of those encountered over the
course of the research.

Theme 1: Peace, Love, Unity, Respect (PLUR)

The essence of the rave movement (and it is a movement on not only a
global but cosmic scale) can be well summed up in four simple letters;
PLUR. For those who haven't already heard, PLUR stands for Peace,
Love, Unity and Respect. (newsgroup discussion, anonymous, 13
November 1995)

It's all about breaking down barriers, losing preconceptions, expanding
the mind and feeling the vibe. (interview, male raver and university
student, 1995)

The unity of good people is the only scene that exists. (interview,
male raver DJ and tattoo artist, 1995)

The MC kept saying, "Peace, love and ecstasy. There's no attitude with
us here. We are good vibes." (field notes, 4 November 1995, words of
MC talking to ravers at party promoted by Good Vibes company)

The "peace, love, unity, and respect" (PLUR) ideals and philosophies
were evident in all areas of my data collection. While comments like
those above were commonplace in the study and are the crux of the
data presented in this section, PLUR-related views and expressions
were also articulated in the rave flyers that advertised the parties.
Since these parties were often organized around certain rave-related themes, the flyers offer insights into widely consumed versions,
symbols, and interpretations of the rave doctrine. Often included in
these flyers were descriptions of the "rave philosophy" as expressed
by someone from the promotional company who organized the rave,
and a rave party-title that reflected these views. Some ravers and
promoters referred me to these flyers to help explain the ideals of
the rave movement, thus affirming that the flyer at least tentatively
reflects or guides the perspectives of some ravers. The following are
examples of the names and themes of some rave parties:

Unification of a Peaceful Nation (rave put on by Aqua promotion company, 4 November 1995)

Love, Peace, Unity, Hope: Take an Oath to Your Essence (rave put on by Eden promotion company, 27 October 27 1995)

Good Vibes (rave put on by Good Vibes promotion company, 4 November 1995)

Many ravers described explicitly how these philosophies – PLUR and related ideals associated with "expanding the mind" and "breaking down barriers" – can be brought into everyday life. One raver, a male university student, referred me to excerpts from an underground rave magazine article that he was co-author of to help explain these ideas:

It [raving] is learning about the nature of the environment around you, which includes everything from paying attention to your body to learning to care for the planetary environment ... It's up to us to pick up the pieces of a post communist/capitalist, us/them "dominator" culture world and transform it into a "partnership culture world" of global unity with respect for cultural diversity. It can be done, but it will take work, most likely all of our lifetime. But when all is said and done we will leave to our children an intact planet which will be on the road back to prosperity ... The choice is ours now, as we gather together in our dance ritual to build the feeling of togetherness, instill courage and break down emotional and mental barriers. (*Subterrane* magazine, 1995)

Other interviewees explained how lessons derived from their rave experiences can be applied outside the rave: "It [the rave] introduced me to a lot of new people who take this 'vibe' from the rave and they exercise it as a practice in their life. Where they try and avoid preconceptions of people on the street and they try to generally be nicer to people ... I think that is the real good that can come from raves" (interview, male raver and university student, 1995).

The PLUR philosophy manifested itself in various ways at raves that I attended. At no time did I feel physically threatened at a rave. Often people would smile or offer me a cigarette. When people would bump into me accidentally, they would often say "sorry" and smile – a contrast to the macho norms of many nightclubs. Other times, ravers performed friendly acts, such as giving away marshmallows, cotton candy, and homemade stickers with cartoon depictions of ravers. Another created a cooling spray that he would offer to ravers who were hot and sweaty from dancing.

I did not sense that this "vibe" (meaning collective feeling of positive energy) was present at all the rave parties I attended, however. It seemed to depend on the extent to which people who were attending the rave were actually "committed ravers" and whether or not I was at a rave or rave club, such as the now-defunct Industry Nightclub mentioned in chapter two. For example, sometimes people would come to the raves because the bars were closed and they still wanted to "party," not because they had any interest in the rave community or respect for its norms. As noted later in this section, major tensions existed within the rave scene about whether outsiders should be discouraged from entering the scene.

Theme 2: Technology and Futurism

The music is amazing. A lot of people blast it [put it down] because it's technological and it's not produced by live musicians and that it takes away from the talent involved. But technology can do things to the music. [It can] make things that people can't make ... Some of the melodies and baselines that are intertwined are above the human level. They have a consequent effect on the people who listen to it, a really intense effect. (interview, male raver and university student, 1995)

Underlying the rave doctrine was a reverence to and celebration of technology, and an implicit and explicit belief in "progress through technology." Rave music is generated by computer or synthesizer. Rave parties are advertised over the World Wide Web, and were advertised this way before the recent and rapid rise of the Internet. Rave flyers often include references to the future (e.g., names of raves included "Progress Forward" and "Knowledge in a New Dimension") and included futuristic-looking computer images (e.g., images of outer space or science fiction–like cities). Perhaps the best example of rave's positioning as a pro or high technology culture is the increasing occurrence of virtual on-line raves. Although virtual raves take many forms, they generally include live video of DJs playing music that can be viewed on the event's Web page and an accompanying chat room where virtual ravers can interact. One of the innovators of virtual raves in Toronto, a DJ and university student, explained the event in the following invitation that was sent to a rave newsgroup:

Well, I'm doing it again. In the summer I did a live-to-internet "concert" of sorts from my basement. I'm doing the same thing this Saturday, but from my residence on the Ryerson Campus ... I'll be playing a live set from about 11:00 to 12:00. The whole thing is going out via Real Audio [a computer software programme for audio-downloads – the programme can be downloaded for free off the Internet], and my entire residence is invited as well, although from historical experience they're pretty apathetic about expanding their music tastes. If you're interested in coming, send me an email. If you can't make it out, then you can tune in online ... [The last time I held this event it was] held in conjunction with a party in my residence with public terminals setup so that people at the party in residence could chat with people online. About 120 people listened online, with about 200–300 people through my livingroom during the night. (from the now defunct Web site http://www.io.org/~andrewm/pots)

In addition to virtual raves, there are an increasing number of rave Internet newsgroups where people discuss issues related to the scene, and exchange news about upcoming parties. One Toronto-based newsgroup, known simply as "techno.ca," is an explicitly pro-technology list, as the newsgroup's Web page described:

The technolist was originally conceived as a forum for discussion of techno music and its related culture. There were no restrictions placed on what should or shouldn't be talked about on the list, in an experiment to see how discussion unfolds and to see what topics would be of interest to list members. Once the list had matured somewhat, it was put forward that it should be a place to discuss not only the music and culture that we love [rave culture, electronic music], but also pretty much anything pertaining to technology, its influence on our lives, and its role in changing the face of humankind ... This isn't a rave discussion list, nor is it really meant for debating merits of one religion over another or the perpetual drugs discussion that inevitably comes up. Use your own discretion when posting, but keep in mind that there are a number of very opinionated people on the list who love a good argument and will back it up with intelligent debate. Be prepared to defend yourself and your arguments. (introduction to the "techno" discussion group, from www.techno.ca)

One of the creators of the list discussed how his group of raver, DJ, and promoter friends came to start a Web site that built on the techno.ca concept:

"Tom," and "David" and myself [rave DJs in the Toronto area] started out the chat room basically, where you send messages back and forth, and we decided we wanted to expand on it by making a Web page. The purpose of it is basically to connect people. We found that there's companies and people that are doing things that benefit themselves. We decided we wanted to get friends together. There's a lot of talent in the scene ... I've been pretty lucky to make some contacts but not everybody is ... [On the Web page] will be the distribution of records, an online radio station, [and we will] have people sponsor our show ... The main thing is to get people connected ... We are also going to have real audio capability so if you want to listen to a record or mix tape before you buy it [through the work access of this raver at a Toronto record store] then you can. (interview, male DJ and record shop worker, 1998)

For many ravers interviewed in the study and participating in newsgroups, the use of high technology was a central part of their leisure and occupational lives. Through the Internet, for example, they listened to and bought music, and booked DJs for upcoming rave parties; or they might be working in the computer technology sector.

Rave-related fiction books, which were read by some members of the rave scene who I interviewed and were sometimes discussed on raver newsgroups, often included storylines focused on the positioning of rave-related culture (e.g., cyberpunk culture) in futuristic societies. For example, *Disco 2000* (Champion 1998) is a book of short stories about rave-related culture at the millennium with plotlines focused around an "end of the century party" (i.e., rave) that will take place on New Year's Eve 1999. The back of the book jacket included a précis of the stories' underlying themes that

illustrates and illuminates connections between technology, futurism, and excess. The book is described as "an anthology of cult fiction set in the final hours: The party starts here ... with a cast of crazy
scientists, nomadic DJs, fetish queens, conspiracy theorists, killer
ants, graffiti artists, gangsters, convicts, cult leaders, Netheads, re-
plicants, religious maniacs and ballroom dancers ... It's the last night
of the millennium and anything could happen ... Around the globe,
TV broadcasts end-of-the-world predictions of crackpot professors
and in every city parties are going out of control." It is important to
note in this context that "pleasure through excess," which is intricately and purposefully related to the technology cultures described
in these literatures, is the third philosophical theme that emerged
from the research.

This focus on and fascination with technology was inextricably linked with the raver interest in advances in communication –
particularly the Internet. In this way, the Toronto scene influenced
and was influenced by global rave developments. For example, interactions on this rave "world level" were evident through a Web site
called "hyperreal" (http://www.hyperreal.org), a site often referred
to by interviewed ravers. This widely available information source –
which at the time of the research had both European and North
American based sites – offered insight into rave culture that was
consistent with the data I was gathering locally through interviews,
local zines, local Web sites, and newsgroups.* This connection was
explained on the site as follows: "[Through] online connections;
information is exchanged, a loose community evolves. Technology
fosters communication: Interacting on the internet helps bring us
together" (http://www.hyperreal.org/raves/spirit/plur/PLUR.html).

Pro-technology and pro-future views were not equally integrated into the everyday lives of all ravers. Although some ravers
actively and vehemently supported these views, including the tech-
no.ca raver group, others emphasized aspects of rave culture that
had little to do with technology when discussing "why they raved."

* Not all ravers I interviewed were necessarily informed by this site – some
ravers, such as techno.ca members, were likely more web-savvy or web-reliant
than some others – although at least indirectly this site appeared to be an
important reference for understanding rave philosophy as it existed in Toronto
and abroad.

For example, a portion of those interviewed focused exclusively on the pleasure aspect. Others pointed out that being pro-technology should not mean "losing humanity." As one male DJ suggested: "When I spin records and put together my sets, doing things that a band couldn't do, I acknowledge that all I'm doing is arranging their hard work. They made the music. I mix it. Realizing this, DJs shouldn't get their heads too big" (interview, male raver, DJ, and tattoo artist, 1995). Despite these sentiments, ravers, whether they were conscious of it or not, were inextricably linked to high technology in the music they listened to, the designer drugs they took, the images they were exposed to, and the themes of the parties they attended.*

Theme 3: Pleasure and Excess

The best [rave] that I've been to was the Science Centre rave [a rave that was held in Toronto's Science Centre] ... .We smoked on the way there. I know we did shrooms [magic mushrooms] in the parking lot. I was doing good on that for awhile. And then I did acid, a couple of those, and that took me up until about six o'clock. It was so much fun. I can't even express to you how much fun it was. It was the best night of my life and I've had a lot of good nights. It was everything, everything was there. Like when I think of drug use I think it brings you back to childhood almost. Everything seems simpler, everything seems brighter and so good. Going there [the Science Centre] you had a chance to play on all the exhibits, and that was a lot of fun 'cause you're so messed up and everything seems so interesting ... It's so friendly. They had a Lego land, that was so cool ... The music was really good, there were like four different rooms, a ton of people. But the things that's best about raves is there's no "attitude." Like if you go to a bar, there's so much attitude, you've got your little honies and their trying to pick up and the guys are horny as hell looking to pick up and their testosterone's going and they're thinking "Let's get in a fight tonight." There's none of that [at a rave]. (interview, female raver and university student, 1998)

*See Gilbert and Pearson (1999) and Wilson and Atkinson (2005) for more elaborate discussions of links between dance music culture and technology.

The rave is an exceptionally conducive space for decadent, indulgent "partying" – in other words, for using usually illegal high-energy amphetamine drugs, and for uninhibited all-night dancing and socializing. This emphasis on the joys of unrestraint and excess was evident in discussions I had with many ravers about their favourite raves and typical "good rave nights." A standard rave night for one female university student is evidence of this:

First, pre-party at someone's house ... This would include getting dressed up as fun as we could, smoking weed, and listening to music ... Then at around twelve or so we would go to the rave ... we always drove so shuttle buses [that take ravers from a central meeting point to a rave party] weren't in the agenda. We would scope out the party, find our crew and whoever they were with ... do the introductions because there were new people coming in every weekend – the family we had grew weekly. We usually already had our E and other substances but if we didn't we would find one of our dealers and get what we needed and then we would take our drugs and dance the night away into the morning light. Usually we would judge how good the night was by how much "rug we cut" [dancing we did]. Then we would go to an after party and do more drugs and if it wasn't any good we would think of something to do like go to the airport and feel the natural bass the air-planes would make as they flew over the car ... or hang out in front of a huge religious building and discuss whatever topics came to our minds ... deeply. Depending on who we were partying with, we might go to their house and chill there until we came down. There was also a peri-od where we would go home, shower and then go to the Sunday night party at the Subway Room and do more drugs till Monday morning ... It's weird to think how much I actually did now that I look back at it. (interview, female raver and university student, 1998)

Others interviewees focused exclusively on the relation-ship between rave parties and drug use:

[On a typical rave night] meet my friends early and try and be at the party around midnight or so, ingest psychedelic drugs immediately before entry if possible. Listen and enjoy the music until (a) I get so tired and I want to leave or (b) wait until my ride or friends I'm with leaves. (inter-view, male raver, campus radio DJ, and university student, 1998)

I basically got involved in raving because I like drugs a lot. I still see it as a place where I can do drugs and not worry about things. (interview, female raver and university student, 1998).

For the most part, however, interviewed ravers indicated that the pleasure aspect was only part of the broader philosophy behind raves. That is to say, excessive partying was ideally not to be an end in itself, and should be viewed as a sensual and symbolic escape from and a form of subtle resistance against the "*un*PLUR" aspects of everyday living.

Introductions to the Scene, Learning to Rave
Interviewees offered several reasons for their initial interest in attending raves. These included that it is a relatively safe place to do drugs; it is a place where the drug experience is often optimal; and they were encouraged by a friend who was already involved in the scene. Some indicated that they first came to be involved in rave culture only because they liked the music, but then found themselves swept up by "raver attitude": "I have come to really enjoy it. There's hope in that community, there's very little violence. I saw the way people came closer together and the way you could expand your mind" (interview, female raver, 1995). Others explained how they were looking for some sense of community and heard that raves were a welcome place for "outsiders," people who were on the margins of social groups in high school. Yet, according to many ravers this reason for attendance has become less applicable in recent years since the rave scene has became increasingly "cool," mainstream, and sometimes cliquey – and ironically, therefore, a less open and accepting cultural space.

Interviewees often found out about raves from other ravers because of common interests in music, dancing, or drugs (the process of "seekership" according to Prus 1994):

Initially I was listening to dance music ... because I love to dance. I've always loved to and I met a friend, who is now my best friend, and we had a common interest in drugs. We smoked drugs the first time we met, and we got along great ever since, and he introduced me to the style of music, the techno music that they play there, and then ... he took me to a smaller event that happened during the week the first time I went, and it was called "Explode" … I went a couple of times and I liked it so much that I wanted to go to the real thing and I went to my first rave … and it was a great time and I went ever since. (interview, male raver and university student, 1995)

One raver discussed the dynamic of rave recruitment in high school: "In a high school it's easier also to get people to go, because you're in classes with them, you trust them, you're on a different level with them. There are a lot of people recruited into raving through high schools and I think that has produced an element where there's younger and younger people going to raves" (interview, male raver, 1995). Still others are drawn in by the ever-increasing media promotion of rave events: "Don Burns [whose radio name is Dr. Trance – a DJ with a rave-based radio show on the Toronto station Energy 108 at the time of the interview], the reason he has his radio show was because he wants the people to hear the music, he wants to expose as many people as he can. It's not his position to educate the people about the rave scene. A lot of people go to raves because of that" (interview, male raver, 1995). As discussed later, many ravers expressed concern about how this mass recruitment of ravers has impacted "the vibe" of the rave scene.

For the most part, people I spoke with seemed to acquire rave-related values, and PLUR, in particular, from people they knew or people they had met in the scene. Although not all ravers acquired or adopted these values, according to the "mature" ravers I spoke with, neophytes to the rave community are ideally educated by more experienced members of the scene. Interviewees offered several approaches for educating neophyte ravers:

If you are educating, as a mature raver, you could tell them your experiences as a mature raver, as a person who has done it and as a person who understands … you talk about the vibe, you talk about the social differences between the clubs [no violence at raves, not the same cliques]. It's not just the music, it's the magic, the magic of a rave. I can think of several parties where I have simply walked into a room and been overcome with a feeling of total abandon, "all right, go out, have a good time, it doesn't matter." (interview, male raver, rave underground zine publisher, university student, 1995)

You tell the people what it's about. You tell them to try and leave people their space at the raves and go and dance and you can be in your own little world if you want to but try and go out and meet people because maybe you will meet a mature raver and he will greet you and it will start a snowball where you go out and you talk to more people and you know more people and eventually you lose some of your preconceptions. (interview, male raver and university student, 1995)

The Internet and newsgroups were also common places for neophyte ravers to seek information about rave philosophy and etiquette. Below appears a newsgroup commentary by a Toronto raver and promoter about rave etiquette in the scene. This exposition usefully identifies renowned rave traditions, emphasizes which traditions are "good and bad," and why, and which ones have become lost or de-emphasized:

When I first started partying I tried E right off the bat. It wasn't necessary. It may not have been right but at the same time I was taught about the messages and the hugs and the candy and about bringing a blanket to sit on and about dressing the way you feel like ... Along the way I think I forget to tell others about PLUR and what not and I stopped bringing candy and I stopped offering messages and I became a dirty old man but maybe it's time to revert back to the happiness of yesteryears traditions ... I think its time to look at our rave traditions and see which ones have a place and which ones we shouldn't be teaching the newcomers. [For example]:
[1] Bringing Candy
    • Gives you sugar and energy
    • More sociable than a smoke and your breath don't stink afterwards
    • Comes in cool packages and shape and sizes
    • Great for sober people and people on heavy drugs too!
    • Cheap to give away and makes you and the receiver feel good when you do. Tell your friends to bring more and more and always bring some yourself give them away. GOOD TRADITION
[2] VICKS Inhalers
    • THE JOKE IS ON YOU HA HA
    • VICKS used to contain ephedrine (i.e., speed) in Canada and the smell was there to prevent the gag reflex when snorting the shit, heating them up with lighters was to get more of a speedy hit, basically they've been a placebo for years already and we're just crack heads for

using them. Maybe the time has come to drop them.

[3] Soothers

  • For when you grind your teeth when dancing. GOOD TRADITION

[4] Running Shoes

  • Comfy easy to wear and dance in and when you step on someone's toes they don't hurt like fucking combat boots. GOOD TRADITION

[5] ROAR [Right of admission refusal]

  • A sign to all that trouble is expected

  • Redundant if you have big security dude(tte)s

  • BAD TRADITION. Maybe we're giving ourselves a bad rep by advertising this one.

[6] HUGS

  • Relax you

  • Feel Good

  • Great way to be introduced to someone

  • GOOD TRADITION

[7] WET NAPS

  • Relax you

  • Feel Good

  • Great way to be introduced to someone

  • GOOD TRADITION

(male raver and promoter, quoted from newsgroup discussion, October
1998)

Tensions in Rave: A Popularized Scene and a "Maturing" Raver
Although the rave doctrine appeared to be widely known among
both long-time ravers and relative neophytes, there were disagreements and tensions surrounding the application of these perspectives. This was particularly true as the rave scene was increasing in
popularity, with more people regularly attending rave parties – a
phenomenon fuelled by the actions of many rave promoters and DJs.
This primary ideological tension was between those who felt that
rave should be open to and inclusive of all willing participants, and
those who believed that rave should exclude those who do not
understand or support the rave philosophy. Underscoring the latter
view was a belief that in a fast-growing scene, neophyte ravers are
not receiving the proper education about rave philosophy and etiquette, learning instead from cursory descriptions they might have
read in popular media reports. The following raver articulated this
ambiguity:

I feel two things. I feel its bad that there are so many people coming into the scene now so quickly that there is not time for the mature ravers, the people who have been doing it for a long time, to take them under their wing, and teach them what it's all about. And they come and they create their own culture, "vibeless" if you will and it's like a big club, a big dance party – it's not a rave anymore. And there's a lot of people out there, like the mature ravers that feel lost, and they feel like they have been robbed. At the same time if those people who are going to these parties are there for the right reasons, not just to do the drugs but for the music, then that is good, because that is the point ... It's kind of like a double-edged sword. (interview, male raver and university student, 1995)

On one side, then, are ravers who felt that with more people in the scene there is greater potential for positive social change. Two of the ravers that I spoke with drew on their understandings of witchcraft to explain this possibility: "I'm a witch. I do rituals with large groups of people. We raise a bunch of energy and we send it to something. We use that energy for something ... whether it's to heal a particular person or place on the planet to try and create something to happen, in a larger political context. I see all these people at raves and they have this intention of community. They're raising all this energy. If somebody could just take that a step further and that could be really powerful" (interview, female raver and nurse, 1995).

On the other side were ravers who were less tolerant of this influx of "uneducated" outsiders who attend raves with less progressive goals in mind: "I like everything about it [the rave parties] except the increase of bad attitude and the 'fear' that I sense at parties when hard-hittin, gangsta style ginos show up lookin for a piece of ass and maybe a fight" (from Internet discussion group, anonymous, 1995). Interviewees also suggested that rave was receiving too much "vibeless" publicity that was intended to attract large numbers of youth consumers to raves, not to promote the rave philosophy per se. An excerpt from a Toronto-area magazine called *Club Scene* demonstrates this trend:

Those of you who already experienced the rave scene know exactly what I'm talking about. For all the rest who do not, I make it my personal goal to introduce and inform you about the existing Toronto rave companies, what to expect from them and encourage you to attend.

Now, I myself have overheard all the crazy rumours circulating about raves. I would like to assure everyone that raves are not completely composed of crazy freaks that only come out after midnight. In fact, ravers are mostly people who have a deep passion for underground music, good clothes and are generally looking for something to do on a Saturday night. (Kinga 1995, 14)

Many ravers were critical of this sort of publicity because it appeals to people who are "looking for something to do on a Saturday night," not necessarily those who are looking to expand the mind and support the community.

Other problems associated with the mainstreaming of rave were embodied in discussions about the opening of rave clubs. Rave clubs, which are distinct on a number of levels from conventional raves (e.g., conventional raves are not in stable locations and are not held regularly, while rave clubs have weekly, often alcohol-licensed events) were a source of friction for those who felt that these clubs exemplified the negative movement from an underground rave culture or movement to a mainstream, "sell-out," dance culture. Other ravers were more upbeat about rave clubs, however, arguing that they are a great place for "mature" or older ravers to continue to enjoy electronic music and a friendly, if not quite "ravey," atmosphere with people their own age (twenty-five years plus).

I addressed this tension about "club" raves versus "real" raves, and more general issues to do with subcultural authenticity and rave, in the following field note excerpt written following a night when I attended a club rave and a conventional rave – the club rave until 4:30 AM, the conventional rave from 6:00 AM until 9:00 AM:

Chris [a raver who had been in and out of the rave scene since the early 1990s] and I went initially to Industry [the club rave] and then to the "Clockwork" rave party put on by the promotion company PHYRL at the Masonic Temple (an abandoned temple that was now rented for events – acknowledged to be a great venue). Both of these venues were high energy. However, Industry, where we stayed until about 4am, still had a bar feel to it. People were facing the DJ, dancing like at a rave, but few people were really lost in the dance beyond cheering at a good song (many people were drinking which no doubt played into this). There were only a couple of people I noticed doing the "flowy" rave dancing which I've only seen at "authentic" raves. People were still enjoying themselves – a "vibing bar" as opposed to a "vibing rave."

At the Masonic Temple, where we arrived at about 6am, there was a place where people could paint pictures and put them up on the wall, there were psychedelic projections on the wall behind the DJ. Even the music was more ravey (the name of the DJ was Neuromancer, a DJ in from Sweden, playing hard techno), and people were obviously feeling the music, dancing in that fluid, almost break-dance style. Chris suggested that the difference between the places was likely a combination of atmosphere and venue, but also underlying drug use. Chris explained that "really fluid" dancing at 7am is usually an indication of being wired on ecstasy. Chris also said that this party was almost exactly the same as the parties he used to go to a few years ago in Toronto. For him the lack of development and change actually symbolized a *lack of authenticity*. The idea that raves appeared to be the same as they used to be, but because it's 4 years later, it CANNOT BE THE SAME as it used to was the point I took from that. I've heard this kind of sentiment before from ravers who appear to be "on the way out" of the scene and had become disillusioned. (20 December 1997)

Crucial here is the overlap of rave politics, subcultural authenticity/evolution, and raver interpretation. The tensions surrounding the loss of authenticity in the scene which are played out in both the "club versus rave" debate and in the concern that rave culture is too stagnant are interestingly mediated by the interpretations of ravers who, depending on their relationship to the rave scene at any given time, tend to assign contradictory meanings to the relationship between subcultural evolution and authenticity. A vicious circles emerges where, for some ravers, rave parties should not change to rave clubs or they lose authenticity, and yet for others, rave must change or evolve into something else or it loses its authentic positioning as a hip, dynamic culture.

Other ravers expressed concern that the popularization of rave culture has led to political tensions associated with the business side of the scene – tensions that are manifested in the competition among promoters (for rave attendees) and DJs (for gigs). One raver explained how the politics have "killed the vibe" for him:

Once you've lost the magical, the "wow" of raving, then you start to understand the politics and there are politics. And that's because at the

same time people are in there having a good time there's people making money from it. And so long as somebody's making money, they're
getting power and politics and power go hand in hand, I guess. Right
now in Toronto, if I were to speak specifically, there is a rave company
called Pleasure Force that was the staple of raving for a long, long time
and every party they'd throw, just put their name on the flyer, 2,000
people guaranteed. And they started to raise the ticket prices and that
created a price war where other companies who wanted to throw parties would either have to match or lower their prices, I guess. Then,
with the expansion of raving, there's so many more people now, you can
have two parties every weekend. There's a lot of different companies,
some that are big, some that are small. If someone plans a party on a
specific date, they'll say "we don't like those people, we'll throw a party
that weekend to spite them and that has happened a couple of times."
(interview, male raver and university student, 1995)

Others expressed similar sentiments:

The second money comes in, it sucks the spirituality right out of it.
(interview, female raver and tattoo artist, 1995)

The politics generate a lot of animosity between certain people especially in the scene and it reflects in the attitudes of the ravers. When
the big people are having problems, that compounds the little people
feeling bad that the big people are having problems. (interview, male
raver and university student, 1995)

Over the course of the study, the topic of rave politics became more pronounced in interviews and newsgroup discussions.
Respondents often voiced their concern that "money-hungry" promoters were putting "pro-rave" promoters out of business. For example, pro-money promoters were sometimes accused of throwing a
rave on the same night as another company in an attempt to bring an
insurmountable loss to the pro-rave, non-profit promoters, who were
usually students. These sorts of tensions were particularly evident in
newsgroup discussions between rival Toronto rave promoters. The
following letter posted to a Toronto rave newsgroup, written by a promoter for the Destiny rave promotion company, was a response to a
series of public accusations made by another promoter that had been
spread through newsgroups and other rumour mills in the Toronto

rave scene. The issues had to do with the promotion of drugs at raves, unethical advertising practices, and DJ and venue booking practices. The controversy related specifically to a New Year's Eve event. New Year's Eve is a time of high tension for rave promoters because almost all of these companies tend to throw raves on this same night. In many cases, "teams" of three or four promotion companies will collaborate, pooling their resources to throw one rave party.

Dear Rob:

I am writing this letter to you in an attempt to find out why you find it necessary to continue your "con" job on the party people of Toronto. I told [you] from the outset that I was not interested in getting involved in mud slinging or low-ball tactics when it came to our events this New Year's, but you continue to make these your main focus of your marketing campaign.

1. [In response to an accusation that Destiny advised Skydome not to rent to the "accuser's" promotion company] You know as well as I do that we NEVER attempted to book Skydome and NEVER even spoke to them regarding your party in any way. I'm sure if you had any sort of relationship with them at any time you could easily confirm this fact.

2. [In response to an accusation that the advertised DJs for Destiny's New Year's Eve event would not actually perform at the event] If you have spoken to the various agents of our DJs as you say you have, then you know for a fact that we have purchased flights for Eric Davenport and Anne Savage for New Year's. Anne is playing Ottawa and Toronto the same night and Eric is doing the same with Montreal ... .[and] 3. You know that Czech [a well known DJ from Vancouver] is playing our afterparty (as stated on the flyer) ... [and] 4. You know Mark Oliver is exclusive to us on New Year's, not you. Mark has been attempting to remove his name from your line-up ever since you placed it on your pre-flyer without his knowledge.

5. [In response to the accusation that the rave promotion company is linked with the sale and promotion of drugs] Finally, any attempt to link our event with [the drug] crystal or any other illegal substance is the most ludicrous thing I have ever heard. If you had been in the scene from the early years as you claim to want to take it back to, you would know that Destiny led the way with anti-crystal information on our flyers, in our mail-outs and even in newsletters handed out to all

those who attended our events. Maybe you should look at your own financial backing before making suggestions in this direction.

I hope that you take what I have said to heart and don't assume it is some sort of attack on you or your company. This is not my goal. I only hope that you decide to remove yourself from spiteful and hurtful marketing practices that help nobody and only damage a scene we have all worked hard at creating and maintaining for so many years.

Thank-you and Sincerely,
Ryan Kruger
Destiny Productions (public letter posted on newsgroup,
17 December 1997)

There was more general evidence to suggest that *some* promoters do deceive and defraud. A notorious instance was a rave called Ravestock that was being advertised for May 1999 at Canada's Wonderland entertainment park in Toronto. Tickets for this event could only be purchased through a Web site. Follow-up by other promoters in the Toronto rave scene who telephoned Canada's Wonderland because they were suspicious of this unknown promoter revealed, apparently, that this was a money-making hoax. Ravers were subsequently warned via radio – on the Global Groove Network radio show in a commentary by Don Burns, a.k.a. Dr. Trance – and on newsgroups to not buy tickets.

Generally accepted and widely used pseudo-deceptive advertising practices include hiring international DJs, particularly from Europe or at least from outside the Toronto area, who are either inexperienced or are not prominent artists in their home country or city. These DJs are then marketed as "big names coming to Toronto" since there is inherently more subcultural capital associated with attending raves with DJs from other countries, particularly when the DJs are from Britain, Chicago, Detroit, or New York City because of these cities' links with the origins of the rave scene. Since this practice occurs in other cities and scenes as well, some local Toronto DJs who were interviewed joked that it was sometimes easier to "get a gig" outside of Toronto or internationally than in their home city.

Some disgruntled DJs talked about raves where promoters "disappear" during the party (i.e., leave Toronto and not return) without paying the people hired to work, including DJs. A New Year's Eve rave held on the Canadian National Exhibition (CNE) grounds called Skyhigh put on by the promotion company KIND – dubbed "unKIND" by some ravers after the event – gained notoriety for this. A brief newsgroup exchange in January 1998 about the incident follows:

Well, go figure … After a great party (albeit, not as well attended as some individuals would have hoped for) and a number of fantastic performances (Alex Patterson's set was mind blowing) it seems the inevitable has happened. All those that performed at SkyHigh, New Year's Eve have been stiffed. I'm not (and won't) go into detail as I refuse to feed the rumour machine – however it is extremely uncool (and unKIND) to issue everyone bum cheques because "investors took the money at the door and disappeared." I'm sure you'll all be hearing more about this in the days to come.

[Response to above note] Guess what I found out recently? That [the] promoter of KIND … has done exactly the same thing in his past business ventures as he did this New Year's Eve. That is, get in a business, make some money, then fuck everyone else around him … The cheque that I was paid with (and every other DJ/act) was for an account that was closed. And the bastard gave it to me with a smile on his face … he even looked me in the eye. I guess he has a lot of practice in lying … Anyway, if anyone ever runs into [him], or knows him (he has somehow "disappeared") kick him in the shins for me.

The Waning of Idealism

These various tensions surrounding the popularization of the rave scene contributed to a "waning of idealism" (Haas and Shaffir 1991) for many ravers over their careers as subculture members. A comment by one DJ and tattoo artist who has been raving in the Toronto scene since the early 1990s exemplified this sentiment:

When the rave scene first started here, there was only one promotion company, called Chemistry. They were great. It was cheap. They had parties with swimming pools, soap suds, crazy stuff. Once the scene got publicized, they had one last great party and then got out. They were great parties. People weren't getting baked and running around like madmen. When Chemistry folded, I think it was the beginning of the end for the rave scene. As for the future of the rave scene, if it keeps going the way it's going, the scene is gonna be sickly. Black-eyed fourteen year olds sniffing powders and going home to the wrong address under the guise that they're having a good time. (interview, male raver, DJ, and tattoo artist, 1995)

Similarly, a female interviewee talked about how her perspective became tainted as she gained more knowledge of the scene over time:

When I first started going to raves, I was on top of the world. I insisted that everyone I knew who hadn't experienced it were missing out and had to do it in order to find true inner peace. It was a purely spiritual release for me (the drugs were a major part of that) and I loved the people and the whole philosophy that went along with it ... The music was like I've never heard anywhere in my life and the way it made me feel was so intense that I had trouble describing it but was constantly trying. It was fresh and new and very exciting and I wanted to be a part of it. Now I think that my ignorance was bliss. I know a lot more about the politics of the scene and I have seen many people who seemed like amazing people at the rave when they're on all kinds of E but have turned out to be very different outside. I saw a lot of hypocrisy and bad people feeding bad drugs to innocent young ones. I found that as it was turning into a fad – people were losing the meaning of the ritual and it was being tainted by those who were trying to make a profit out of it. I became more attached to the musical aspect of it and stayed away from the "scenesters and partiers." Now raving does not mean much to me at all. I care only about the music and few parts of the scene ... I do believe there are still some very special parties that still go on with the same philosophies that were present in every person (or so I thought) that is in attendance ... but they are few and far between. (interview, female raver and university student, 1998)

The most common changes in perspective, however, in-volved interpretations of drug use. Many experienced ravers explicitly described the process of getting involved in ecstasy use and other drug use, becoming caught up in the drug, and then becoming disillu-sioned as they experienced the problems associated with overuse.

The Symbolic Use of Dance, Music, and Drugs: Activities at the Rave

The primary activities in raves are listening to music, dancing, and doing drugs. Below, I describe the various ways that people learn about and perform these activities, illustrate how these activities are linked to one another, and show how they are viewed and evaluated by subculture insiders.

Music

For me, listening to the music is the single most important thing. For example, if you take away the drugs and the dancing, people would keep on loving the music. People who love the music would keep on raving without the drugs. And if you took away the flashy lights, people would still go. If you took away all the weird clothing and perhaps even all the good feelings and good vibes associated with raving, people still would go because they love the music. I like the music and I think that is the most important thing. But I like the other things, too – don't get me wrong. (interview, male raver and university student, 1995)

Once in the rave, listening to music is the one activity that never stops. However, people consume the music in several different ways, depending on the desired mood. At many of the earlier raves I went to (all of those attended in 1995), there were two different mood rooms defined by their distinct styles of music and atmosphere. The slower ambient music in one room was associated with relaxing or "chilling out," and faster techno music in the other room, with intense dancing:

I walked into the "chill-out" room. There was a black cloth hanging down over the entrance to the room. The music was what is called Ambient – it is akin to some of the "New Age" music that is very popular. Ambient still has a strong beat, but it is much slower and more flowing, not intense and heavy-beated like Techno music. In the room, the smell of marijuana was strong. The room was filled, but not with people dancing. People were all sitting on the floor or on easy chairs or couches that were dispersed throughout the room. The people were alone or in circles. Basically everybody was smoking something, either a cigarette or a joint ... After buying an Evian at the smart bar, I spotted an easy chair that I strolled over to and sat down ... Also in the chill-out room, in full view of my easy chair, was a unit of televisions. When I say unit, I mean that it looked like a solid structure which had several TVs built into it. There was a total of 6 televisions, 2 across and 3 down. There were cool-looking computer-generated images on the screen. (field notes, 14 October 1995)

The music in the straight ahead room (the "hardcore" room) was hard techno or a variation thereof (characterized by a heavy and fast beat). Although the beat was always very fast, there were a couple of "mixes" where the beat picked up to a frenetic pace. These were crowd favourites [I later learned that this buildup was often meant to help the raver get a euphoric feeling or "rush" from the drug ecstasy]. The music was very very loud, pumping out of large speakers that surrounded the dance floor. People were dancing all over the place – the dance floor, beside the dance floor, everywhere. (field notes, 21 September 1995)

Many of these music genres have evolved and fragmented from the early 1990s to the present. For example, "techno" music – one the original forms of electronic, fast-paced, heavy-beated, rave-related music – has segmented into a more melodic electronic genre known as "trance," and into even faster-beated types known as "hardcore," "Rotterdam," and "gabba." In fact, many rave party-themes are intricately related to the party's dominant music genre. These musical divisions are inseparable from the emergence over time of different sub-scenes and related taste hierarchies. For example, some interviewees described how older, more experienced and "sophisticated ravers" tend to listen to more soulful house music and more subtle, "minimalist" techno music. These same ravers are also, apparently, more likely to prefer ecstasy as their drug of choice. Members of the techno.ca newsgroup tended to have (or at least talked about having) these "urbane" subcultural tastes. The arguably less refined and usually younger crowd (fourteen to eighteen year olds) were believed to prefer listening to music with an ultra-fast and unvarying beat known as "happy hardcore," and using the more intense, dangerous, and less expensive amphetamine drug crystal meth. Experienced ravers explained how, over time, one learns to appreciate the nuances of "less raw" techno music styles, while becoming less enamored with the speed and power of more intense forms. The "sophisticated" and "less refined" groups were not empirically this distinct or divided, however. In fact, many interviewed ravers crossed over between scenes, and enjoyed various genres of rave music.

Drugs

There was a clear relationship between drug use and music consumption. Smoking marijuana to "chill out" or relax was preferred by many ravers when listening to slower, ambient music. Ecstasy, and to a lesser extent crystal meth, were the amphetamines of choice when it came to fast dancing. Interviewees described how certain techno music tracks were structured around the effects of a drug. For example, some tracks include a "buildup" stage, where the beat gets fast and faster, followed by a "plateau" stage, where the beat remains consistently fast. This structure is apparently conducive to an optimal euphoric feeling or "rush" for those on ecstasy.

There were mixed views on drug use at raves. Most ravers felt that the use of ecstasy and marijuana is acceptable if you are educated about them. A health counsellor in Toronto who distributes information at raves about the dangers of drug use and the need for responsible and educated drug use for those who choose to use drugs referred me to an information guide describing the goals and objectives of the "Toronto Raver Information Project" (TRIP), a community service programme that focuses on educating the rave community. The following are passages from that guide:

Objective [among others]: To increase ravers' knowledge regarding drug use harm reduction practices.
Health Risk Profile: Drug use is common among this group of youth, however the drugs commonly used are of the "non-addictive" variety: LSD, MDMA (ecstasy) and Psilocybin. Crystal Methamphetamine (speed) is also used and is addictive. Alcohol, opiates, barbiturates, and crack cocaine are not currently used within this community. Opiates, however, are increasingly used within the rave scene in other localities. While the drugs of choice for ravers may be currently mostly non-addictive, they do present other risks for harm. For example, LSD, MDMA and Psilocybin can increase tactile sensitivity and reduce emotional barriers between people. These effects in themselves may

reduce the likelihood of practicing safer sex, especially in combination with the difficulties youth experience negotiating safer sex when high.

The guide went on to stress concerns about the quality of the drugs at raves, and the potential dehydration and overheating that have accounted for drug-related deaths at raves. Ravers themselves often talked about the importance of "trusting your [drug] source."

This need to be educated and responsible about drug use was often emphasized by interviewed ravers. An example of responsible drug use is the practice of being someone's "E-Mother" (i.e., ecstasy mother or guardian) – meaning staying with someone and watching over them for their first experience with the drug. As one female explained: "My 'E-mother,' she would sit me down and explain things to me [before a rave], and explained that no matter what happened I could count on her" (interview, female raver and university student, 1998).

Despite these practices, it was clear from the interviews and from Internet discussions, as well as sensational mass media reports, that irresponsible drug use in the scene is the major concern:

Around 9am, at *Delirium* [the name of a rave party] in Toronto, one of the girls who was dancing collapsed. She had taken something, possibly E and ended up flat on her back. By the time I got there, people were attending to her, but nobody really knew first aid. Not even the security guard that was present. So I stepped in. She was in bad shape – her eyes were rolling back in her head, she was semi-conscious, her mouth was bleeding, supposedly from biting her tongue. We kept her conscious and warm till the paramedics arrived. She slowly drifted back to coherence, but her vital signs were worrisome. They took her to the hospital. As one of her friends was leaving, I said to her "I hope you'll be a good friend and not allow her to end up like this again." I admit, I am against drug use – I have never touched it, I don't smoke or drink, but I don't condemn others if they do. All I strive for is education. My message to all of you is this – you better believe how much it hurt me to see this seemingly mature individual in such bad shape, all because of a bad trip. I've now seen firsthand what the risks of recreational drug use are, and frankly they scare me. I'm not saying all of you should quit drugs cause I know you won't. But please, please BE CAREFUL. Don't end up like this poor girl did. Thank God she was alright, but she could well have not been. The safest drug is your own pure, internal E. The energy and adrenaline that comes from within you and radiates to all those around you. (newsgroup, anonymous, 1995)

While acknowledging that unsafe drug use in raves is relatively common, most interviewed ravers de-emphasized this aspect of the rave, pointing out that the links between drugs and rave culture are too often the focus of exaggerated mass media reports. Veteran ravers I spoke with also recognized that their current views on drug use were, in large part, gleaned from their own and others' positive and negative experiences with drugs:

From my perspective being older and such I can honestly say I have done it all and reached every limit possible and sometime[s] to the point of almost checking out. It is sort of a "did that, done that" attitude now. I mean now to me drugs are just not that important to me and I know no matter how much I do, I will always fall short of what it used to be like with me, so I say why bother. Kids that "abuse" drugs are young and I was too, when I was hard-core. Everyone runs around and thinks it is the coolest thing going on to trip your ass off, or tweak or roll but in time even those kids one day wake up and go "is this really worth it." I see people who are letting drugs control them tell me "I'm fine, serious" and I them and I say "Dude you're not, trust me." If they could only see themselves through my eyes. In short, drugs should be treated with respect and caution. I mean I have lost friends to drugs and I have almost lost myself to them. Drugs also stagnate your life growth. When you are abusing too much, life just passes you by and at that age you are living the best days of your life, it would be much nicer to live them and enjoy them at least sober most of the time. Some people might be surprised and really enjoy it. (comment in newsgroup discussion, male raver and promoter, November 1998)

Despite these concerns, many interviewed ravers also commented on the *benefits* of drug use at rave parties when they're done safely:

Besides the ecstatic feeling that you get from it ... it breaks down barriers. It breaks down preconceptions, it makes it easier to meet people, it creates an ecstatic feeling more intense than anything most people have ever experienced, and you couldn't experience it without the help of the drug. And if you're experienced with it, rather than just going with it because it is so overwhelming your first couple of times, consciously you think about certain things while you are doing it. You think about how it changes you and how you feel while you're on it as opposed to how you feel when you're not and you try and take the feeling that you get when you're high and relate it to your own life. Do you really need social barriers? Do we really need the defenses that we have and would life be better off if we didn't have some of the defenses that we have? Would it be easier to meet people, easier to communicate? It all comes down to communication because there is a lack of communication obviously in our society. (interview, male raver and university student, 1995)

Ecstasy is a drug that minimizes your problems because you are in such a happy, lovey state. It keeps you awake and energized. It doesn't make you hallucinate, but it gets you really into sensation. So if you're at a club, with really loud music, house music, the sensation of music is way more intense, the lights are way more intense. (interview, male raver and coffee shop worker, 1998)

Many of these pro-ecstasy interviewees were highly critical of what were perceived to be the unfair and often-uninformed labels put on drug users and drug use, specifically the assumption that all ravers are drug abusers. Sometimes underlying this critique was the view that those who unconditionally denounce drug-users are hypocrites:

Anything in excess can be life threatening, including coffee. It depends on how you do it. The bad aspects of the drugs is that people can't control themselves and like the feeling so much, they have to do it all the time. That's like anything, alcohol, computer addiction. My dad needs a drink every night before he goes to bed. My friends get wasted three or four nights a week at the bars. Once a week I use E and have a really positive time. I go to school and have a good job. Who's the bad guy here? ... You can go spend forty dollars on ecstasy and do it and party the whole night, or you can spend fifty dollars, get loaded [on alcohol] and get violent, act like a retard and get sloppy all night. (interview, male raver and coffee shop worker, 1998)

Drug use was viewed in various other ways as well. Some ravers enjoyed the drug-induced feeling and the rave party, but were sensitive to and concerned about the stigma associated with drug use. For example, an interviewed female university varsity athlete was concerned about her teammates finding out about her raving and, for this reason, actively hid her raver identity at school. Another university student and raver indicated that she was becoming more interested in the campus bar scene as she got older – and now interpreted drug use as still enjoyable, but anti-social in the context of her university-based peer group.

Dancing

Although most ravers described dancing as a sensual and aesthetically pleasing activity whether combined with music and drugs, or just with music, the dance experience and performance were sometimes viewed in contradictory ways. On one hand, respondents discussed how dance is empowering and liberating:

At a rave you can dance in your own little world or you can dance with someone else or you can dance with a group of people. A lot of the people who go to the raves love dancing and that is why they are there. But that is like an offshoot of the music. Because after you listen to the music for a little while, the dance becomes an outward expression of how you interpreted the music" (interview, male raver and university student, 1995).

Experienced ravers I spoke with described how one tends to acquire a sense of ease in one's dancing over time as a raver. This process of becoming in tune with the rave – with feeling "the vibe" – was described by one respondent who outlined how people become more relaxed with the music and dancing as they go to more rave parties:

When you go in originally, most people prefer the faster music because it's different, and they'll stay in that stage for a couple of months, and once they realize what is going on, they'll start to groove a little more which is a more relaxed [dancing] style. After awhile you can really tell. And then you start to develop you own style. A lot of the older ravers you can tell because instead of being like a club style dance, it's really like a flow" (interview, male raver and university student, 1995).

On the other hand, it was apparent that dancing was often an activity "on display," both for good dancers who enjoy being watched and for novice dancers who are concerned about being watched. Although only one interviewee (a male raver who was a long-time member of the scene – and apparently a good dancer) admitted that he likes dancing "for attention," the positioning of some ravers "on stage," literally and metaphorically, at more recent rave parties is evidence that the display of dance prowess is desirable for at least some ravers. This seemed to be inconsistent with the purist view of rave dancing as an activity for escaping reality or "exploring one's essence," and unveiled a contradiction and tension in rave dance culture, since these overt dancing displays are often linked with concerns about the popularization of the rave scene, including, for example, the increased popularity of rave clubs that sometimes feature "go-go" dancers. The most highly criticized example of mainstream rave-related dancing is the well-known Toronto dance-television show Electric Circus (shown on Canada's music station MuchMusic and on CityTV), which often features renowned local and international rave DJs who "spin" music while dancers perform for the camera. According to many interviewees, the show is an extreme example of the vanity, superficiality, and cheesiness that are hallmarks of the negative mainstreaming of the scene.

Of course, embedded in these findings which show both the meanings that ravers give to the varied activities they are involved in and how these activities are interpreted at the distinct stages in a raver's career, there are also issues of identity and "identity-performances." They are the subject of the next chapter.

4
Making Impressions, Making Investments
Identities, Relationships, Commitments, and Rave

the capacity to define a situation as one sees fit and to make a role as one chooses is far from unlimited, for the individual continually bumps into others, their definitions, and their purposes. (John Hewitt, *Self and Society: A Symbolic Interactionist Social Psychology*, 1994, 177)

All the world's a stage and all the women and men merely players (William Shakespeare, *As You Like It*, 2.7.139–40)

In his classic book *The Presentation of Self in Everyday Life*, Erving Goffman uses the theatre as a metaphor to help describe how people play roles and present themselves in distinct ways depending on their situations and audiences. Key to this "dramaturgical" lens on social life is the notion of "impression management," a term adopted to illustrate how people strategically manage their behaviours and appearances in the hope of impressing others. An important nuance to this framework is that people tend to alter their roles and identities as they become more familiar with and trusting of their audience, and as they gain more experience in a social group. Identity changes are not only observed by audiences, of course. They are also internalized by the actor who is more or less invested in the performance as time passes.

　　While this metaphor and perspective, in itself, is a compelling guide for this chapter's discussion of the types and evolution of identities, relationships, and commitments within the rave subculture, it also coincides with understandings of subcultural style and symbolic expression that emerged and developed in the work of Dick Hebdige (1979) and Hall and Jefferson (1976) at the cccs. That is to say, style is meaningful for subculture members who are managing their impressions and physical appearances for their peers and for outsiders (such as adults), as Goffman would argue. At the same time, as Hebdige would argue, style, when understood as a symbolic means for expressing dissatisfaction, is a political form of identity work.

Trying to "Feel the Vibe": Identities and Reputations in the Rave

As with all social groups, and despite rave's idealist goals of "losing preconceptions" and "breaking down barriers," impression management was a central concern for those in the rave subculture. Various players in the rave scene negotiate identities and manage reputations as part of their occupational and cultural role in the scene. To be regularly employed by promoters, DJs – the celebrities in the rave scene who control the music and in part the mood or vibe of the party – must establish reputations as being technically proficient at smoothly mixing records ("beat matching") as well as being emotionally "in tune" with the audience so they can inspire highs and lows without over or underexerting dancers and listeners. Similarly, it is important for promoters to establish their ability to throw a party that has a good location (e.g., a unique, well-decorated location with reasonable acoustics, a large dance area, and a sufficient "chill-out" room), interesting props (video screens with intriguing images, dry ice or bubble machines, "sensual areas" where ravers can, for example, paint pictures), and excellent DJs. These issues are especially evident in the style-related identity negotiation and development of ravers themselves, as I demonstrate in the following section.

Looking the Part: Comfort and (Symbolic) Style in the Rave

Adidas (the athletic apparel company) clothing appeared to be the label of preference. Many people wore Adidas shoes, Adidas jackets and Adidas pants. Other apparel companies were also evident, usually Converse or Nike. However, the apparel was generally "old style," meaning clothing that is (or appears to be) several years old. For the most part, the clothes worn were very baggy, shirts not tucked in and loose pants. Although many other ravers did not wear "old style" Adidas apparel, most still adhered to a "nostalgia" look, with older looking golf shirts (long and short sleeve), sneakers of any sort (old and new), and baggy pants (jeans or cords). For the most part males and females dressed in similar ways. (field notes, 21 September 1995)

Various styles and looks were adopted by those who attended raves, including the "return to childhood" look, the "sporty" look described in the field notes excerpt quoted above, the "outrageous costume" look, the "psychedelic look" (e.g., tie-dye shirts, colourful head-bands, small sunglasses), and the "nothing special" look. Although the meanings that ravers assigned to these various looks, both their own and others', usually included references to "openness, accept-ance, and uninhibited self-expression," more extreme identities and styles in the scene, particularly the candy-raver identity or style – a radical version of the "return to childhood" look – created some ten-sions among those who viewed these styles as short-term strategies to get attention, not representations of a commitment to PLUR and the rave movement.

Some interviewees were emphatic about the symbolic meaning of the clothes they wore. The "sporty" style was often con-sidered to be a dancing-style, while the neo-hippie look (tie-dye shirts) embodied the PLUR philosophy. The "childlike" look symbol-ized a temporary return to innocence for some ravers, a meaning consistent with these ravers' interpretations of the rave as an es-cape. This look for many female ravers included wearing pigtails, a baby pacifier in their mouths, and a "school girl" skirt. Males might also have pacifiers, wear bright colours, and in many cases wear baggy pants (a.k.a., "phat" pants) and tee-shirts with cartoon pic-tures or phrases or words that are meant to be funny or silly. At raves and raver hangouts, such as certain record shops and coffee shops on Queen St. in Toronto, I observed male and female ravers carrying teddy bears. One young female who I saw at two raves looked to be around seventeen years old and wore a white skirt, a white shirt, and a tin foil halo designed so that it sticks up over her head – an obvi-ous attempt to represent the "angel-like" innocence of a child. Another female raver explained her "return to innocence" look and what it means to her: "When I go to a rave, I have a little kid persona. I take 'Jezibel' [the name of her rave persona] out to play. I dress in a school girl outfit. [At this point the female raver began to speak in a 'little girl's' voice, saying silly, funny, childlike things about raves. Then, returning to her normal voice,] the child is very liberating ... there is potential for these liberating acts in the rave scene. You have to exorcise your demons" (informal interview, female raver and tattoo artist, 1995).

Candy Ravers: Tensions Surrounding an "Ideal Type"
The subgroup of ravers that have adopted an extreme form of the childlike-style and persona are labelled "candy ravers" by the rave community. Although candy ravers are only one group in the diverse rave scene, they are an intriguing case study of a raver subgroup that has, in the opinion of many ravers encountered in the study, become "too into" their rave role. In general, males and females who are affiliated with this group adopt extreme childlike props as part of their costume, including sparkles on the face, plastic toys and bracelets, glowsticks, and bubble-blowing kits. While I saw variations of this look and these props at all raves that I attended, the candy raver style is the dominant style at raves that feature the genre of electronic music known as "Happy Hardcore" – a fast-beated, upbeat music, often with a young female voice accompaniment. In Toronto, this subgroup was most often associated with raves put on by the promotion company Hullabaloo, a company run by, among others, a well-known happy hardcore DJ called "Anabolic Frolic." The following excerpt from a flyer for a Hullabaloo rave titled "Foreverland" demonstrates some of the views of this subgroup: "Dress up and get ready to return to the world famous *Hullabaloo* atmosphere as we present you a very special party. Remember, once you grow up, you can never go back! ... No drugs, thugs, markers, attitude or frowns. If you feel you can't contribute to the crazy *Hullabaloo* spirit, then stay away!! Happy ravers only!!" (17 April 1999).

Many who I interviewed found the candy-raver identity to be "try-hard" and irritatingly childish: "These kids with their glowsticks and their sparkles. My friends and I look at them being all 'so into' their glowsticks and their toys and think 'ya, right'" (interview, female raver and university student, 1998). One raver expressed his mixed feelings about disliking candy ravers because of his commitment to the rave philosophy of "respect and acceptance":

As a raver am I expected to feel the overriding sense of unity and thus support for portions of our "scene" that I personally find repugnant ... Keep in mind that the way that everyone makes fun of Ginos across the board is very very similar to how people make fun of Candy Ravers ... I personally have yet to decide whether Hulla's [Hullas are the candy ravers who attend the "happy hardcore" music raves put on by the rave company Hullabaloo] are my ultimate dream or my ultimate night- mare. Candy ravers add colour to what might otherwise be a very dark and bleak scene, however at times I can understand the beauty of black. Candy Ravers are a riot to watch and a lot of fun at parties but on the same token it calls into question the integrity of the whole thing, are they really this happy? Are techno snobs really intellectual? Do trancers have any soul? Or the bigger question, does it matter? ... Is the concept of PLUR just that a concept or is it ultimately expressed by Hullas? (newsgroup, male raver, January 1999).

Another raver offered insight into the evolution of rave clothing, and how a distorted nostalgia for the "original rave scene" of the 1980s and early 1990s has been played out in the candy ravers' style:

In the progression of "raves" into this whole "candy raver" thing, the def- inition has changed. When I went to raves [in the early 1990s], there were nice people dressed oddly. Now you have what is termed "candy ravers" because they go out of their way to give you stuff (candy) and dress like kids. They used to wear Dr. Seuss hats and etc. They didn't try to con- fuse people into thinking they were 3 [years old]. While the PLUR aspects of the rave scene have not been lost, the imagery that surrounds it has. It's mutated into something rather humorous. Even before that, with warehouse parties (and I don't mean a rave thrown in a warehouse – I mean it like it was meant in the 80s), they didn't even dress like those crazy ravers from "back in the day." (newsgroup, male raver, 1998)

Comfort Zones and Rave
Just as the ravers seemed to become more in tune with their activi- ties as they gained experience in the scene, so too they seemed to become more comfortable with their identities and appearances within the subculture over time. The long-time ravers I spoke with

suggested that as they gained more rave-related experience, they did not see a need to "show off" their raver status to others:

At my first rave I thought I had to have a costume of some sort and after that I just went and didn't worry about it anymore because I realized you don't have to dress a certain way to be a raver ... I don't have any special clothes that I wear to raves. I don't go crazy with my hair or do anything wacky. I just go and enjoy myself. There are people who go all out in terms of costumes and that sort of thing ... and that's one of the neat things about it – you can't tell how long someone's been raving based on their costume or based on their outward appearance or how much they understand about raving based on their outward appearance. There are some people who dress differently because they think this is part of what they should be doing. (interview, male raver and university student, 1995)

Others suggested that the rave is a place where people can be themselves without feeling ostracized: "Tamara came to the interview wearing sparkles on her face and wearing a short top that appeared to be made out of a towel. She said, 'This is what I'll wear when I go to a party ... I love that once a week you can just be accepted and dress free.' Clearly, Tamara felt free to dress a little outrageous other times, but at raves this was culturally accepted and encouraged" (from field notes following interview with female raver and university student, March 1998). Tamara went on to explain how she made her shirt out of "terry towel" because it is comfortable to dance in "when you sweat and everything" and it feels "soft and fuzzy" on the skin – especially when you are on the sensual ecstasy drug. Others discussed how they would make unique and fun outfits for parties. A female raver and university student who I interviewed in 1997 would often make clothes so that she could match them with her dyed hair – bright red at the time of this interview. This was evident in a follow-up interview where her hair had been dyed jet black so she could wear "more formal" looking black and white clothes with her hair colour. A male interviewee and journalist talked about wearing "cool" second-hand clothes like a "bowling shirt with someone else's name on it" or "old Adidas track jackets." More optimistic ravers suggested that while outrageous raver "uniforms" – symbolic expressions of openness – were celebrated, they were not required to "fit in." Less optimistic ravers felt that some of those who attend raves are not as accepting of these unique looks and styles. Tamara also talked about one time when she went to the washroom at a club rave: "there were two other girls in there who I could see in the mirror were looking at me like 'she's so weird.' It bothered me and it didn't. I go to raves to get away from that, but that doesn't happen very often" (interview, female raver and university student, 1998).

Overall, and while raver style was not emphasized as a method for making public statements – as it was for punk rockers, for example – there is clearly a sense that clothing was both a homologous expression of rave values (e.g., be yourself, be comfortable, be free and innocent for a night) and a display for peers. Of course, and as mentioned throughout this chapter, there were also divisions in the rave scene over music preferences that at least partially defined the identities of specific style or attitude groups (e.g., the link between happy hardcore music and candy ravers). However, this passage from "neophyte" and sometimes "try-hard," to "authentic" and more comfortable, to mature and experienced, and often cynical, appeared to be a consistent developmental process.

Feeling and Sharing Energy: Relationships and Bonds in the Rave

The thing that I like most is the vibe that you get from the people. It is an immeasurable feeling that is very difficult to describe. You can feel it if you recognize it just by walking into a room full of people where the feeling exists and it can be described from my point of view as a total release from preconceptions ... it's all in your reaction, if someone was to bump into you at a club, they would expect you to turn around and apologize to them and they would threaten you with violence. But if you bumped into someone at a rave where this vibe exists, they might turn around and introduce themselves, apologize to you for being in your way and then smile at you and ask if you are having a good time. (interview, male raver and university student, 1995)

The relationships in and around the rave scene are intricately connected to the underlying "vibe" that ideally is the impetus of the rave party. This section outlines the types of bonds that people in the scene have with one another, the ways they develop these bonds, and the implications of these relationships.

"It's a gathering of like-minded people": Developing Bonds in Rave Culture

Many ravers indicated that they had initiated and solidified friendships through shared rave experiences. Two ravers and DJs who I knew of – one was interviewed – were housemates who had met through DJing. Another raver indicated that he had made his best friend at a rave where they talked initially about their shared musical interests. A female raver explained how the intimate experiences she shared with people at the rave will stay with her forever. These relationships were also evident from the snowball sample that evolved from the interviews, as some of those interviewed referred me to friends they had met at rave parties. As one male raver put it, "It's a gathering of like-minded people" (interview, male raver and DJ, 1995).

This raver/DJ's statement is particularly insightful and useful in this context because it implicitly acknowledges that friendships in the rave scene emerge and are maintained because of shared interests, and not necessarily or exclusively because of a mystical, religious, or spiritual bond that some pro-rave commentators have alluded to. Moreover, the extent to which relationships were maintained appeared to be related in many cases to the longevity of the shared interest or activity. This understanding sheds light on why the newsgroup friendships that were formed around music and technology appeared to be ongoing and intense. For example, friendships forged through the techno.ca newsgroup included not only ravers who regularly met to attend raves, but also people who had raved in Toronto, moved away, and then remained part of the newsgroup so that they could stay in contact with techno-friends from southern Ontario. This also provides some insight into why several interviewees described how their drug-inspired friendships were often transitory, a point elaborated on later in this chapter.

Race, Gender, Sexuality, and Age in the Rave Community

To some extent, the bonds people formed at the raves they attended appeared to transcend racial barriers. While the raves that I went to were populated predominantly by "white" youth, with some minority presence, there was no apparent animosity or segregation, and certainly no violence. An experienced raver that I spoke with suggested that there was a large contingent of minorities at raves that he had been to. He attributed this large cross-section of people to the "open mind" philosophy of the rave community:

It's the province of minorities: there are many black people, Filipinos, a lot of homosexual people, at raves a great many more than you would find in any cross section of people. Going along with raving, the lack of prejudgments and the lack of preconceptions makes it easier for minorities to be accepted and to find their own place in the rave scene which is good, and it makes them feel comfortable. I've got a lot of black friends that rave ... the combined culture makes it so that as long as you like the music and your comfortable with what everybody else is doing, you'll be accepted. (interview, male raver and university student, 1995)

All I can say is I'm surprised that such a person is able to tolerate the cosmopolitan, open nature of the bona fide rave scene. (one of many Internet newsgroup responses to a racist comment made by a participant in a rave newsgroup discussion, 15 November 1995)

Subterrane, an underground rave magazine that one interviewee published, provided a specific statement on this acceptance: "As a group we are incredibly diverse. We are multi-racial, multi-ethnic, multi-talented ... In many respects we are the results of the goals of the 60's. We have learned to interrelate, communicate, and party with each other across lines of race, gender, class, and sexual preference ... We come together for a ritual such as a full moon rave on a remote beach."

Race was seldom the focus of conversation except in discussions about the unity of the scene, as in the above quotations. Although most of the formal interviews were with what I perceived to be "white" youth, those minorities who were interviewed were equally focused on the rave as a PLUR space, and did not discuss racial tensions. For example, the interviewee who defined himself as "Black Canadian" responded to an e-mail interview question about his parent's socio-economic background in the following way: "It's not your parents that are important. It's your own status. How you identify with society. That's what rave culture is more and more about. The identity of self. Either by hiding in the rave scene garb or using it to stand proud and saying you are an individual" (interview, male DJ and former university student, 1998).

This kind of response was reflective of most "still optimistic" ravers' perspectives on the rave scene as being a place where there are no preconceptions, or at least none that are overt. This is not to suggest that these tensions do not exist in the scene, only to indicate that in the observations and interviews conducted in this study, rave culture appeared to be a place of conditional empowerment for any marginalized groups, and particularly for youth who defined themselves as outsiders in high school.

In more recent discussions, some ravers suggested that the "jungle" music scene was more racially divided, it being a scene and musical style that is more explicitly associated with reggae and rap music cultures – cultures which are generally associated with their Caribbean and urban African-American roots, respectively.* In my earlier research, however, done before the rampant fragmentation of rave culture into various somewhat distinct music scenes, this kind of division was not evident. Even in the later stages of my research, I saw no obvious racial divisions such as obviously segregated race-related cliques and crowds when I observed jungle music rooms at raves. However, I did not attend any jungle-music-only parties. It would thus appear that issues of race should be considered in future studies that focus more specifically on the fragmented late-Canadian rave scene. This is particularly important to consider because, although racism and racial segregation were clearly against the rave doctrine, the overall lack of discussion about these topics might also be interpreted as meaning there has been a relative silence about these potentially hidden issues, or ignorance of them.

Sexuality was often referred to in conversations about the openness of the rave scene, but was seldom discussed in any depth. From the few newsgroup discussions on the topic and from probing in the interviews, it appeared that ravers emphasize the importance

---

*It would be remiss to not acknowledge that these forms of music have both been incorporated in ways that have sometimes weakened these associations, a point discussed by authors like Lipsitz (1997). In an article I wrote with Ben Carrington, we explored related issues around conceptualizing race and dance music in subcultural theory (Carrington and Wilson 2004).

of accepting people with all backgrounds and orientations to the rave scene, but acknowledge that the "gay dance club crowd" was seldom integrated with the mainstream rave crowd except when certain DJs drew a more diverse audience (apparently the early Toronto dance scene in the 1980s was extremely integrated, as discussed earlier). The following newsgroup participant made an interesting perceived distinction between the cultural values associated with the different scenes – with the gay scene apparently focused more on fun and hedonism, and less on the progression of music:

I used to love gay House (music). A while back I used to frequent a night called "Joy" in Toronto. Then I got really tired of gay house and the gay scene. I got tired of it because gay house isn't about pushing the limits of music, it is more about pushing the limits of hedonism. But if you are really into gay stuff, go to the Church St. gay ghetto in Toronto. On Church between College and Welsley and look for flyers. There are tons of gay parties every weekend that are more or less unknown by the "raving" population and they always get good turnouts and bring in well known international DJs. I never understood why the gay and straight scenes don't mix too much in Toronto. Jr. Vasquez [an internationally renowned DJ from the New York house music scene] really brought those two scenes together when he was in Toronto. (newsgroup comment, male raver, June 1999)

Although I do not have any direct empirical data to confirm or contradict this observation, one male raver and coffee shop worker who attends both gay and straight raves upheld the view that these are relatively unintegrated scenes. This trend toward segregated scenes is consistent with developments in other cities and countries and would be interesting to study more explicitly in the Toronto rave scene.*

Unlike the research on race and sexuality, for which the findings are limited, particular attention was paid to the way PLUR values, especially "respect," were played out in male-female interactions. In all interviews, ravers talked about the differences between the "pick-up culture" of bars and the more friendship-oriented relationships at the rave. Many ravers described interactions at rave

*See Lewis and Ross's work on this topic in the Australian context (1996).

parties as "sensual as opposed to sexual," since hugging and mas-saging are central parts of the culture for many ravers.

There were situations where those attending raves were insensitive to the PLUR doctrine. Individuals who were disrespectful were usually assumed to be either (a) people who had no interest in being part of the rave culture and were intentionally destructive of the vibe – a.k.a., "toxic ravers," as they are called by one of the female ravers quoted below – or (b) uneducated ravers:

At the community meeting, the young speaker (a female raver, eighteen years old) talked about how GHB (the "date rape" drug) was becoming increasingly prevalent at raves. She talked about how some people take it for pleasure at parties, but it also has meant problems for females who go to raves and are put in difficult situations. The speaker went on to explain how she escaped what she believed was a danger-ous situation with a male because she recognized the early signs of GHB coming on (which must have been slipped to her) and got out of there in time. (field notes from community meeting about raves and drug use, North York, Toronto, 19 February 1999)

There are some guys who go to raves to try and pick up stoned young girls. I call these guys "toxic ravers." (interview, female raver and tat-too artist, 1995)

I danced in this one spot for about a half hour with this guy in front of me who wouldn't leave this one poor chick alone. He kept touching and grindin' her even though she kept on pushing him off. Where the fuck did this ... loser come from. (Internet newsgroup, anonymous, 14 November 1995)

Furthermore, most interviewees talked about how the rave was a welcome place for those who are "outsiders" to the popu-lar/cool cliques at their high schools. One relative neophyte, a female raver and senior university student who had been raving for about one year, talked about how the rave saved her from the depression and poor self-image that plagued her through high school and on into university:

When I hit university, I had no money but I was drinking and getting fat. My clothes were out of style in high school because we didn't have that much money. When I walked into the rave for the first time and saw

what everybody was wearing and doing I was like, "Shit, I'm home."
I went through high school, through university in residence, I've been
searching for funky neat people that I fit in with and it was like, god,
there's thousands of them right here. Where have I been hiding? It really
changed my life. At the end of first year university I was 170 pounds
from drinking, pretty much alcoholic ... When I was drunk I felt a bit
looser and felt like I could fit in with the other people. It was totally
opposite of that. I was all bummed out, I'm like, ah, I'm fat. There's no
cool people here, like, I was miserable. That was at the end of first year.
I get down sometimes, but since I started raving and all the people
I've met through raves, I feel way better. I am healthier, I lost weight.
(interview, female raver and university student, 1998)

Some male ravers talked about how they and their friends were marginal to the "cool crowd" in high school because they were "too
intellectual" and "geeky" – "too into" video games, computers, and
fantasy games. For example, a raver and graphic-designer who described himself as a "hyper-intellectual" spoke about how he has
few close friends outside the rave because he is too intense for many
people to talk to. In the rave though – a place where he felt able to
connect with like-minded people – he established relationships with
relative ease and made a few close friends. However, it is difficult to
discern from the research findings whether these friendships were
short-term, which appears to be characteristic of bonds formed
exclusively around rave-related drug use, or if they were lasting,
such as those formed in the techno.ca newsgroup. Whatever the
continuity of these relationships, it would be fair to say that for many
ravers a sense of community and empowerment was found at least
temporarily in the rave scene.

Having said this, certainly not all of those interviewed indicated that they were seeking community, and not all found community to the same extent. Furthermore, some have argued that as rave
has become a "cool" thing to do, it has also become less welcoming
for the marginal. However, the transition that apparently took place
during the 1990s and beyond – from "welcoming rave community" to
"bad attitude dance club" – was not nearly as complete as a few
ravers suggested. That is to say, rave developed into a hybrid and
complex scene – not just a scene that was exclusively "bad" or
"clubby." In fact the extent to which rave was perceived as being a
cohesive and supportive community appeared to be related to the

amount of experience that a raver had in the community, if we remember the "waning of raver-idealism" described earlier.

Moreover, and despite the rave community's apparent openness, it is still in some ways a *gendered* scene, there being only a few female DJs or promoters. Only two females had semi-regular DJing gigs in the Toronto scene at the time of the study, and there existed one all-female promotion company in the city in the early and mid 1990s – a renowned pro-rave company called Transcendence. Aside from these examples, there was very little female involvement at the level of promotion that I or other ravers were aware of. The extent to which females were excluded from these roles was seldom an expressed concern, whether in interviews or in the usually male-dominated newsgroup discussions. In dialogue that did take place, strategies for achieving equal representation in these occupations were not discussed during my years as a newsgroup member. One male DJ and record store worker who I explored this topic with in 1998 felt that females were often better DJs because they were more "in tune" with the audience and the mood of the party. Another male newsgroup participant suggested that the female DJs who were in the scene should not by revered just because they were female: "I don't care what sex a DJ is ... that is all! I don't understand why it is hyped up so much whenever a female DJ (or mc) comes to Toronto ... This practice should be finished now. Personally I think that their music (or MCing) should speak for itself. In DJ Rap's [a female DJ] case I think that's true. I loved her set" (newsgroup comment, July 1995). Another participant in the same discussion argued that internationally recognized female DJ Anne Savage is actually not a very good DJ "but her looks make up for it" (newsgroup discussion, male raver, 6 January 1999). Clearly, there were mixed and often masculinist views on the topic. Overall, and although these social-structural issues about female occupational status in the rave business are not the focus of this research, it is important to consider this issue as it relates to the masculinist culture of DJing and promotion, for the very existence of this culture brings an element of hypocrisy into the supposedly "open" rave culture.

The clearest demographic division within the scene, however, was *age-related*. This difference was amplified with the development of club raves as ravers generally need to be of drinking age to attend such raves. Underscoring this difference was the assumption that older ravers were more "sophisticated" music and drug connoisseurs: the belief essentially being that younger ravers are inherently more interested in the faster, high energy music and drugs, whereas more experienced, older ravers would tend to seek more subtle and nuanced music and experiences. Underlying the latter assumption was a belief that younger ravers are often too immature and inexperienced in the scene to adequately understand the complexities and implications of the culture, including, for example, using rave-related drugs responsibly. Other ravers pointedly disagreed with this argument, suggesting that at the more "vibing" raves, age is not a barrier. Several examples of ravers who became friends despite age differences (ravers in their mid-twenties becoming friends with teen ravers) were cited in this context.

Relationships with Outsiders

It sometimes takes the "outsiders" not understanding and poking fun at our society to make us grow strong. It also shows us that we do have a society, however divided, that hopefully is based around, peace, love, harmony, brotherhood, acceptance, and unity ... keep striving towards our Utopian society 'cause I know it's out there, I've seen it. (rave newsgroup discussion, male raver, 1995)

Underlying the earlier comments about "toxic ravers" was a dominant perception that "outsiders" in and around the scene create problems with their bad attitudes and inclinations toward picking-up. Despite these concerns, ravers appeared to have and maintain relationships with those outside the scene. Simply put, rave subculture members are not isolated from outside, mainstream culture – unlike classic subcultural groups such as punks, skinheads, or especially hippies, who sometimes co-habitate and/or "live the subculture." The ravers that I spoke to had lives and friendships that were completely separate from the rave scene. DJs and promoters, two groups most closely linked via their occupations to the rave scene, usually worked other jobs as well (although sometimes these jobs were in music shops), or were students. So, while the focus of a raver's social time was often on rave-related activities and relationships –depending on how committed the raver was to the scene – many ravers emphasized the importance of "maintaining a balance" while remaining true to the rave spirit.

Giving Back to the Scene: Commitments to the Rave

The 50 raver volunteers ... that support the TRIP project [the Toronto Raver Information Project – a community outreach group to educate ravers about safe sex and drug use] illustrate the acceptance of a harm reduction project of this kind. Many of the volunteers have indicated that TRIP offers them a way to give back to the rave community, to try and foster the original ideals of community that the rave scene offered. (from an information package for the "Toronto Raver Information Project")

Many interviewed ravers described how being involved in some activity that supported rave culture was a personal priority. In this section, I assess the intensity of these involvements and examine the ways in which, and the extent to which, some ravers organized their lives around the scene.

Many ravers I spoke with contributed to the rave community by volunteering in a variety of ways. One male raver designed stickers and t-shirts with rave characters on them (i.e., cartoon caricatures of males and females in typical rave garb) and gave them out at raves. This same raver invented a "cooling spray" that he used to shower people at raves who were getting hot and dehydrated from dancing. Another person I spoke with had promoted a non-profit rave, charging only enough to cover the costs, and DJed for free at some raves. Another was working as a health counsellor for ravers, which, while a paid position, nonetheless required a high degree of commitment. Newsgroups and information Web sites also contained advertisements for a variety of anti-drug, raver-driven campaigns and support groups, such as "Ravesafe." Other contributions and commitments included the following:

After a while of doing it [raving] ... I decided that I wanted to give something back and I was just playing around with the idea of a magazine and I asked John if he would get involved and he said yes and it got off the ground ... we named it first and then we went around and got a lot of

articles ... it turned out to be something really big, we produced 500
issues our first time, and then 700 and then 1,000, and the last issue we
put out was 2,000. (interview, male raver and university student, 1995)

Someone had put some serious time into decorating this place. The
decorations looked like they had been done by hand. The personal
effort that must have gone into some of these was incredible (this suggested to me that the people who volunteered or the people who put
on the rave were really into making this a good party) [I came to learn
that the promotion line for raves often encourages ravers to come out
and help – and several often do, with incentives like free admission].
(field notes, 14 October 1995)

Although many ravers appeared to use raver values construc-
tively in their everyday lives, experienced ravers at times expressed
concern that some youth were overly committed to their raver role,
attempting to *completely* escape from life's challenges and problems by partying:

Some people use it as a full lifestyle and they try and use it to escape
from real life. Which you can't do because at some point you have to
deal with people, you have to get a job. And if you're hair is blue, and
you have six earrings in your nose, and you wear clothes that people
are going to call different, that's going to cause problems for you when
you try and relate to people in real life. You have to have a careful balance between the raving lifestyle and your own lifestyle and how you
relate that to your own life, and a lot of people have problems balanc-
ing that out. (interview, male raver and university student, 1995)

In other words, "giving back" to the scene is applauded by
rave culture idealists, while avoiding life's responsibilities through
raving is condemned. The following passage from the now-defunct
Toronto-based underground rave magazine *Subterrane,* referred to
earlier, embodies these sentiments:

Raving has always been a place to escape to for many people. Young
and old, Black and White, we have managed to disregard our differences, come together ... However, I've noticed lately that many are trying to escape from something or someone, instead of escaping *to*

raving. I realized that my problems were still there when I woke up Monday morning and that they were beginning to take away my experience on the weekend. So here's some advice as publisher and friend: 1. Make raving a reality instead of a fantasy. Get involved and spread the values into your everyday world. 2. Reexamine why you rave. If you can't have a good time at a rave when you're sober, don't go. Using raving as a tool to procrastinate from life responsibilities will dilute the experience and cause more problems than it solves. May the force be with you.

Perhaps the most telling and complex example of rave-related commitment took place in the aftermath of a threat by Toronto mayor Mel Lastman and city council to make raves illegal in June 2000. The reaction by the rave community unveiled both the ambivalence of ravers to political causes, and a strong pseudo-political commitment by ravers when faced by a serious threat: there was poor attendance at an initial rally to protest the potential anti-rave law, but when the reality of the loss of raves set in, a subsequent and successful pro-rave rally with up to 20,000 people took place in Nathan Phillips Square. Issues around rallies, rave, and politics are discussed further in the next chapter.

The Life World of the Rave: Conclusion and Departure Points

The findings described in this and the previous chapter showed PLUR (peace, love, unity, and respect) to be rave's dominant group perspective, and the activities of dancing, doing drugs, and listening to music to be the embodiments of this perspective. The identity development of ravers was evident in their tendency to become increasingly comfortable as they developed relationships within the scene, and to at the same time make varying time and resource commitments to it. In a similar way, as ravers moved through their careers as subculture members, they experienced a "waning of idealism" that was attributed to increased knowledge of rave politics and a greater understanding of some of the hazards associated with drug use.

Over the course of this study, on a macro level, the rave subculture arguably moved from an underground culture to a "sub-mainstream" culture, something I distinguish from a "full on" main-stream culture because of the successful resistances of some groups to this transition. For example, more intimate, underground parties that only some "in the loop" ravers know about still took place at the end of the study period. Regardless, this movement toward main-stream culture created both tension and excitement in the rave com-munity. The different reactions to this tension within the community illuminate the various perspectives, interactions, and commitments of ravers, many of which appear to be predicated on the individual raver's experience in the scene. In the following two chapters, these experiences and dynamics are considered for their relevance to existing theories of youth and culture.

PART 2

Reading Rave, Interpreting Youth Culture

5
Fight, Flight, or Chill
Reconsidering Youth Subcultural Resistance

When flies get stuck on flypaper are their efforts to flutter free evidence of struggle and resistance or merely part of a scripted death in which the strength sapping efforts are part of the script? The pessimist will breathe a melancholy "aaahh"; the optimist will shout "people are not flies!" The optimist will point to the few who perhaps escape; the pessimist to the many who don't ... the optimist is quite correct; people, of course, are not flies. But they do seem like passive role players much of the time; it's what we call social order and are grateful for it more often than not ... Relative autonomy? Active agency? These may reproduce the structure of domination and subordination as often as they undermine it. (Bennett Berger, *An Essay on Culture: Symbolic Structure and Social Structure*, 1995, 148–9)

Many scholars have dealt with this fundamental tension between "individual freedom and structural constraint" by adopting a classic compromise position where individuals, whether youth or otherwise, are considered to be "relatively autonomous" or active within certain social constraints. Karl Marx's aphorism "human beings make their own history, but not in the circumstances of their own choosing" is the clearest articulation of this position (1963, 15). Over the years there have been many attempts to provide a more sophisticated framework that bridges the structure-agency gap, including structuration theory (Giddens 1984), the negotiated order perspective (Strauss, Schatzman, et al. 1963), social network analysis (Fine and Kleinman 1983), and mesostructural theory (Maines 1982). The difficulty with many of these integrated perspectives is that they do not adequately theorize the structure-agency relationship in a

way that acknowledges the oppression and struggles of marginalized groups. Also, these perspectives are generally not equipped to
deal with the increasingly complex and contradictory relationship
between social action and social structure in a global, mass-mediated society, and/or they fail to adequately theorize the place of dominant and resistant *culture* in this relationship (Lull 1995). These
concerns and questions are embedded in a series of debates that
continue to exist in youth cultural studies – debates about how much
"credit" youth should be given for being creative and proactive in
their subcultural expressions, and about the extent to which youth
subcultural activity is essentially passive and unreflective.

My research in the Toronto rave scene acts as a departure
point for demonstrating how existing explanations of youth cultural
activity as described in chapters one and two tend not to adequately account for the *range of ways* that young people interpret and use
subcultural activity at any given time, and the variety of ways that
subcultures are understood and experienced by youth during their
careers as subculture members. In offering a more encompassing approach, I attempt to not only honour the actual subcultural experiences of young people as reported in chapters three and four, but
also to illustrate how binaries such as micro-macro, agency-struc-
ture, and social action–social systems, while useful for helping us
conceptualize links between social contexts and cultural activity, are
inherently insensitive to the nuanced and multifaceted aspects of
social life and its micro and macro levels. In a similar way, I hope to
bring attention to the potential for disruption, social change, and
collective resistance and action that youth now possess in an age of
Internet technology, a topic that is only beginning to be pursued in
youth cultural studies.

Rave's Continuum of Resistance

there is no truly untheoretical way in which to "see" an "object" ... Even
the most "naturalistic" of accounts involves deconstruction of native
logic and builds upon reconstruction of compressed, select, significant
moments in the original field experienced. (Willis 1997, 248)

In the most general sense, the previous chapter showed that rave is
a complex scene and culture that is comprised of a variety of inter-

pretive groups, cultural spaces, and sub-communities. On this basis, I argue here that the findings of the study I undertook offer simultaneous support for optimistic, ambivalent, and pessimistic interpretations of rave culture. Although this stance could be viewed as fence-sitting, my feeling is that it reflects instead the complex reality of an extremely diverse culture – a culture of youth who give a variety of meanings to their subcultural experiences, and whose experiences, as Paul Willis suggests in the above quotation, are interpreted in diverse ways by theorists.

Underlying this inclusive approach to theory is implicit support for a "multiperspectival approach" to understanding youth – an approach that draws on a range of analytic procedures in order to attain a comprehensive and balanced understanding of social phenomena. Douglas Kellner (1995) described and rationalized this approach as follows:

A perspective ... is an optic way of seeing, and critical methods can be interpreted as approaches that enable one to see characteristic features of cultural artifacts. Each critical method focuses on specific features of an object from a distinctive perspective: the perspective spotlights, or illuminates, some features of a text while ignoring others. The more perspectives one focuses on a text to do ideological analysis and critique – genre, semiological, structural, formal, feminist, psychoanalytic, and so on – the better one can grasp the full range of a text's ideological dimensions and ramifications. It therefore follows that a multiperspectival approach will provide an arsenal of weapons of critique, a full range of perspectives to dissect, interpret and critique cultural artifacts. (98–9)

Of course, there are potential problems with approaches like Kellner's, not the least of which is the underlying assumption that "the more viewpoints we include the closer we get to the truth." The problem is, this can only be an assumption. What about viewpoints that are ideological fronts for particularistic interests? Why does including more perspectives necessarily reveal ideological ramifications rather than reinforce and mystify them further? Although there is no concrete solution to these issues, what researchers can do is be explicit about the unifying logic that led to their choice or combination of perspectives. In this book, the perspectives offered on the rave phenomenon were introduced and interrogated as preparation for an exploration of "freedom and constraint" in youths' lives – an exploration of the meanings that young people give to their cultural experiences and the role of broader structural constraints and circumstances in social life. That is to say, the arguments and analyses made in this and the next chapter draw on both a micro-sociological approach to understanding the emergent and serendipitous nature of group life, and a macro-sociological approach that is attentive to the power relations that exist between dominant and marginal groups, and the historical circumstances in which these relations take place.

Five Theses on Rave Resistance

There are a various ways that rave could be interpreted from the data – as a weekend escape, as an intentional resistance movement, as an unintentional form of deviance, and so on. To summarize these interpretations, I developed a rave-specific conceptual continuum that is sensitive to the broad finding that youth cultural behaviour is sometimes active, intentional, and resistive, and at other times passive and unintentional – and most times a combination of these. An abridged version of this continuum appears below in table 1. Following table 1, I elaborate in greater detail on each of the "five theses on resistance" that were conceptualized – theses that represent the range of resistances referred to above. The forms of resistance presented in the table are also described with reference to existing theoretical approaches to youth and rave. The forms are "purposeful-tactical resistance," "reactive-adaptive resistance," "trivial resistance," "self-aware and oblivious non-resistance," and "reproduction of the dominant culture." These various conceptions of rave culture reflect not only the diverse sub-communities that exist in the rave scene and the variable meanings that youth give to their activity, but also the variety of possible interpretations of youth behaviour that can be manufactured by theorists and researchers.

   Acknowledged in this analysis is that the forms of resistance described in the five theses are in many cases "analytically close" and open to multiple alternate interpretations. This raises important questions about interpreting youth cultural activity. For example, when young people engage in a symbolic form of resistance, such as displaying shocking hairstyles, are they simultaneously reproducing dominant cultural norms? In other words, are they reinforcing their own exclusion through the shocking hairstyles? Similarly, when this symbolic resistance is seemingly consented to by dominant cultural groups, does this then make the youths' resistive behaviour trivial or empty? Put another way, is resistance that "makes no difference" indeed resistance? By the same token, when youths are coping with the sometimes oppressive circumstances that define their everyday lives by attending (escaping at) a rave, is this an adaptive form of resistance, or is it a form of non-resistance (i.e., blind consumption)? Is pleasure-seeking behaviour "reactive and adaptive" resistance, or "self-aware non-resistance," or is it "oblivious non-resistance"? In the following analysis, I cannot resolve these definitional ambiguities, only make attempts to untangle and organize them. What I have done then is to offer a series of empirically and theoretically informed interpretations of a complex data set, and provide suggestions for relative points to which this data might be anchored. The hope is that by making analytic distinctions that are based at least partially on the meanings that youth give to their activities, a more grounded understanding of rave cultural activity – resistance-related or otherwise – might then be approached.

Table 1: Five theses on rave resistance

Thesis 1: Rave is a form of symbolic "purposeful-tactical" resistance – or "quiet" resistance.

At certain times in their subcultural careers, many ravers view their own behaviours as being symbolically and tactically resistant to dominant norms and groups. Although these resistant strategies are sometimes spectacular (i.e., noticeable, outrageous, and often public), they are best viewed as tactical and "quiet" because they are done as part of a private ritual, not a public display. This ritual of quiet resistance is a concrete form of what Michel de Certeau (1984) would view as "tactical resistance." This finding of a spectacular, quiet resistance provides a basis for alternate interpretations of conventional "spectacular" versions of the resistance thesis that seldom distinguish between the meaning of subcultural style as *public versus private* display (e.g., Hebdige 1979). In the same way, the findings inform recent re-interpretations of the tactical resistance concept that have focused largely on resistance as "unspoken pleasure" (Malbon 1998 in his work on club culture) as opposed to "planned retaliation" (which this study found, at times). This model is distinguished from thesis two's adaptive-reactive model because this model is about purposeful subversion, as opposed to incidental deviance.

Thesis 2: Rave is a form of "adaptive-reactive" resistance.
Rave culture includes communities of "techno-ravers" who embrace technology and future-oriented culture in resistive ways. For example, techno-ravers are "resisting through hyper-adaptation" – that is to say, they are leading a pseudo-mainstream social movement within a postmodern culture that is, for many commentators, oppressive or alienating. Although these developments can be theorized in a Jean Baudrillard– inspired model of resistance that emphasizes "subversion through over-consumption" and in a Michel de Certeau–influenced model of "tactical resistance," I argue that the most adequate model here is a classic subcultural adaptation perspective. This subcultural adaptation, or "adaptive-reactive" resistance model, is a toned down version of the classic CCCS spectacular resistance thesis that acknowl-edges the class-based reaction to postmodern conditions – in the case of rave, a specifically middle-class reaction. The proposed model is distinguished from subtle resistance models that are overly focused on escapism (thesis four), as opposed to this thesis's emphasis on conscious adaptation.

Thesis 3: Rave is a form of "trivial" or "hollow" resistance.
What is often defined as "resistance" by some members of the rave community (e.g., PLUR) is, for the most part, superficial, *dis*united, and unable to alter broader social consciousness, even symbolically. So, while rave culture in its ideal form would be "quietly resisting," and thus supporting McRobbie's subtle-resistance thesis, the empirical findings suggest that this conception of rave resistance would be more accurately defined as "hollow" or "trivial" resistance – that is, a "resistance that makes no difference." Based on this notion of a "hollow" resistance, I argue that an adequate macrological explanation of rave culture can be drawn from a classical understanding of the "hegemony" concept – a concept often ignored in analyses of rave culture, likely because of the rave's popular positioning as a "postmod-ern" culture. This view of "trivial resistance" is in many ways akin to thesis one because it is a purposeful resistance. However, the resist-

ance here is characterized by the ravers' false and romantic sense
of being part of a social movement, whereas the ravers described in
thesis one understand the modest implications of their actions.

Thesis 4: Rave is a form of self-aware or oblivious non-resistance.
This study showed that some ravers did not give resistive meanings to
their activities. These ravers include pleasure seekers, hedonists, toxic
ravers, and "willing dupes." These findings act as a departure point for
informing and criticizing models that theorize pleasure as a resistive
behaviour (Pini, McRobbie, and Malbon) and for informing and supporting Reynolds's cynical model of rave as an "autistic" culture. Furthermore, the "willing dupes" are examined as a group that is self-reflective
and critical of dominant ideological practices, but still "chooses" or is
positioned to not resist. This apathetic cultural group is examined in
relation to two models of non-resistance: an ideological model (Abercrombie et al.'s "dominant ideology thesis") and a postmodern model
(Muggleton's nihilistic view of contemporary youth culture). Although
neither position is privileged in this analysis, the discussion tries to
demonstrate the importance of considering these other interpretations
of the "escape through pleasure" hypothesis – interpretations that do
not require viewing youth as either passive or resistive.

*Thesis 5: Rave culture supports the reproduction of aspects of the
dominant culture.*
Ravers reproduced the dominant culture in two ways. *First*, many
ravers still distinguished themselves and their rave-related tastes from
mainstream culture, while symbolically detaching themselves from
outsiders who "buy into" the commercialized version of rave culture.
In this sense, raver culture was in many ways about seeking out and
preserving "cultural capital," the same capital that mainstream youth
and adults seek in other settings – only for ravers, what is termed
"subcultural capital" (Thornton 1995) is the most valued symbolic
commodity. In the same way, the rave values of "acceptance" and
"no preconceptions" were clearly and ironically contradicted through
ravers' attempts to protect and attain subcultural capital while exclud-
ing the mainstream "other" from the upper rungs of the "hierarchy of
cool." *Second*, and moreover, the occupational structure of rave culture
supports and reflects mainstream, exclusionary, masculinist, "gender
ordered" norms. Again, and although the rave culture effectively

upholds gender-related issues of respect and "breaking down barriers" on one level, the seemingly systemically male-dominated DJ and promoter cultures reproduce broader societal norms that are hegemonic and masculinist.

Thesis 1: Rave is a form of symbolic "purposeful-tactical" resistance – or quiet resistance

There was evidence that some ravers were symbolically, subtly, and purposefully resisting mainstream value systems and culture. For example, the promotion of the PLUR philosophy and emphasis on "breaking down communication barriers" were considered crucial corrections to the violence and alienation that in their view represent the status quo. Similarly, rave-related drug use was for some ravers a subtle (i.e., not overt or "on-display") reaction to a hypocritical mainstream critique of drugs and reverence of alcohol. Other ravers suggested that respectful rave partying is a strategically symbolic reaction to the mainstream norms of a nightclub or bar culture that is notoriously gendered and racially segregated. For those ravers that interpreted their activities in this manner, subtle resistance was an active form of resistance – or a concrete form of "tactical resistance," as opposed to such passive forms as McRobbie's "escape resistance."

These findings also showed that spectacular youth cultural forms are not necessarily meant for public display. That is to say, although sometimes sensational styles (e.g., the candy-raver look) and activities (e.g., frenetic, often drug-induced dancing) were adopted and practiced, they were not necessarily meant to garner attention from those outside the rave scene and certainly not to appall or shock – although, when the styles are carried over into everyday wear that can stand out as peculiar. This absence of an element of public display in rave culture is an interesting appendage to conventional understandings of "spectacular" subcultures, such as those of punks and skinheads. Furthermore, the finding that youth gave resistive meanings to their activities is useful as an empirical confirmation of what are often purely theoretical readings of subcultural groups. This is not to say that resistance must be verbally articulated for it to be authenticated; however, research findings that include this kind of "first-hand" evidence supporting the thesis that subcultural activity is intentionally or strategically oppositional are less vulnerable to the common criticism that youth studies theorists "seem to have discovered resistance virtually *everywhere*" (Gruneau 1988, 25), or that they tend to theorize resistance without any insight into the actual meanings that youth give to their activities (Tanner 1996).

In the same way, my view of some ravers' cultural activities as subtly or tactically resistant contrasts Malbon's (1998, 1999) understanding of rave-related sensual pleasure as being a form of unspoken tactical resistance. What Malbon views as tactically resistant – seeking and experiencing pleasure – is, according to the definition I am offering here, a form of "trivial resistance" or "escape resistance" (i.e., resistance that makes no difference). Moreover, and without overemphasizing the difference between unspoken escapism and spoken tactical resistance, the point here is that this distinction "counts" when theoretical anchorage points are sought. Returning to the findings of this study, to be clear, not all ravers gave subversive meanings to their activities at any given time, and ravers' views of their activities as being more or less resistant varied over the course of their rave subculture careers – a point recognized in the theses to follow. Underlying these observations and others made throughout this section is the point that these *middle-class* ravers are not reacting with the sense of anger or discontentment that tend to characterize the activities of such spectacular working-class subcultures as punks and skinheads. Perhaps the PLUR philosophy, from this perspective, could be considered at least a partial reflection of the more "comfortable" realities that are associated with economically and culturally privileged backgrounds and lifestyles.

Thesis 2: Rave is a form of "adaptive-reactive" resistance
According to many commentators, the high-speed, ever-accelerating technological and cultural evolutionary process that is associated with the turn of the millennium is threatening and oppressive, as the influx of popular books about coping with and/or resisting an increasingly "digital society" demonstrate.* Yet, rave culture is not only liberated from these constraints, but has embraced technology in profound ways, having integrated "high tech" into leisure consumption so extensively and seamlessly that rave culture could be

---

*See, for example, Brook and Boal (1995) and Tapscott (1997).

interpreted as being resistive both to mainstream skepticism about "postmodern" technological developments and to conventional perspectives on "how technology should be used."

This resistance is manifested in three ways. *First*, the tendency of some ravers to *over*-consume and *over*-embrace technology could be interpreted as itself subversive and excessive, as resisting by not resisting – a stance akin to one taken by Jean Baudrillard (1983a; 1983b). It is worth noting, however, that the ravers I spoke with about this topic seldom interpreted their behaviour in this way. Their view of technology was, on one hand, an extension of the argument for "breaking down barriers" that underlay the PLUR-inspired rave doctrine , and on the other, about progression, experimentation, and pleasure. In this sense, as many of these youth did not view their activities as "oppositional" per se, a Baudrillardian stance does not cohere with the youths' actual interpretations of their activities. It is evident, however, that the excessive consumption of technology by some ravers clearly falls within the parameters of "deviant" as defined by many mainstream commentators on youth – commentators who have disapprovingly used the term "screen-agers" to describe media, computer, and technology savvy young people. Although this argument is overly presumptuous about what constitutes resistance, it is a useful counterpoint to conventional concerns about "today's troubled youth."

Second, "techno-ravers" in particular – those who belonged to the techno.ca group – are resisting through hyper-adaptation, rather than through hyper-consumption, as the Baudrillard-style argument above suggests. They are leading (sub)cultural figures in a pseudo-mainstream social development. They have, in a small but real way, reversed the ideological power structure of technological usage, flow, and manipulation. Rave culture resists the tendency to be paralyzed by fear of accelerated socio-cultural change. *Third*, and similarly, while taking leadership in this movement, ravers are also using technology in unintended, subversive, and tactical ways – having virtual parties, spending endless hours downloading, listening to and creating computer-generated music, and developing rave-related personal Web pages. These latter two arguments about rave cultural resistance are most closely aligned with Stanley's interpretation (1997) of the rave as a "wild zone" – a subversive space existing in a broader context of over-regulation.

The same findings, however, are also arguably consistent with classic subcultural models that emphasize the relationship between social class and resistive capacities. Put another way, working-class youths' propensity and ability to cope with changing social conditions in 1970s Britain using the resources and skills that were available and of interest to them is akin to the "coping" of many ravers at the millennium in Canada. Ravers in Toronto are for the most part a middle-class group which, according to the pro-PLUR rationale provided by many ravers, is increasingly alienated by such pre-millennium fears as global warming, AIDS, racial tension, the apocalypse, and so on. The crucial difference between the punks and skinheads of 1970s Britain and the ravers of 1990s Canada is that Canadian middle-class youth have different "coping resources" than did their working-class counterparts in 1970s Britain who were victims of oppression that was more clearly class-based.

Thesis 3: Rave is a form of "trivial" resistance

In theory, rave culture is about temporarily escaping, but also gradually reversing the perceived societal norms of oppression, segregation, and poor communication. The rave party is intended to act as a micro-society where raver values (e.g., PLUR, openness, acceptance) can be practiced homologously through, among other things, dance, music, and drug use. Ideally, ravers bring these values from the rave to their interactions with others in their day-to-day lives. So, in theory, rave culture is about changing society in non-offensive, subtle, but real ways. It is supposedly about more than coping with and escaping from the multiple pressures of everyday living at the millennium. In its ideal form, then, rave is a "quiet" social movement and raving a depoliticized form of resistance that can progressively alter everyday practices, as McRobbie (1993, 1994) has argued.

However, the current findings showed that the "rave doctrine" is somewhat abstract and open to multiple interpretations, and that PLUR, in particular, was decoded in distinct, and often non-resistant ways – and at times was not interpreted at all. Moreover, and without discounting the importance of considering and highlighting the variations of rave resistance noted throughout this section or the empowerment that can be gained from raving, it is crucial to be sensitive to the multitude of ways that a social or youth "movement" can be interpreted by theorists, and the related potential for these commentators to overstate the actual resistive potential of the group. Similarly, it is necessary to be attentive to the numerous ways that resistance can be defined (e.g., as "subversion" or "deviance," as opposed to social opposition). As noted previously, Malbon's and McRobbie's "subtle resistance" thesis might be usefully reinterpreted in a way that emphasizes how the pleasure that youth gain from the "rave escape" is empowering, but constitutes little more than a "trivial" or "empty" form of resistance, or, as Cloward and Ohlin (1960) would suggest, a form of retreatism. That is to say, while rave's PLUR revolution might allow some youth to temporarily "feel better" about themselves, in the end, what was intended to be a meaningful, united, social movement is little more than a false sense of resistance for many ravers. Furthermore, underlying rave-related practices that are supportive of this doctrine are tensions, contradictions, and complexities that undermine any "real" resistances that might take place beyond those existing in small pockets of the rave scene.

In the context of classic hegemony theory, it would seem then that the use of rave culture for coping and symbolic pleasure would be readily "consented to" by the dominant groups being opposed because the rave movement, in its present form, is unlikely to threaten the authority that maintains mainstream commercial culture. In other words, the rave is not a counter-hegemonic force. In fact, those aspects of rave culture that are considered most threatening to the dominant group – those related to the group's "underground" status – have been effectively diluted through "strategies of neutralization" (Baron 1989a; Hebdige 1979). These strategies included *incorporation* of the rave into mainstream popular culture (e.g., the movement toward club culture), the *trivialization* of the group (e.g., through portrayals of rave culture as a "neo-hippie" group of "fun-loving" youth), and *moral panic* (e.g., mass-mediated concerns about drug use and drug-related deaths at raves). As many commentators have pointed out, moral panic led to the early *censure* of the rave subculture – a censure that resulted in the closure of some rave parties by police, costing rave promoters money. This led promoters to start using legal venues and increasingly more stable locations. This was the beginning of the movement toward mainstream rave clubs which, in effect, completed the neutralization process. As the culture had now become effectively incorporated and commercialized, rave resistance had been effectively neutralized.

What is left, arguably, is a PLUR-related resistance that makes no difference, which is to say that the "resistance" actually perpetuates
the consumer culturalist agenda, while providing only a temporary
sense of empowerment for raver revolutionaries.

In making this argument for understanding rave in a classic
model of hegemonic relations, it is important to note that the underlying power structure assumed in this analysis is not as straightforward as might be thought, largely because the boundaries between
underground and mainstream have become increasingly blurred – a
process that does not clearly benefit either ravers or incorporators.
Consider, for example, the ambiguous relationship that rave promoters have with mainstream and underground culture. While rave
promotion is big business for many (e.g., it can entail investing thousands of dollars to fly in DJs from overseas, renting rave venues,
advertising events, hiring security etc.), other rave promoters con-
centrate on "giving back to the scene" by throwing non-profit parties.
In many cases, then, the underground and mainstream collide in the
form of "pro-money" versus "pro-rave" promoters. Yet even this conflict is not so obviously dichotomous, since many promoters struggle
with their alignments – are they "promoter-ravers" (money-oriented
but somewhat sensitive to the state of the scene), or "raver-promot-
ers" (exclusively non-profit, or reinvesting all profits into the next
rave party)? In this context, the subculture versus dominant ideological culture model is problematized because representatives of the
dominant group are sometimes indistinguishable from the subculture members. What is left is a movement defined by its "partial
incorporation." It suffices to say here that despite the widespread
movement toward interpreting rave culture in postmodern frame-
works, Gramsci's hegemony perspective and Hebdige's neutralization
model both still provide balanced and comprehensive macro-expla-
nations of developments in the Toronto rave scene.

Thesis 4: Rave is a form of self-aware or oblivious non-resistance
For many of those interviewed, rave was about seeking pleasurable
and sensual experiences. For these individuals, raves were viewed
as relative "safe spaces" for drug-use, places where one can dance
with reckless abandon, watch and enjoy favourite DJs, meet new
people, and spend time with friends. These ravers did not interpret
their behaviours as subtly, symbolically, or overtly resistant – instead focusing, quite simply, on how rave is a "good time." Consider

also the finding that experienced ravers tended to retrospectively suggest that in their early days of raving, when they "lost themselves in the partying," *they were actually lost* – a contrast to Malbon's assertion that rave is the practice of "losing yourself to find yourself." These kinds of arguments problematize the idyllic "pleasure as resistance" thesis espoused by Malbon and McRobbie.

The point here is that empowerment, coping, and pleasure – among other benefits that are sometimes read from rave culture – can be analytically distinct from resistance, subversion, or transgression. As many of the more actively "pro-PLUR" ravers noted, too much pleasure is empirically akin to "too much escape," and often enough to "too many drugs" and "too much commitment" to rave culture. For these ravers, excessive pleasure in this context, interpreted this way, actually reverses the rave value system and undermines the rave doctrine. In this sense, the current study provides conditional support for Reynolds' view (1997) that, although rave is a pleasurable space for experiencing "sensation without pretext or context" in ideal circumstances (i.e., when rave's "desiring machine is running smoothly"), the inevitable tensions and mainstream developments in the scene have led rave from "a way of life" to a situation where ravers should "get a life" (Reynolds 1997, 110).

However, this research also demonstrated how Reynolds's view is, for the most part, too extreme. Although rave may have lost some of its revolutionary potential (if it ever had any), it was clear from the current findings that for many youth rave participation is empowering, if not resistant – as Pini, Malbon, and McRobbie correctly pointed out – and not an exclusively escapist, hedonistic, and problematic space. For example, while some ravers were excessive and self- or scene-destructive in Reynolds' sense, others were seemingly aware of the destructive potential of rave's "desiring machine turned fascist," but participated in and embraced the pleasures that rave had to offer anyway. In fact, for some interviewees who were interested in a weekend escape at the rave, there appeared to be neither a view toward conscious resistance nor toward blind passivity. It would seem presumptuous then to assume that attendance at raves and participation in the excesses of rave signal either resistance or gullible adherence.

With this background, I offer two "middle-ground" interpretations of rave behaviour. The first is an updated version of Abercrombie, Hill, et al's neo-Marxist "dominant ideology thesis" (1980);

the second is a similarly balanced position akin to a more post-modernist approach proposed by Muggleton (1997, 2000). On one hand then, self-consciously excessive, non-resistant rave participation could be theorized in a model developed around the idea that consent to the dominant order is less ideological and more about a dull compulsion toward passivity. This argument is akin to the contention of Abercrombie et al. (1980) that working classes are critical of and question the credibility of the dominant group, but because of the "iron cage" created by the bureaucracies of modern society, and the "dull compulsion of the economic" which requires compliance in the workplace, there is little energy or motivation for resistance. For raver youth, who debatably exist in the postmodern "iron cage" of mass-media images, education, work, and suburban life, it could be argued that the complications and efforts required to resist are not "worth it." These ravers purposefully, consciously, non-resistantly, and temporarily escape through excessive pleasures.

That is to say, youth who are conscious of and reflective about their decision to "escape through pleasure" at a rave should not be viewed as resistant. Instead, their decision should be viewed for what it is – complacent and perhaps pragmatic. In fact, Muggleton's challenge to scholars to consider how a postmodern consumer "beholds the world with a knowingness that dissolves feelings and commitment into irony" (1997, 200) is the postmodern, non-ideological equivalent of Abercrombie et al. Together, these two positions, while distinct in their assumptions about the world we live in, articulate how interpretations of rave do not require a view of youth behaviour as an either/or dichotomy of resistance or passivity.

Thesis 5: Rave culture actively supports reproduction of the dominant culture

In the process of becoming mainstream and commercialized, rave also came to reproduce many of the inequalities and attitudes that, in theory, it opposed. Most notably, the segmenting of the rave scene into hierarchies of taste clearly supported Thornton's view (1995) of the dance club as a place where youth seek to attain subcultural capital in the form of cool clothes, white label (underground) records, and so forth. In the same way, Thornton's work, which insightfully outlined the labelling process that operates within the British rave and club scene – where "authentic" ravers distinguish their values from mainstream, commercial, "pop" values – were akin to the current study's finding that youth were critical of the "inau-thentic" movement toward rave clubs, of the Electric Circus dance television show, and of most other rave spin-off industries. The current study also extends and informs Thornton's work by providing insight into how ravers' interpretations of what is "cool" or "hip" changed over time (i.e., with many ravers experiencing a waning of idealism, as well as an increased comfort level in the scene).

This research also showed that, despite postmodern tendencies in rave culture, rave can still be usefully theorized in a structure-agency framework that presupposes classic conceptions of ideology, resistance, and hegemony, and hegemonic masculinity specifically. Consider, for example, the way ideological and political economic relations are played out in rave promotion – in target marketing in a segmented rave scene, in strategic rave flyer distribution, in the move toward commercialized raves – and consider also the ways that gender inequalities are systemically embedded in the rave DJ and promoter occupational structure, and, more broadly, the strategies of neutralization imposed by various dominant groups. These findings inform and subtly contradict Muggleton, Redhead, and others who have argued that rave culture can no longer be understood in a "depth model" (i.e., in a theory of ideology) of subcultures. For example, Redhead's argument that rave is characterized by shallow-ness, flatness, and "hyperreality" does not account for the clear examples of ideological relations noted previously, although his view that there is a decreased possibility for resistance in the classic sense of British subcultural theory is largely supported by these findings. Clearly, though, there is a need to be cautious about pro-claiming the "end of youth culture" (at least in Canada) considering the structures at work in the Toronto rave scene.

Seeking a Sixth Thesis: What Rave Is and What It Could Be

Underlying these five theses are questions about how rave influences the lives of those who are part of the culture and/or how it impacts people and structures that exist outside the scene. I am referring here to the range of ways that "politics and rave" can be understood. Below, I examine issues to do with politics and rave, focusing on ways that rave is and could be an agent of social change.

Music, Social Protest, and Rave

Many scholars of music have been attentive to ways that social or political actions have been associated with musicians and music cultures. Notable in this context is George Lipsitz (1997) who, in his book *Dangerous Crossroads: Popular Music, Postmodernism and the Poetics of Place*, draws on the writings of renowned social movement theorists Manual Castells and Alain Touraine to inform his discussion of, first, the political potential of music-related cultures; and, second,the ways that, and extent to which, local cultural expressions or events are influential on a global scale. Central to Lipsitz's argument is the view that music-related social movements, such as those associated with hip hop (i.e., a culture associated with rap music, graffiti, and break dancing) and other forms of diasporic African music, are, on one hand, locally-based and territorially defined, and on the other hand, cultural disseminators that effectively raise the consciousness of people around the world about race-related social issues (Lipsitz 1997, 33). In expanding on this point, Lipsitz delineates the relationship between music, youth culture, and politics:

At a time when African people have less power and fewer resources than at any other time in history, African culture has emerged as the single most important subtext within world popular culture. The popularity of hip hop reflects more than cultural compensation for political and economic domination, more than an outlet for energies and emotions repressed by power relations. Hip hop expresses a form of politics perfectly suited to the postcolonial era. It brings a community into being through performance, and it maps out real and imagined relations between people that speak to the realities of displacement, disillusion, and despair created by the austerity economy of post-industrial capitalism. (1997, 36)

Two points from Lipsitz's argument are especially relevant to this study of rave. The first is that music cultures can be viewed as privileged sites for "transnational communication, organization and mobilization at a time when the parochialism of trade unions and

political parties leaves those institutions locked into national identities" (1997, 34). That is to say, the *global* flow of music has enabled
the dissemination of pro-movement information that is the foundation for social action. As evidence of this, Lipsitz points to the influence that Jamaican reggae singer Bob Marley's music had on both
the formation of a "Black power" movement in Australia and on liberation movements in South Africa in the 1970s.* In the same way,
and as described in chapter two, early, pre-rave dance-music venues
and cultures were vital precursors to the emergence of the gay liberation and pride movement (Garratt 1998).

Secondly, and as pertinently, Lipsitz uses the term "identity
of passions" to describe the affective connections that are established and exist among diffuse people who have mutual opposition-
al-political aspirations. According to Lipsitz, cultural phenomena
such as music are crucial for evoking these types of passions and
aspirations. Of course, Lipsitz's understanding of the conditions
around and processes of subculture-driven social resistance raise
questions about the extent to which subculture members actually
share a "sense of struggle" that enables a collective consciousness
and "identity of passions," and the extent to which meaningful socio-
political resistance or opposition results from these connections. In
the context of this study of rave, it also begs the question, does Lipsitz's interpretation of contemporary hip hop culture, a culture that
engages and embodies issues related to race, class, identity, and
postcolonial struggle, help us understand rave culture? That is to
say, is rave in any sense a political and social movement, and if so, to
what extent is it influential beyond a local level?

My response is that the rave culture I observed in Toronto
from 1995 to 1999, while "anti-establishment" in many respects (in
embracing technology; in attempting to bring certain values from
rave to everyday interaction) was neither political, influential, nor
"movement-like" in the ways described by Lipsitz. In fact, being
"apolitical" was, according to some ravers, part of the subculture's
ideology and is a reflection of a socio-historical moment – that of the
late 1990s and millennium – that encourages escapist cultural behaviour rather than overtly resistant behaviour. This position was

*See also Bennett (2001) and Eyerman and Jamison (1998).

articulated in an article written by raver DJ "Pezboy" that appeared in *Future Harmonix*, a Portland Oregon–based rave webzine:

Rave culture has never been, nor ever will be, a coherent social move-ment. Up until very recently I thought that it would be possible to moti-vate ravers to join together and become politically active. Not so. At first this realization disheartened me. Now I see that this very lack of cohesiveness is what gives rave its power. In the ten years the culture has existed, rave has never made any claims. Rave has never chosen sides. Rave has never dictated an ideology. Simply put, rave is whatev-er you (that is, the individual) wants it to be. It is, in fact, a complete escape from any and all establishments. Again, this is what makes rave so vital in today's age. Human society is quickly spiralling toward a new era, a new age. This is what I refer to as the "post-historic age." An age when things happen so quickly, and change is so constant, that history ceases to be a relevant factor in motivating people's interac-tions with the world around them. An age when it is irrelevant to choose sides, because the sides are always changing. An age when very survival will come down to whether or not a person can navigate through the world in the present-tense. (http://www.futureharmonix. com/resonance/electronic/raveolution.html)

In his recent book *Rave Culture: An Insider's Overview*, Jimi Fritz contradicts Pezboy's suggestion that we live in an age "when it is irrelevant to choose sides." In fact, Fritz described how the 1990s and post-millennium socio-historical backdrop are inextrica-bly linked to the emergence of geographically-dispersed "Protest (Rave) Parties" around North America – events not acknowledged by Pezboy. Fritz explains:

In recent years rave culture has developed a keen social conscience and we are seeing a marked increase in events designed to bring awareness and raise money for community groups of all types. A party called Rave for Choice recently donated its proceeds to local abortion clinics and a national pro-choice women's group. In Boulder, Colorado, rave for the Rain Forest raised money for a number of ecological organ-izations. A group called Rave to Benefit AIDS has raised $75,000 to date by staging parties in Detroit and New York and a San Francisco party called Unleash the Queen was specifically designed to raise awareness of homophobia. Events like these are now taking place worldwide and are a good example of rave's commitment to creating a healthy community. (225–6)

Fritz also describes a Vancouver-based, non-profit, pro-rave community called B-Side that regularly holds protest events in front of Vancouver's downtown public library. The group aims to bring awareness to the anti-war values embodied by the rave community (Fritz 1999).

In my view, Fritz's examples are not so much proof that rave is a political culture so much as they are evidence that *pockets of the scene in different cities are political at specific times and under certain circumstances*. This argument is reminiscent of one made by social movement theorist Doug McAdam (1982) who, in his classic work on the black civil rights movement, described how collective action is tied to many factors that are external to the potentially resistant group. One of the key factors identified by McAdam is "political opportunity," or a set of conditions that allow or inspire a group to effectively mobilize. In a similar way, Marx and McAdam (1994) suggest that movements arise in response to collective concerns about a social change (or "social strain") of some sort. In a departure from these more functionalist-oriented perspectives, Buechler (2000) describes how interactions and struggles between movement members and those representing key social structures are often driven by political-economic considerations, a point that is especially relevant in the case of rave culture.

Political Opportunity and Raving in Toronto

As a way of reflecting on these theories, I examine two key moments in the recent history of the Toronto rave scene. Both moments took place in the aftermath of a proposal in May 2000 by Toronto's Mayor Mel Lastman to ban raves from city-owned public property, a proposal that closely followed an Ontario coroner's inquest into a drug related, rave-related death of a university student (Hier 2002). During the first moment, two unsuccessful pro-rave rallies took place. Both rallies were organized by Toronto's Dance Safe Committee – an organization composed of ravers and concerned individuals from the health community. McCall (2001) describes these failed efforts:

While Ontario's rave scene was under close scrutiny by the government, the Toronto Dance Safety Committee pleaded for support to hire a lawyer to defend rave culture's interests at a coroner's inquest into a rave-related death. Sadly, the bulk of the funds came from the city's largest promoter, who obviously had the most at stake. Furthermore, only a small number of ravers were actually present at the inquest. The same week a benefit called Rave Against Rage was held at a small Toronto club and it was almost empty. (145)

The second and subsequent moment – referred to earlier in chapters two and four – was an extremely successful demonstration against the over-regulation of raves in Toronto. It took place on the grounds of Toronto's city hall on 1 August 2000. This demonstration was jointly organized by the Dance Safe Committee and the PartyPeopleProject (another organization of concerned ravers and promoters). Hier (2002) described the political impact of the protest in his study of media reports surrounding the event:

With an estimated attendance of 12000–20000 people, the protest rally was orchestrated as a symbolic confrontation to city council's pending vote [on whether raves would be sanctioned in city spaces] ... Not only did the rally place on display several aspects of rave culture and music in Toronto – reinforcing the universal philosophy of Peace, Love, Unity and Respect (PLUR) – but through the many speeches, flyers, posters and information tables made available at the rally, a discursive subpolitics served to symbolically challenge in an explicit fashion termination efforts and present rave in a favourable – and victimized – light. (51)

As a supplement to this public demonstration, a thirty-six page report was submitted to city council (Hier 2002, 48). The report questioned and challenged the city's position that endorsing rave events was an attempt to "reduce risk." Hier explained the challenge on three fronts to city council's position, highlighting attempts to involve other stakeholders that would be affected by such a decision:

The report contested ... [city council's ruling to outlaw raves on city spaces] on three fronts. First, in attempting to delineate the parameters around what constitutes a rave, the Ontario government defined rave as "a dance event occurring between 2:00am and 6:00am, for which admission is charged." But raves, the report suggests, cannot serve as the object of spatial regulation, as there is no sound way to separate raves from wedding receptions or other events into the early mornings.

Indeed, such was the case when the proposed rules for rave were publicized and organizers representing Caribana Committee and Unity 2000 (an organization representing the annual Gay Pride Week festivities) voiced their outrage at such a wide ranging and indeterminate mandate ... The second point of contestation called attention to the fact that the [proposed anti-rave policy] violated ravers' rights as Canadian citizens under the Canadian Charter of Rights and Freedoms ... And third, the most powerful overriding argument to emerge from the report was that the over-regulation of raves would drive raves underground subsequently amplifying the risks associated with raving in Toronto. (2002, 49–50)

Ultimately, the efforts of ravers, promoters, and concerned others were successful. On 2 August 2000, Toronto city council voted 50–4 in favour of sanctioning raves in city spaces, a vote that came only three months after raves were banned from these same spaces. It is notable that over the three months since his initial proposal, Mayor Lastman had become a strong advocate for the re-sanctioning of raves, a radical stance-reversal on his part.

Certainly, this triumphant protest is evidence of the ways that a "social strain" – in this case, the clear and present threat to the lifestyles of ravers in Toronto and the occupational lives of those working in the scene – is a precondition for a successful collective action. As notably, however, this social response and protest is an example of an interest group taking advantage of political opportunities. By positioning city councillors so that they would appear responsible for rave-related risks and drug-related incidents if the scene was driven underground, the group had astutely and opportunistically captured the moral high ground on a key political issue – one that elicited a "damage control" response by city council. As importantly, by emphasizing and publicizing an issue that would have an impact on other interest groups with strong political voices in Toronto (the Caribana Committee and Unity 2000 gay-community representatives), city council was required to think about much more than upsetting the young raving community when making its decision.

Reconsidering Rave, Political Economy, and Social Resistance Movements
This successful protest notwithstanding, there are reasons to be hesitant about labelling rave in Toronto as being either "political" or

a "social movement." First, and as both McCall and Hier noted, the funding by key rave promoters was fundamental to the success of the movement. In other words, what might appear to have been a grassroots movement by "cause-motivated" ravers could, alternatively, be viewed as an economically-inspired reaction by business people who had a vested interest in saving the rave scene. This suggestion is consistent with an argument made periodically in this book, namely that political and economic concerns and issues underlie much of what takes place in the realm of youth culture (a point pursued in depth in the next chapter).

Second, the Toronto City Hall rally provides an intriguing basis from which to consider whether rave is a social movement that is concerned with youth rights and freedom of expression, or an "interest group" whose members are motivated by their desire for personal pleasure and "the party." The evidence described here – the two "moments" of resistance to the anti-rave law – seems to point to the latter, more pessimistic view of ravers as apolitical and self-serving. That is to say, although ravers came together to oppose the anti-rave bill proposed by city council, it would seem that the successful collective effort only materialized when many ravers appeared to realize that they might not be able to maintain their weekend dance-drug lifestyle. McCall (2001), in arguing that ravers tend to be insensitive to environmental concerns during and after their dance parties, supports this more cynical stance:

Unlike hippie culture that embraced a grassroots way of living stressing environmental concerns, some rave communities are arguably symptomatic of a 1990s anti-environmental mentality. Any snapshot of a rave space after an event is evidence of the culture's wasteful nature. The floor is strewn with empty water bottles and flyers, soon to be tossed in the garbage rather than the recycling bin. Even at outdoor parties, it is typically the promoters who are left to deal with the carnage that patrons leave behind because they were too high to care about where they littered. (139)

Of course, the problem with adopting an overly pessimistic viewpoint such as this one is that it assumes that rave is somehow a coherent group with a singular ideology and set of social practices. As I have argued throughout this book, such a position does not acknowledge the extent to which rave is a complex and contradictory subculture. A more accurate depiction of the scene would show the following: (a) that some ravers are overtly political and use rave as a forum to promote their views on "how the rave doctrine, if taken seriously, could improve society"; (b) that other ravers are associated with certain causes under specific circumstances; and (c) that others simply "enjoy the party," without investing anything in the scene except for the price of admission to the rave. This is not meant as a critique of ravers who are apolitical so much as it is a recognition that what many ravers are most passionate about and will fight for under duress is their right to be apolitical – their right to "escape" to their temporary utopia once a week.

The Internet and Rave's Political Potential
Although authors like Lipsitz describe the often transnational political influences of music cultures, there are surprisingly few articles or studies that consider the potential for more widespread or "global" forms of youth-driven cultural resistance – music-related or otherwise. While authors like Mellucci (1996) might explain this disparity by pointing to the overall lack of youth movements either locally or globally since the 1960s, this argument does not hold up in this age of on-line technology, where global connections and movements enabled by the inexpensive and wide-reaching Internet medium have emerged and developed in near unprecedented ways (e.g., worldwide protests against the US movement into Iraq in 2003; orchestrated anti-globalization debates at various World Trade Organization summits). Against this background, the surprising lack of research on youth movements pales in comparison to the disparity of work considering how on-line communication might enhance young people's abilities to resist and express on a global (cyber)stage (Wilson 2002).

Supporting this view are authors like Downing (2001) who in his book *Radical Media* suggests that the links between the rise of the Internet and the increased effectiveness of social movement efforts are strangely understudied, considering the striking relationship that has been shown between the development of new, interactive forms of communication and the enhanced abilities of marginalized groups to organize themselves.* The most renowned

*See also Castells (2002), Kedzie (1997), and O'Neill (2002).

advocate of this perspective is Manual Castells (2002). In his book *The Power of Identity,* he describes how the resistive capacities of environmentalists and a Mexican pro-democracy indigenous group were enabled by the Internet, and attributes the success of these groups largely to their ability to draw support from sympathetic *global* audiences. A fundamental part of Castells's argument is that a relatively small number of individuals – who might even be an unrepresentative fragment of a larger group – can still have influence on a global cyber-stage.

This latter point is particularly relevant to this discussion of rave because it in some way contradicts an argument made throughout this book that rave in Toronto was not a movement or political force per se because of the fragmented and contradictory nature of the scene and its members. Yet, in reflecting on Castells's point, I acknowledge that there is evidence that *some* ravers are intent on speaking out on a global stage (e.g., about issues related to war, community, health risk, and social inequality), and that these fragmented voices can be influential. When this understanding is considered alongside my finding that there is a relatively long-standing connection between rave and Internet technology, it is difficult to not recognize that there is immense *potential* for ravers to incite social change on a global level – although a uniform desire or motivation for change is not present among those in the scene.

Pre-Political Formations, Public Spheres, and the Micro-Politics of Rave

In his book *Zines: Notes from the Underground*, Stephen Duncombe (1997) argues that, while subcultural groups might not be socially active or "making a difference" at the present moment, many of these "pre-political" groups are in the process of finding a language and strategy for expressing their underlying political positions and aspirations – aspirations that will eventually become political actions. In a similar way, Gilbert and Pearson (1999), drawing on the classic works of Stallybrass and White (1986), suggest that carnivalesque events such as rave have historically been precursors to collective actions – actions that emerged out of the excess and unrestraint that are enabled in these social contexts. Gilbert and Pearson (1999) explained that "the playful irreverence of carnival can easily shade into a more serious challenge to authority" and described how negative reactions to the carnivalesque, and to its largely work-ing-class participants, by the ruling classes are evidence that the potential threat was recognized (162).

In these ways, Duncombe and Gilbert and Pearson provide an important counterpoint to those (myself included) that are some-what dismissive of the links between the more escapist or symbolic versions of rave-related activity and the potential for "real," counter-hegemonic political practices and actions. What is especially ad-mirable about Duncombe's and Gilbert and Pearson's arguments is that they are not overstated. That is to say, they both acknowledge that many seemingly apolitical (sub)cultural activities are far re-moved from any kind of collective resistance, while at the same time pointing out that these same activities have historically been part of an elongated process that *sometimes* cumulates in counter-hege-mony and social change.

In a similar way, authors like Bennett (2000) argue that social commentators who are critical of subcultures like rave be-cause they are apolitical tend to understate or be unaware of the identity politics that play out in youthful venues or scenes. From this perspective, dance spaces should be viewed as alternative "public spheres" where gender, ethnicity, race, class, and age-related identi-ties are negotiated and reformed. In this sense, dance music spaces and communities that are based, ideally, on respect and communi-cation are themselves political spaces that represent a new kind of youth cultural unity.

Extending this position beyond issues to do with race, eth-nicity, class, gender, and age, Angela McRobbie argues that legi-timate forms of micro-politics are embodied in the youth-driven second-hand clothes industry – an industry that undermines the dominant capitalist logic of cultural consumption and production. McRobbie suggests, for example, that the buying and selling of retro-clothes and the "recycling ethic" that is associated with them "do not just produce 'retro' images on the streets: they also provide a counterpoint to overpriced high street fashion" (1994, 162). McRobbie goes on to argue that by working in the retro-fashion busi-ness, these young people have "relatively unprofitable but per-sonally rewarding" employment – employment that challenges the conventional work ethic of the Thatcher conservatives and con-tributes to a hidden or alternative cultural economy (1994, 162).

McRobbie points out that "do it yourself" music productions by rave DJS (e.g., on home computers) and underground rave and club promotion companies reflect similar "alternative capitalist" values.*

In sum, while the rave scene described in this book initially appeared to exist within and be driven in many cases by the economic and escapist values of some ravers, hope and potential do exist. In the next chapter's discussion of rave, community, and political economy, I continue to pursue and examine this topic and its surrounding tensions.

*For a more elaborate discussion of the dance music scene, subcultures, and economic developments, see Chatterton and Hollands (2003) and Smith and Maughan (1998).

6
Marketing
"The Vibe"
Community, Nostalgia, Political Economy, and Rave

Words have meanings: some words, however, also have a "feel."
The word community is one of them. It feels good: whatever the word
community may mean, it is good "to have a community," "to be in a
community" ... "Community" ... promis[es] pleasures, and more often
than not the kinds of pleasures we would like to experience but seem
to miss. (Zigmund Bauman, *Community: Seeking Safety in an Insecure
World*, 2001, 1)

Although the term "community" is often used by ravers who are
describing the sense of connection that is felt between those deep
in the experience of the dance party – those who are "feeling the
vibe" – the concept has far wider application. Authors like Benedict
Anderson (1983) describe community in terms of the "imagined"
connections between people who share an interest or devotion, to,
for example, a country or sports team, but will never meet. Other
theorists examine connections between people that transcend conventional social structural boundaries (e.g., class, gender, race, eth-
nicity, and age), connections that are the basis of what Victor Turner
(1969) called "communitas." Still others, like some marketers and
cultural theorists, refer to "communities of consumption" when
describing population segments that tend to purchase the same sets
of products or to participate in similar leisure activities (Schouten
and McAlexander 1995).

Sociologists like Joel Best and David Luckenbill, in their
book *Organizing Deviance*, use the term in research that examines
and describes the "level of integration" that a group has – with an
extremely integrated and self-reliant group being a "community." In

this context, Best and Luckenbill refer to the gay community and gay neighbourhoods as groups and spaces characterized by a high level of integration. More loosely connected groups of people with similar interests, habits or pursuits are, according to these same authors, a social "world." Authors like Bennett (1999, 2000) and Malbon (1998, 1999) use the terms "scene" or "neo-tribe" to describe transient (but more local) groups, whose associations are based on periodic gathering at a dance party or sport event. Theorists like Hakim Bey (1991) take the neo-tribe concept even further, describing periodic, spontaneous, and often hedonistic communal formations – raves, for example – as "temporary autonomous zones," as parties or gatherings that explicitly challenge mainstream value systems associated with consumption and social order by virtue of their status as unsanctioned get-togethers in illegal venues.

As with portrayals of social resistance, these depictions of community range from more positive renderings of cultures where people are united, mutually supportive, and concerned with each other's well-being to more pessimistic representations of a society where relationships tend to be more instrumental and contractual, and where social cohesion is relatively low. Underlying much of the more pessimistic work – especially the early writing of Tonnies (1957), Weber (1978), and Cooley (1967) – is the view that modernization, and associated developments aimed at making labour practices more efficient and bureaucratic, have led to a situation where functionality and emotional detachment have become a way of life. That is to say, these theorists expressed concerns about the impact of late nineteenth- and early twentieth-century developments on the nature of societal relationships. Surratt (1998) summarizes this position as follows: "modernization is equated with the progressive loss of human community, which provided personal ties, a sense of group membership and loyalty within small communities. The social world of the community was circumscribed in space as well as in its way of life; modernity erodes such possibilities" (20).

In this chapter, I use the research findings presented in chapters three and four as a departure point for critical reflection on, first, the various depictions of community noted above and then, more generally, on the nature of contemporary subcultural communities. In doing so, I make the specific argument that rave, while embodying the *potential* for transcendent connections among its members, has become (with notable exceptions) a business that exploits glorified and nostalgic images in order to "sell" the dance party to youth.

Communitas, TAZ, and Rave: Linking Community and (Micro)Politics

In the previous chapter, I was somewhat critical of the work of Angela McRobbie, Ben Malbon, and Maria Pini because of their tendency to equate subcultural resistance with escapist behaviours, and to overstate what young people gain from the rave experience (e.g., that ravers "lose themselves in order to find themselves"). In this section I will reconsider their positions in attempting to understand how the temporary "communal experience" might be both empowering for young people while at the same time being a symbolic reaction to the "loss of community" that according to some sociologists characterizes late century and post-millennium culture – although my position that these forms of expression are not "counter-hegemonic" remains unaltered. Two bodies of work form the basis of this analysis. The first is the writing of Hakim Bey (1991), as it was adapted by Simon Reynolds (1998) to understand the potential and meaning of alternative forms of rave-related community. The second is the work of Victor Turner (1969) and a more recent version of Turner's position offered by Ingham and MacDonald (2003) in their examination of sports fans and community.

The first strand of theory is embodied in Simon Reynolds's work on the UK rave scene and his writings about the time he spent with a rave-related group called Spiral Tribe. Spiral Tribe is a counterculture dedicated to living an alternative lifestyle and raving "outside the law." The group's vision was expressed in the following way by its leader Mark Harrison:

We keep everything illegal because it's only outside the law that there's any real life to be had. The real energy in rave culture comes from the illegal dance parties, pirate radio, and white-label 12 inches [records] that bypass the record industry altogether. Rave is about people creating their own reality. Last summer we did a party that went on for fourteen days nonstop. It's a myth that you need to sleep. Stay awake and you begin to discover the real edges of reality. You stop believing in anything that anyone told you was true, all the false reality that was hammered into you from birth. (Reynolds 1998, 168)

Reynolds viewed this type of illegal, free party movement as being akin to what philosopher, revolutionary, and "anarcho-mystic" writer Hakim Bey has called the Temporary Autonomous Zone or TAZ – a "separate, self-governing [event] that take[s] place between the cracks of society's fabric" (from http://hyperreal.org/raves/spirit/), an event that is an "advance glimpse of utopia" (Reynolds 1998, 169).

Bey's 1991 book on the topic, *T.A.Z.: The Temporary Autonomous Zone, Ontological Anarchy, Poetic Terrorism*, includes an intoxicating synopsis of the potential and meaning of the TAZ. The book's thesis is underscored by Bey's position that the spaces inhabited by "bands" of people who share anti-establishment affinities – people who collectively refuse to be part of "cultural sinkholes" like stable work environments and the nuclear family (104) – are in themselves zones of and for resistance. In building his argument, Bey describes the resistive potential that exists when people/bands spontaneously organize and participate in a "festal culture removed and even hidden from the would-be managers of our leisure" (105). This culture is, according to Bey, reminiscent of "sixties style 'tribal gatherings', the forest enclave of forest eco-sabateurs, the idyllic Beltrane of neo-pagans, anarchist conferences, gay faery circles ... [that] are already 'liberated zones' of a sort, or at least potential TAZs" (106).

Reynolds views rave as a powerful "real world manifestation" of the TAZ. That is to say, Reynolds feels that the nomadic and hedonistic characteristics of rave are akin to Bey's view of a festal culture that gains its power from spontaneous events. This spontaneity, according to Reynolds, allows rave to subvert mainstream regulation and incorporation – at least in theory. Most pertinently, Reynolds (1998) sees the broader rave culture, with all of its technological connections (e.g., pirate radio broadcasts, electronic music, and designer-drug use), as being consistent with Bey's "vision of TAZ as a temporary power surge against normality" where the raver audience is "shocked out of the living death of normality, as opposed to a doomed attempt at permanent revolution" (245). In this way, Bey's utopian vision of a space where "celebration is celebrated" is at least temporarily played out.

This reverence of the temporary and impermanent is in contrast to arguments made in the work of Victor Turner and in subsequent works by Ingham and McDonald, who examined and commented on human associations they describe as "communitas."* Ingham and McDonald (2003) define communitas as follows: "A special experience during which individuals are able to rise above those structures that materially and normatively regulate their daily lives and that unite people across the boundaries of structure, rank, and socioeconomic status" (26). In his book *Ritual Process*, Turner (1969) differentiated the following: (a) the spontaneous and temporary form of communitas; (b) the ideological affirmation of this spontaneous, temporary form; and (c) the more permanent form. Turner went on to describe how certain forms of ritualistic activity contribute to social cohesion and to a sense of community, a sense of community that has been dwindling over the twentieth century. In an inadvertent departure from Bey's celebration of temporary associations or festivals, Turner lamented both the loss of a more permanent form of communitas, and the lack of continuity and meaning in more temporary gatherings. This view of a movement "away from community" is especially pertinent for this study in light of work by authors like Furlong and Cartmel (1997) who have noted the increasing sense of dislocation that young people have felt over the course of the twentieth century and into the twenty-first century.

The reason that Ingham and McDonald's version of Turner's work is instructive for this analysis is that they consider the possibility that, even in an era where more permanent forms of "communitas" are a near impossibility, groups like sports fans *might* still experience some sense of community through shared commitment to a professional sports team that represents a city – even if this commitment is a partial result of the effective marketing practices of the sports team. Applied to rave, individual ravers would experience community through their group's shared commitment to the subcultural rave doctrine and through their collective adherence to rave-related values at dance parties, even if this commitment and adherence is in part attributable to the marketing practices of some profit-hungry promoters. Ultimately, however, and despite this guarded optimism, Ingham and McDonald concluded that this type of community

---

*Reynolds himself includes skeptics' views on TAZ as part of his discussion.

is not feasible in the contemporary context – a conclusion that raises important questions that can inform an understanding of rave and community. Consider Ingham and McDonald's (2003) position:

The crucial question is whether representational sport remains an effective vehicle for the manufacturing of "community," or whether it can merely serve momentarily in the generation of spontaneous communitas. We argue for the latter. The die-hard fan may be there no matter what, but spontaneous communitas requires something above the mundane – a league championship or equivalent … Only the exceptional can provoke spontaneous communitas. But spontaneous communitas is fleeting and cannot form the basis for community per se. Community involves time and social commitment, and the investment of social capital. Community, in the Utopian sense, involves trust and obligation, and representational sport, especially in North America, provides no such basis for such. (28)

In essence, Ingham are McDonald are making a judgment about what people gain from their passing associations with a cultural group and whether the capitalist structures that are in place to facilitate a sense of community are, in fact, meaningful and significantly empowering for participant-consumers.

In considering these issues as they relate to rave, there once again arises a stark contrast between more optimistic and pessimistic understandings of the culture. Looking through a more cynical lens, rave would appear to be a largely incorporated group that is driven less by the rave doctrine and by the values espoused by authentic pro-rave visionaries – like Mark Harrison of Spiral Tribe – and more by the marketing strategies of promoters. From a more optimistic perspective, such as that offered by Reynolds in his discussion of Spiral Tribe, the potential for at least "pockets of community" to exist outside of and to challenge mainstream sensibilities and business practices seems to exist.

My own findings in the Toronto rave scene demonstrate that, in fact, *an Ingham and MacDonald–influenced understanding of rave is consistent with Reynolds's optimistic portrayal of a countercultural rave group*. Reynolds's suggestion that there are merely pockets of young people who are temporarily empowered by working outside the mainstream subcultural system – a system that remains dominated by images of an idealized, utopian rave that are especially appealing for new recruits to the scene – does not contradict Ingham and McDonald's perspective. That is to say, marginal resistance groups easily, and perhaps necessarily, exist within a predominantly incorporated culture. Simply put, if TAZ is understood as a subaltern and almost negligible presence in the rave scene, then a view of rave as being driven in large part by political economic motives is in no way undermined.

Globalization, Political Economy, Nostalgia, and Rave

The extent to which Toronto's rave culture is and was influenced by developments in Britain and/or New York is a contentious issue. At the very least, there are interesting parallels between the evolution of the rave scene abroad and the scene's development in Toronto and area. For example, both scenes originated in the gay community and were subsequently incorporated into an underground but less marginalized culture. Both scenes evolved into various sub-scenes or sub-communities that were defined largely by music genre, but also by age and drug use (e.g., the two Chicago house music scenes are akin to the sophisticated "techno" scene and the less refined "happy hardcore" scene in Toronto). There were also undeniable influences on the seminal developments of the Toronto rave scene by early promoters who attempted to simulate the British rave in the Toronto context. In fact, the authenticity of the original parties in Toronto were judged by their perceived similarities to the British raves, in the same way that current raves in the Southern Ontario scene are judged against nostalgic versions of early Toronto raves.

However, if we consider Reynolds's and Redhead's historical treatments of the rave scene, and their insights into the problems with the scene even in its purest form, then it makes sense to be at least somewhat critical of these idealized memories of early raves. Consider Smith's (1979) argument that nostalgic or mythic reconstructions of the past often offer "the illusory hope of escape from social conflict into an idyllic past that never was, and can never be" (202).* Work by Ingham, Howell, et al. (1987) on sport and nostalgia is relevant because it embodies concerns expressed about the potentially

*See also Nauright and White (1996) for a discussion of ways that nostalgia images have been used to "sell" ideologies around sport.

insincere motives of those who privately benefit from the use of nostalgia in campaigns to promote sports teams and other seemingly public entities in ways that financially benefit only a few; or, as the authors suggest, a past that perhaps never existed is sometimes used "not only to promote a sense of 'we' that does not structurally exist, but also to promote a mythical consensus that blurs the distinctions between private profit and public good" (453).

These arguments have particular relevance to the Toronto rave scene at the millennium since constructions of the "ideal rave" culture represented by the past – for example, as described in several retrospective testimonials provided by veteran ravers – are used by promoters to advertise rave parties. For instance, the rave promotion company Better Days, whose name can be interpreted as either a reference to the future or the past, threw a party in London, Ontario, on 15 March 1997 called "Back to my Roots" which was advertised as a "blast from the past," a revisiting of the roots of the scene in London, England, and as an "evening of nostalgia." The irony of nostalgic constructions of rave in Toronto is that *its rave parties might be, on some levels, more British and more aligned with the revered summer of 88 than the British raves ever were.*

Consider how this nostalgia-sensitive reading of rave is an implicit critique of classic subcultural evolution perspectives that theorize the linear development of youth subcultures from underground to mainstream, and from resistant to commercial. If the above argument that rave is characterized by distorted, decontextualized "memories" of better, more authentic days past is understood along with the finding that individual ravers, regardless of when they entered the rave scene, experience a rave career characterized by a waning of idealism, then the idea that subcultures progress over time and that experiences within subcultures vary according to the "state of authenticity" (i.e., closeness to the subculture's point of origin) is brought into question. This is particularly so since studies of inauthentic cultures, such as the commercialized rave scene or non-British spinoff rave scenes like Canada's, presume that there actually was an authentic, untainted starting point.

On this basis, the case study findings presented in chapters three and four both support and contradict Redhead's criticism (1990) of the tendency for academics and journalists to inaccurately view subcultural development from 1945 on as both progressive and continually authentic. To provide some additional context on this point, Redhead argued that "pop [culture] time has, in many ways, been circular rather than linear: the speed of what comes around again may change but the cyclical motion is embedded in pop's genealogy" (1990, 24–5). He clarifies this position in the following excerpt:

Beginning, initially, with the teddy boy style in the mid-1950s, working class subcultures are retrospectively mapped back on to British cultural history every few years. The mods, seen to spring from a more semi-skilled and white collar social base than the teds, explode on to the youth cultural landscape to clash, metaphorically and literally, with unskilled rockers. Greasers, bikers and other variants emerge, though with nothing like the legendary menace of American Hell's Angels. Skinheads, metamorphosed "hard" mods, are spotted "taking ends" at football grounds in the season after England's World Cup victory in 1966, before they splintered, eventually, into crombies, suedeheads and other groupings by the early 1970s ... These youth subcultural fashions were read as white styles; some urban black styles, rudies, rastas, B-boys did however receive a similar kind of treatment in youth cultural histories on a parallel time scale ... Subsequent revivals, for instance, of teds, mods, skins, hippies, and greasers, failed to disrupt the impression that what stood out in this evolution of post-war youth styles was continuity rather than circularity. (23–4)

This "end of (or lack of) youth culture" thesis is akin to Baudrillard's argument (1987) that "we have reached the end of history" – "where history has stopped meaning, referring to anything ... [where] we have passed into a kind of hyper-real where things are played out ad infinitum" (21).

While it is in some respects supported by the current study, I suggest that Redhead's argument for the "end of youth culture" is too extreme. That is to say, although aspects of rave were characterized by the circularity that Redhead refers to – e.g., the waning of idealism and the movement from underground to commercialization back to underground – rave culture is still historically important and specific. For example, while some ravers are reacting to current social conditions through subcultural participation, they are doing it in ways that are distinctly relevant to the cultural world they inhabit

at the millennium, as in their embrace of certain forms of technology and communication associated with the Internet. So, while traditional understandings of youth culture as a linear project are flawed
in some respects, history remains a crucial consideration when interpreting the strategies youth use for subcultural reaction, subversion,
and resistance. Also, it is important to consider how Hebdige (1979)
and others, whose portrayals of youth cultural development were
critiqued for being "too linear," actually did acknowledge the circularity of subcultural development. For example, Hebdige refers to
the "strategies of neutralization" employed by the mainstream –
such as moral panics, trivialization, and incorporation – strategies
employed on a recurring basis with the goal of neutralizing the resistive potential of any threatening subcultural groups.

Consider also how the British scene and the Canadian
scene's subsequent evolution can be understood in the context of an
increasingly globalized world. Maguire's broad description (1994) of
the "processes of globalization" is instructive for attempts at understanding the flow of rave culture from its various origins – New York,
Chicago, Detroit, Ibiza, Britain – to locales like Canada:

In the global flow of goods, services, and culture, indigenous groups
are active in interpreting what they receive. People – whatever the
unequal power relations – are not blank sheets on which transnational
corporations imprint their commodified tastes. In the multiple identities that compose a person's biography, involving class, gender, and
ethnic dimensions, a dynamic interweaving occurs between the local,
national, and transnational. A sense of place ... coexists with visions of
"other" places ... There is no *single* global flow; in the interweaving of
global scapes, disjunctures develop and cause a series of diverse, fluid
and unpredictable global conditions and flows. (402)

Maguire's argument can be extended to include situations
where local audiences both embrace cultural colonization, as with
rave, and are at the same time inevitably bound by local socio-cultural conditions that on some level modify the ways that any cultural form is interpreted and adopted.* In a recent article I wrote with
Ben Carrington (Carrington and Wilson 2002), we were guided by
this understanding of cultural flows, and especially by a classic arti-

*See, for example, Appadurai (1990), Lull (1995), and Wilson and Sparks (1996).

cle written by Arjun Appadurai (1990) that described "five dimensions of cultural flow." Our article examined the development of an
increasingly globalized rave dance culture that maintains distinct
local flavours and scenes. In doing so, we outlined a number of factors that have contributed to the evolution of this "glocal" culture,
including the rise of a "rave tourist" phenomenon, the evolution of
mass and alternative media, and the development of a more flexible
economy that allows and inspires ravers themselves to promote
their own music, parties, and scenes over the Internet.

Following these arguments – especially those that emphasize the importance of being sensitive to the ways that local cultures
reinterpret and modify "foreign" messages – it would seem that the
problem with lending too much credence to an understanding of the
Toronto rave scene that is overly focused on "British influences" is
that the rave movements in each country took place in somewhat
distinct social contexts. The movement from "raves to clubs" in Britain was largely because of the Criminal Justice and Public Order Act
of 1994 that essentially outlawed and criminalized raves in Britain
(Brown 1997; Redhead 1997). Although the law has been a factor in
the movement of raves from illegal to legal venues in Toronto, this
process was much more discreet and has arguably been initiated by
promoters who were tired of taking financial losses from rave parties
that were periodically closed down by police.

Consider also how the New York club scene in the 1970s
was originally a gay and ethnic movement, and how the Detroit techno scene was a supposed cultural and symbolic reaction to the decay
of an urban centre. While the rave in Toronto has been shown to be
a gathering place for marginalized youth, and the pro-technology
flavour of Toronto's rave culture to be a hyper-adaptation to increasingly postmodern conditions, to argue that the rave scene was a
social reaction akin to those in New York and Detroit would be over-
stating what took place. In fact, the British and Toronto scenes could
be more aptly viewed as examples of scenes that appropriated or
incorporated music and traditions in ways that might *disempower*
groups whose formerly resistant cultures have been pillaged in so
far as the resistant potential of their symbolic form has been diluted
by changing the symbol's meaning. Lipsitz (1997) discusses this
transformation in his work on popular music, postmodernism, and
"the poetics of place":

Like other forms of contemporary mass communication, popular music simultaneously undermines and reinforces our sense of place. Music that originally emerged from concrete historical experiences in places with clearly identifiable geographic boundaries now circulates as an interchangeable commodity marketed to consumers all over the globe. Recordings by indigenous Australians entertain audiences in North America. Jamaican music secures spectacular sales in Germany and Japan. Rap music from inner city ghettos in the U.S.A. attracts allegiances of teenagers from Amsterdam to Auckland ... These transactions transform – but do not erase – attachments to place ... [For example] electric-techno-art music made in Germany serves as a staple for sampling within African-American hip hop; Spanish flamenco and paso doble music provide crucial subtexts for Algerian rai artists; and pedal steel guitars first used by country and western musicians in the U.S.A. play a prominent role in Nigerian juju ... This dynamic dialogue, however, does not necessarily reflect relations of reciprocity and mutuality. Inter-cultural communication does not automatically lead to inter-cultural cooperation, especially when participants in the dialogue speak from positions of highly unequal access to power, opportunity, and life chances. (4)

While the adaptation of rave from Ibiza to Britain and Britain to Canada does not necessarily reflect unequal cultural positionings, the adaptation of 1970s club cultures into disco within the United States (i.e., the adaptation of a gay, Black movement into mainstream) does. In a more subtle way, Toronto's incorporation of house dance music into raves and rave clubs might be interpreted as a mainstreaming and threatening of the gay club scene, which is largely separate from the Toronto rave scene.

Stability, Transience, and Rave: Reconsidering Subcultural Membership

As noted previously, commentators like Malbon (1998) and Bennett (2000) suggest that rave is a "tribal formation" characterized by regular group meetings, but an unstable group membership. That is to say, while the rave party, and especially the rave dance club, are rel-

atively stable gathering spaces, individual ravers tend to move between dance music scenes and venues, and in and out of the scene
altogether. In many respects, my findings in the Toronto scene affirm
this UK-based perspective. For example, my interviews, which usually
included retrospective discussions about rave involvement, showed
not only that ravers' musical tastes evolved over time – which neces-
sitated attendance at different parties associated with distinct musical sub-scenes – but also that as ravers became disillusioned with
the scene or acquired other non-rave interests, they would halt or
limit their attendance at parties and clubs.

The problem with this sort of analysis, however, is that it
tends to overlook the cultural patterns that do exist in rave, especially in the subcultural lives of group members. That is to say, while
the rave space is relatively transient, ravers' perspectives on and
involvements in the scene seem to evolve in somewhat stable ways.
For example, many ravers experienced a "waning of idealism" over
their time in the scene, a waning that begins and elevates as ravers
learn more about the politics of rave and become more cynical about
the positioning of drugs as a cultural mainstay of the scene. Another sense of stability that is not fully accounted for in a neo-tribal
framework is the ongoing involvements that many ravers have in
rave-*related* activities, involvements that do not require and are not
defined by attendance at raves. For example, while it may appear that
rave is a transient scene because many ravers cannot be "counted
on" to attend parties on a regular basis (with subcultural neophytes
continually taking veteran's places on the dance-floors), many
seemingly absent or retired ravers remain involved in music-making,
or participate in rave-related technology newsgroups. Put simply,
young people's careers as subculture members are, in fact, patterned, and these patterns can be discerned by researchers who
remain actively engaged with a scene over time and/or those who
attend to ravers' retrospective understandings of the scene and their
involvement in it.*

---

*For examples of arguments supporting this position, see Becker (1963), Prus
and Sharper (1977), and Haas and Shaffir (1991).

Final Thoughts on Rave, Community, and Postmodern Subcultures

From the post-war days of the jitterbug, demob suits, big bands and ballrooms ... through the Teddy boys bopping to Bill Haley, ampheta-mine-fuelled Mods out on the dance floor every weekend dancing to early Motown and R and B; through the Northern Soul and Southern Funk scenes of the 1970s and to the warehouse parties of the 80s and raves of this decade, dance music has been a focal point of working class youth culture ... Yet, somehow, this has escaped the attention of all those involved in today's rave scene. For these individuals, nothing seems to have existed before 1989 and their belated discovery of dance music and Ecstasy ... And what better way of claiming impor-tance for a music scene than claiming that it is subversive? Thousands of kids united under the "dance" banner, threatening the status quo, dancing to the "underground" music – you know it's underground and "dangerous" because of the slick marketing of the CDs, raves and the slew of promotional items tells you so again and again. (Strongman 1999, from the webzine "Discord" www.discord.co.uk/rave.html)

Controversy remains about the extent to which rave is a postmodern subculture. On one hand, it seems that critics who do not acknowl-edge rave's positioning as a postmodern subculture are also not acknowledging at least one definition of postmodernism, that of it meaning "after modernism," or "maintaining aspects of modernism while having integrated aspects of culture that characterize social life after modern times," which in this case means the aspects of rap-idly evolving mass media and technologies. As Chen (1991) argued: "Postmodernity denotes a 'rearrangement' and a 'new configuration' which have exceeded the boundaries of modernity. Although it is not an absolute rupture, one has to realize ... that no historical era is ever absolute; that 'Stone Age' elements remain, albeit entering new rela-tions with other internal elements" (36–7). If Chen's position is extended from historical period to cultural practice, the rave subcul-ture is surely a postmodern subculture by this definition.

On the other hand, though, the tendency to overstate the po-sitioning of rave as a postmodern subculture is equally problematic.

Work that describes the evolution of rave culture toward a fragment-ed and culturally chaotic group often fails to consider the patterns of meanings that ravers give to their activities. Moreover, models of post-modern culture that emphasize the global and virtual characteristics of the group do not account for or acknowledge how cultures with a worldwide reach are still part of social organizations, even if they have become less easily defined. Other work that emphasizes how rave rep-resents a sensual, emotional, ritualistic techno-community – work that focuses on the affective level of subcultural life – fails in many cases to consider the generic social processes that continue to define all subcultural groups, and that no subcultures are entirely defined by emotional connection.

If we reflect on recent work in youth cultural studies that describes the impact of *post*modern developments on social cohe-sion (i.e., developments associated with globalization, pervasive media, and associated threats to local identities), then these early claims about modernism appear quite ironic. That is to say, contem-porary youth are considered to be increasingly individualistic, pos-sess few ties to their community, are increasingly caught up in the pursuit of lifestyles promoted by pervasive advertising, and spend more time interacting with various media and less with (local) friends and family. For this reason, social commentators often artic-ulate a sense of nostalgia for earlier times, specifically the late nine-teenth and early twentieth century, when participation in local communities and cultures was a central part of social life. A point of irony is that these now-glorified "earlier times" are the same times that Tonnies, Weber, and Cooley focused their criticisms on while liv-ing through them.

Rave culture, because of its popular positioning as the prototypical "twenty-first century subculture" and its tendency to be revered as an atypically open and accepting community, is an ex-tremely instructive case study for considering some of these issues and contradictions. In particular, the timing of rave's emergence and existence, and its relationship to "the past" (i.e., to previous subcul-tures and to the early rave scene) allows for an analysis of, first, the differences, or lack of difference, between modern and postmodern subcultures, second, ravers' perceptions of these histories and how these perspectives have been integral to ravers' experience's in the subculture and, third, the ways that historical images are used to promote the subculture. In a related way, rave's existence during a time of global interactive Internet technology is important to consider when attempting to understand and describe the nature of rave's subcultural and social ties, and the social organization of rave more generally.

conclusion

7
Raise a Fist?
Reflections on Theory, Practice, and Youth (Cultural) Studies

Most academics just ramble. Far too few raise a fist or a voice. Communications professors tell their students everything that's wrong with the global media monopoly, but never a word about how to fix it. Economics professors drone on endlessly about their macroeconomic models while in the real world we live off the planet's natural capital and the backs of future generations ... Nonexperts – regular reasonable people – are disgusted by all this dithering. They already have a good idea what's going on. They can tell by the issues their politicians choose *not* to address ... [by] the way their kids' expressions go vacant by the third hour of television viewing. Abbie Hoffman nailed it when, after being told that academics and experts were busy analyzing the subject of "subversive activity" he said: "What the fuck are you analyzin' for man? Get in and do it!" And Edward Abbey nailed it when he said: "Sentiment without action is the ruin of the soul." (Kalle Lasn, *Adbusters – Journal of the Mental Environment*, 1999, 37)

Critics of books like this one often ask the very reasonable question, "So what?" – a question usually accompanied by suggestions that there is too much theory and contemplation and not enough action in today's academic world, as Lasn articulates above. At first glance, this seems like a compelling argument, especially since Marxist-related critical work, whether on subcultures or other topics, is inherently about making a difference, and yet links between theory and practice are rare. What tends to be forgotten in these general portrayals, however, is that theory is often an "accumulation of practice." That is to say, to describe the ways that previous commentators – be they academics, journalists, or others – have explained a social issue, to offer novel ways of understanding this same issue, to "test" these perspectives and ways through a rigorous and in-depth study, to consider how the various approaches to understanding the issue stand up in light of research findings, and then to offer an updated explanation which researchers and practitioners can draw upon does not seem problematic in my view. In fact, it seems responsible and necessary. In other words, research like that presented in this book – that is critical of and attempts to inform often simplistic mass media portrayals of youth culture and deviance, that attempts to highlight the problems with deceivingly straightforward, no-nonsense solutions or approaches to youth-related issues, that attempts to honour and document the meanings that various individuals give to their experiences within an often stigmatized group – could be viewed as ammunition when attempting to influence policy and programming in areas related to, for example, youth and drug use, youth and leisure, youth and media, or youth and health generally. As importantly, this process also demonstrates that researchers do not have to be activists and that activists do not have to be researchers (although they certainly can be and often are) – assuming that there is a dialogue about how theory and practice can, in fact, complement one another in specific social contexts. In this way, Norm Denzin's call to "make a difference" and to "change the world" in socially progressive ways through social research can be maintained through various levels of social participation (1992, 167).

These tensions between theory and practice act as background for the following commentary that serves as this book's conclusion, a commentary that explores issues related to practical recommendations for dealing with "today's youth" that are prevalent in popular and academic work.

Informing Social Programmes That Target Youth While Remaining Cautious about "Action Plans" and Agendas

This research on youth and rave had various goals that have potentially practical outcomes, including:

- to critique sensational mass media portrayals of "troubled and troubling" youth and, in turn, better inform practical initiatives intended to help youth deal with the issues that are most disconcerting to them
- to demonstrate how social phenomena that are often portrayed in simplistic ways are actually complex and contradictory and deserving of in-depth qualitative study (i.e., before proceeding with politically motivated policy creation)
- to complement existing knowledge about the behavioural determinants of drug abuse by providing insight into the social context of leisure-related drug use (since this study was focused on the ways that drug use was part of the broader rave culture) while showing how drugs were used in different ways for different reasons
- to conceptually guide future research focused on youth cultural experience and the structural circumstances that envelop these experiences
- to contribute to a foundation of ethnographically-informed critical work on youth from which programming initiatives and policy recommendations and responses can be drawn

Additionally, however – and building on this last point – this work was meant to serve as a commentary about action-plans that are focused on creating "high moral standards" for our youth. For example, William Damon's 1997 book *The Youth Charter: How Communities Can Work Together to Raise the Standards of Our Children* is predicated on the idea that, in recent years, standards for youth have fallen, and that people who work with youth need to be better equipped to deal with and reverse this trend. Consider the following statement in the book's preface:

Everywhere I go, parents and teachers complain that the forces influencing children have spun wildly out of control. How can a parent pass on good values when children are exposed to every imaginable form of sordidness through the mass media? How can a teacher pass on skills and knowledge when the popular and peer cultures discourage serious academic motivation? Other citizens, too, express concerns. How can a pediatrician, seeing her caseload bursting with unnecessary teenage health

disorders – suicide attempts, alcoholism and drug abuse, eating disorders, assaults, injuries from driving accidents – do anything effective
about preventing the damage when her young patients refuse to take
her warnings seriously? How can a citizen, seeing his home town
wracked by youth vandalism, theft, and other petty crime, stop young
people from destroying his town – and their futures – when neither the
police nor the youngsters' families seem able to control the youngster's
behavior ... The youth charter is an approach that brings together all
adults who are in positions to influence young people ... in the quest to
define high community standards for youth development ... Many of the
necessary conditions for youth development – solid community, guiding
relationships, clear standards – have been eroded. Young people today
encounter a fractionated society broadcasting messages of low expectations, disbelief, cynicism, relative or nonexistent standards, isolation,
and moral detachment. The guidance many young people need is missing from the usual places. Their families' lives, their schools, their neigh-
borhoods, and religious or other community organizations have been
degraded by conflict or lack of support. The increasingly powerful mass
media impart messages that are mixed at best and corrupting at worst,
further confounding the youngster's developmental quest. (ix–x, 55–6)

My concerns about Damon's position are in no way intended to belittle or trivialize his proactive stance on youth issues. His
goal of making a difference is admirable and he makes convincing
arguments that issues to do with youth violence, drug abuse, and
teen pregnancy, among others, need to be taken seriously. However,
Damon's message is strikingly similar to journalistic calls for something to be done about "today's youth" – calls that create unfounded
anxieties and inspire or support over-reactive policies like "anti-
rave" laws. A question left unanswered in this context is this: Does
sufficient evidence exist that suggests that things are worse now
than they were in years past, as in the "good old days"? In asking
this question, I do not want to imply that youth-related prevention
programmes and support systems are not crucial. I do, however, pro-
pose that the concerns and panics about "today's youth" might be
overblown and overstated, and, moreover, that the labels that are
attached to many youth cultures are not only presumptuous, but
also might create more problems than they solve.

Bibby's large-scale survey reported in his 2001 book on
Canada's teens sheds some light on these issues (the problems with

survey use outlined in chapter one of this book are duly noted here). He collected data about *adult* perceptions of teen behaviour and development; and he identified social trends over time in areas such as teen suicide, experiences with drugs, sex and abuse, alcohol and smoking consumption patterns, and violence. The conclusion drawn from these findings was that, despite some negative patterns (e.g., according to Bibby's work, violence at schools appears to be up and drug access has increased), "most teenagers are neither contributing to these undesirable trends, nor are they directly affected by them" (2001, 258). As he describes in some detail:

our findings show that young people tend to hold values very similar to those of adults, in sharp contrast to the devastatingly negative impressions most adults have of teen values. Beyond just values, our findings on enjoyment, compassion, self-esteem, and outlook, as well as our overall comparison of teen attitudes and beliefs with the three adult generations [i.e., grandparents, parents, and younger adults], add up to an encouraging portrait of today's teenagers. If "the times" are making it more difficult to be a teenager, our findings indicate that most are up to the challenge. (258–9)

A similarly relevant response to Damon's arguments is inherent in Tanner's suggestion that youth behaviour in years past might not be notably different than youth behaviour today:

One of the consequences of imbuing the behavior of the young with important symbolic meaning is that it leads to images of adolescent deviance that do not always correspond with reality ... Simply being young and hanging out with friends on the street or in a shopping mall is often enough to generate negative stereotyping or a deviant label. But appearances are sometimes deceiving, and the fact of the matter is that most young people are not in serious conflict with society, do not hold values that clash with those of the parental generation, and do not engage in the types of deviance that adults find most troubling. (1996, 19)

In the same way, reports that "the media" is a prime culprit contributing to the "problems with today's youth" seldom take into account research on actual media impacts or on the various (sometimes creative and positive) ways that youth use media. Likewise, critiques of mass media on the grounds that it has negative influences on youth implicitly preclude the possibility that *it is adults that are being duped by the mass media* – duped into thinking that youth are, more than ever before, troubled and troubling, and that society and its values are spinning wildly out of control (Onstad 1997).

In fact, some of the data presented in this book support the view that young people have an incredible capacity for adaptation – an argument that could no doubt also be made for previous generations of youth. For example, youth who are part of the current "net generation" (Tapscott 1998), the most technologically advanced generation, should be recognized for their ability to adjust to the changing cultural landscape and for their potential to instruct other generations about the benefits and pleasures of technology. As Rushkoff (1996) suggests in his book *Playing the Future: How Kids Can Teach Us to Thrive in the Age of Chaos*:

The evolutionary experience of culture, as practiced by kids today, directly contradicts much of the traditional New Testament interpretation. It accepts that things keep changing, without a satisfying, determinist ending. It dispenses with storytelling and parable in favour of experiential ... methods of understanding abstraction or divinity. It refuses to treat the discontinuous as anything but natural: the increasing nonlinearity of our media and popular culture is not a heathen retreat from the dualistic morality of God, but the process by which we learn to accept the very natural, organic and complex property of life called *chaos* [original emphasis] ... What I'll attempt to show ... is that the more frightening aspects of a non-apocalyptic future are being addressed today, and quite directly, by the most pop-cultural experiences of children and young adults. Whether it's the Power Rangers showing us how to accept co-evolution with technology, or a vampire role playing game calling for us to accept the satanic beast in each of us, these new forms have the ability to assuage our worst fears, confirm our most optimistic scientific theories, and obliterate the religious and cultural absolutism so detrimental to our adaptation to the uncertainty of our times. Within the form and content of kids' favourite shows, games and social interactions lie the prescriptions for us to cope with cultural change ... So please let us suspend, for the time being, our grown-up function as role models and educators of our nation's youth. Rather than focusing on how we, as adults, should inform our children's activities with educational tidbits for their better development, let's appreciate the natural adaptive skills demonstrated by our kids and look to them for answers to some of our own problems adapting to postmodernity. (12–13)

While I admit that Rushkoff oversimplifies the capabilities of a group as diverse as "kids," his innovative pro-youth position usefully counter-balances the problematic writing focused on the "youth problem." My intention in highlighting this position is not to dismiss the real social constraints and barriers that youth do face, but to show, once again, that youth should be understood for what they are – a transitional, complex, and contradictory social group that is too often portrayed in deceiving and superficial ways.

Appendix 1
Comments about Method and Theory

Underlying the case study of rave was a methodological and theoretical commitment to ethnographic methods and semiotic analysis (both qualitative methods). While the examination of the quantitative-qualitative debates alluded to in chapter one and the discussion of Willis's and Hebdige's influential methodological positions also in chapter one are useful points of departure, there are basic terms and concerns within qualitative research (related to, for example, reliability, validity and generalizability) that require clarification and attention.

Although the largely "critical interactionist" theoretical position developed throughout this book underscores all aspects of the data analysis, the methods used to carry out this study followed closely with classic and recent statements about ethnographic research as a procedure for gathering data (Blumer 1969; Lofland 1976; Prus 1996a; Shaffir and Stebbins 1991; Tedlock 2000; Willis 1978). Ethnographic research (also known as "field research," naturalistic inquiry," "qualitative research," "interactionist research," "Chicago school research," and "participant observation") is concerned with the study of the way of life of a group (Prus 1996a, 103). Blumer (1969) has argued that ethnographic methods are the only methods that adequately enable the researcher to respect the nature of human group life, achieve intimate familiarity with persons in their social world, and develop "sensitizing concepts" from data – concepts developed through what is commonly referred to as a grounded theory and inductive approach, following the work of Glaser and Strauss (1967). Shaffir and Stebbins (1991, drawing on Blumer 1969;

Taylor and Bogdan 1984; and Webb et al. 1981) summarized the central characteristics of this method:

Fieldwork is carried out by immersing oneself in a collective way of life for the purpose of gaining firsthand knowledge about a major facet of it ... Adopting mainly the method of participant observation ... the researcher attempts to record the ongoing experiences of those in their symbolic world. The research strategy commits the observer to learning to define the world from the perspective of those studied and requires that he or she gain as intimate an understanding as possible of their way of perceiving life. To achieve this aim, the field researcher typically supplements participant observation [the primary methodology used by ethnographers] with additional methodological techniques in field research, often including semistructured interviews, life histories, [and] document analysis. (5)

Although definitions of ethnography and participant observation vary (Hammersley 1992; Tedlock 2000), one view is that participant observation is a primary methodology used by ethnographers, a method of research "that involves social interaction between researcher and the informants in the milieu of the latter, during which data are systematically and unobtrusively collected" (Taylor and Bogdan 1984, 15). Acknowledging the advantages of adopting this methodological approach for the study of lived experience, there are several issues and problems related to aspects of ethnography, and to participant observation in particular, as Willis (1978) suggested:

In the preconceptions of the observer, in the artificiality of the observer/observed situation, in the decentration, partiality, inversion or distortion of self-knowledge in the observed, lie many possible sources of error in the participant observation method. Furthermore, replication and proof are impossible and a scientistic concern with technique can never conceal, only impinge and obstruct – the proper workings through of participant observation in its own form of production and work on human meaning. (194)

Embedded in Willis's statement and in other work on methodological considerations in participant observation are concerns with the internal validity ("truth" value), external validity (generalizability), and reliability (replicability) of research findings.* Shaffir and Stebbins (1991, 13–14, drawing on McCall and Simmons 1969, 78) organized some of these concerns as they relate to "doing" participant observation into three categories: (1) the reactive effects of researcher presence on the phenomenon being observed (e.g., when subjects act differently in the presence of the researcher and/or when there is loss of trust between researcher and subject); (2) the distorting effects of selective perception and interpretation (e.g., "going native"; types of relationships with subjects); and (3) limitations on the ability of the researcher to observe all phenomena relevant to the group (e.g., how the sex, age, or race of the researcher might limit access to certain types of information).

Table A.1, adapted from Erlandson, Harris, et al. 1991 and Lincoln and Guba 1985, and others, outlines the strategies that can be used to deal with these issues. Several of these suggestions are at least implicitly referred to in chapter three's report of results.

Table A.1: Dealing with internal and external validity issues

Internal Validity	External Validity
Prolonged engagement: to overcome researcher impacts on context and effects of unusual or seasonal events	*"Thick" description*
Persistent observation: to help distinguish which events and activities are most relevant or central	*Purposeful sampling*: unlike random sampling, purposeful sampling is guided by emerging insights about what is relevant to the study and is focused on providing rich detail about the issues most relevant to the study of the group

*See Erlandson, Harris, et al. (1993), Hammersley (1992), and Lincoln and Guba (1985) for discussion about these terms and related topics.

Table A.1: cont.

Triangulation/Crossgridding of evidence/Clustering (see Denzin 1970; Donnelly 1985; Willis 1978): to help elicit potentially diverse interpretations of group experience, help confirm similar interpretations, provide broader context, elicit alternative explanations	*Reflexive field notes*
Peer debriefing	
Check data with research subjects	
Reflexive field notes	

A few aspects of this table require clarification here. First, the notion of *external validity*, in the context of ethnographic research, is not concerned with generalizability or representativeness in the traditional statistical sense (i.e., where representative samples are selected and generalizations across populations are made within specific probabilities of error). As noted in chapter one, statistical methodological applications break down when more complex meaning or interpretation-based understandings of group culture are sought. In ethnographic research, external validity is satisfied by developing generic social processes that allow comparisons of social life in all its forms across contexts, as Prus (1994) explained:

generic social processes [original emphasis] refer to the trans-situational elements of interaction; to the abstracted formulations of social behavior. Denoting parallel sequences of activity across diverse contexts, generic social processes highlight the emergent interpretive features of association. They focus our attention on the activities involved in "doing" or accomplishing group life ... When researchers are mindful of generic, or trans-situational concepts, every piece of ethnographic research in any realm of human behavior can be used to generate insight into any other realm of human behavior. (395)*

*See also Berger and Luckman (1971), Garfinkal (1967), Lofland (1976), and Prus (1987, 1996a).

Similarly, the use of "thick description" (Geertz 1973) in ethnographic research – or, more accurately, in writing up field notes and research reports based on fieldwork – can effectively allow researchers to assess the potential "transferability" of findings from one setting to another. Denzin (1989) expresses the importance of thick description as a tool in interpretive interactionist research as follows:

A thick description ... does more than record what a person is doing. It goes beyond mere fact and surface appearances. It presents detail, context, emotion, and the webs of social relationships that join persons to one another. Thick description evokes emotionality and self-feelings. It inserts history into experience. It establishes the significance of an experience, or a sequence of events, for the person or persons in question. In thick description, the voices, feelings, actions, and meanings are heard. (83)

On this basis, thick description "permits a willing reader to share the experiences that have been captured" and to "naturalistically generalize his or her experiences to those that have been captured" (Denzin 1989, 83).

Also, adopting a *reflexive* approach to field research is crucial for establishing both internal and external validity. The position taken in this book (following Lincoln and Guba 1985, Woolgar 1988, and others) is that "objectivity" in the traditional "hard" sciences sense is a myth (Berger and Luckmann 1971). On this basis, the ethnography of rave presented in chapters three and four is concerned with the meanings that individuals give to their experiences, while acknowledging that the researcher is partial and subjective when studying groups and interpreting these meanings. Willis (1978) insightfully discussed the way this sort of openness in the research process is beneficial:

I argue for the use of naturalistic comparative techniques [ethnography] to specify more precisely what is the scope and meaning of the essential problematic of the method. Instead of being "problems," the final and "unresolvable" difficulties of the method are its specific resources. These moments concern the ability of the researcher to reflexively analyze the intersection of his own social paradigms with those of the people he wishes to understand. Such an intersection speaks, of course, as

much to the researcher and his world as it does of any other world ...
Usually thought of as unavoidable costs, the "problems" of field work
can be more imaginatively thought of as the result of a fine intersection
of two subjective meaning constructions ... Although the researcher can
never experience another experience – the romantic notion of "empa-
thy" – he can feel how his own experience is minutely locked into
another's: how his own experience is disoriented. The problems of this
method always ask questions. If the researcher feels threatened at
certain points, what is it that threatens him? If the researcher is not
able to join in group activities, what is stopping him? (177–8)

Willis is not arguing that hard, irrefutable forms of data are attained
from this self-reflexive technique, but is instead suggesting that by
identifying and examining various contradictions and problems in
the data "more substantial understandings can be developed"
(Willis 1978, 198). It is interesting to note that Willis's seminal formulations reflect the more contemporary emphasis that postmodern
ethnographers like Dickens and Fontana (1994) have put on the
importance of considering alternative data sources and reflexivity.

Many of these same issues also apply to the use of social
semiotics. In essence, interpreting media "texts," which is the most
common focus of semiotic research (or other texts, such as clothing
styles, hairstyles, or Web pages) is the same as interpreting interview data or field note data – all are texts that the researcher interprets. In all cases, it is crucial to acknowledge one's own social
positioning and potential biases in interpreting data and texts, while
acknowledging that there are multiple potential interpretations of
data. However, this should not exclude the possibility of progressive, meaningful readings of cultural texts, as Duncan (1990) explained: "Responsible textual studies do not assert with absolute
certainty how particular texts are interpreted. But they suggest the
kinds of interpretations that may take place, based on available evidence, and likely interpretations of a particular text. Ultimately
these interpretations must be judged on the basis of the persua-
siveness and logic of the researcher's discussion" (27).

This reaction to the potential methodological and theoretical problems related to a "relativist interpretivist" position are consistent with Hall's argument that despite a "perpetual slippage of the
signifier," social texts, identities, and practices are always "*relatively*

anchored" (Hall 1985, 93) – a position drawn from "articulation" theory. Cowie summarizes this position (1977) as follows: "The endless possible signification of the image is always and only a theoretical possibility. In practice, the image is always held, constrained in its production of meaning or else becomes meaningless, unreadable. At this point the concept of anchorage is important; there are developed in every society decisive technologies intended to fix floating chains of signifieds so as to control the terror of uncertain signs" (22).* What is being referred to here is a critical-realist position that is sensitive to postmodernist understandings of the multiple meanings and interpretations that can be assigned to social texts.

Critical Ethnography and Writing Critical Narratives

Elaborating on these hermeneutic debates, two further points related to doing and writing critical ethnography are discussed here. First, the theory-method connection initiated in Willis's early critical ethnographic work requires emphasis because of the underlying issues related to "power" that are examined in this book – issues that underscore the interpretivist and structuralist theories and methodologies used in the rave study presented earlier.† With this background, I highlight Donnelly's view (2000) of the crucial link between method and theory in macro and micro analyses, and follow his suggestion that methodological concerns are inseparable from issues of theory because "assumptions" and "interpretations" are embodied in both. That is to say, the critical nature of much hermeneutic work is underscored by the assumption, for example, that media messages are designed to maintain an unequal status quo in society, which in turn assumes that a critical interpretation and deconstruction of these messages (i.e., a hermeneutic analysis) is progressive and necessary.

---

*See also McKay (1995).

†Although this book is concerned predominantly with neo-Marxist, structuralist perspectives on power, I acknowledge Prus's fairly recent work (1995, 1999) done in the symbolic interactionist tradition that views power as "intersubjective accomplishment."

Second, the issue of how critical ethnographers represent, in ethnographic writing, the realities of individuals and groups under study requires consideration as a logical extension of Willis's argument for a reflexive method. Denzin's previously noted statement about "thick description" is one presentation strategy that is useful for ethnographers who intend to make comprehensive, empirically informed, historically located, and *critical* statements about the relationship between social structural constraints and human lived experience. Donnelly's argument (1985) for a broader definition of ethnography "that goes beyond traditional forms" is an implicit challenge to ethnographers to access and draw on multiple and varied data sources when (re)presenting the group under study in a written text. Specifically, Donnelly suggested that ethnography should include the analysis of publications put out by subcultural groups, biographies, introductory or how-to-do books, general books, magazine articles written by group members and journalists or freelance writers, fiction, poetry, songs, painting, sculptures, cartoons, and films (1985, 568–9) – to which I add Web sites, Internet newsgroups, and chat rooms. These ideas are reminiscent of suggestions made by postmodern ethnographers like Richardson (1998).*

Foley's paper (1992) on "writing critical sport narratives" summarized the dilemma facing sociologists who attempt to write ethnographies that are accessible and fair to those who these ethnographies represent, *and* are compelling for academic readers who demand the "conventional" methodological rigour that characterizes naïve realist ("scientific") ethnography (Richardson 2000). Foley's argument builds on the critical ethnographic tradition represented by Willis (1977, 1978). Crucial to these authors' approach was the writing of ethnographies in two parts. Part one was written as a personal, reflexive account of and descriptive ethnography of the group under study, or as Foley (1992) put it, "written in a language that expresses my voice and uses metaphors, irony, and comedy" (44). Part two was written as a critical-theoretical examination of

---

*For more developed arguments related to the "crisis of representation" in ethnography, see Clifford (1988), Clifford and Marcus (1986), Geertz (1988), and Marcus and Fischer (1986).

part one, using "the academic dialect that social theorists speak" (44). In both instances, part two also included a more conventional discussion of and reflection on methodological procedure.

Expressing some dissatisfaction with this relatively unintegrated solution to the problem of presenting more authentic ethnographic accounts without losing academic voice, Foley argued that there is a need to find a "middle ground between the extensive poetic experimentation advocated by some postmodern ethnographers" (45, building on Rose 1990; Tyler 1986) and "new, more accessible and quasi-literary versions of the old scientific realist narrative" (45). On this basis, Foley (1992) made three suggestions intended to move toward a more open, relativistic tone in non-positivistic interpretive narratives:

1 Reduce the amount of "generic omniscient ethnographic narrative" and include more impressionistic tales [referring to the use of specific characters and actual events instead of typifications and generic events]. Foley argued that these types of accounts make the researcher more visible and allow for more character development than "bland generic typifications." (45)

2 Do *not* exclude the theoretical voice of the social scientist. Foley suggested that "there is nothing wrong with sprinkling ... more impressionist narratives with some well-marked digressions into the author's theoretical view ... [although] given the somewhat underdeveloped storytelling skills of many social scientists ... these shifts to theorizing mode will be difficult without overwhelming the story being told. (45)

3 Authors of ethnographies must be up-front about their theoretical and personal assumptions.

Although I adopted some of Foley's recommendations in the rave case study described in this book, particularly those related to the integration of personal accounts and storytelling with more generic analysis, and those that support general principles of reflexivity, I am less willing to abandon the style of Willis's (1977) and Foley's (1990) original two-part ethnographies. This two-part approach allows for rich (thick) descriptive presentations of ethnographic data, *while maintaining a commitment to sophisticated critical analysis and theoretical development.** The stance taken here is that the "specificity of the analysis," an analysis that often surrounds and develops underlying conceptual themes, risks being lost or de-emphasized in ethnographies that use "too many sprinklings" of theory at the expense of a rigorous data examination. This stance was reflected in the presentation of the two-part ethnography of the rave youth subculture in this book, with chapters three and four including the data presentation and micro-sociological analysis, and chapters five and six including theoretical reflections on the data through critical, structuralist, and postmodernist lenses.

*Aspects of reflexive, critical ethnography are akin to what some have termed "postmodern ethnography." Postmodern ethnography refers, in a general way, to ethnographic work that emphasizes the need for a reflexive researcher, and is extremely sensitive to the socially constructed characteristics of all texts – including texts that document research findings (Dickens and Fontana 1994; Richardson 1998).

References

Abercrombie, N., S. Hill, B. Turner, and S. Bryan. 1980. *The dominant ideology thesis*. London: George Allen and Unwin.

Acland, C. 1995. *Youth, murder, spectacle: The cultural politics of "youth in crisis."* Boulder, CO: Westview Press.

Adams, M. 1997. *The trouble with normal: Postwar youth and the making of heterosexuality*. Toronto: University of Toronto Press.

Addiction Research Foundation. 1998, June 10. *Snap-shot of raving in Toronto*. Press release from the Addiction and Mental Health Services Corporation. http://arf.org/rave.htm

Akers, J., R. Jones, and D. Coyl. 1998. Adolescent friendships pairs: Similarities in identity development, behaviors, attitudes and intentions. *Journal of Adolescent Research* 13 (2): 175–95.

Alberta Alcohol and Drug Abuse Commission. 2004, September. *Understanding the youth and young adult perspective of raving in Alberta (Technical report)*. Edmonton, Alberta.

Althusser, L. 1971. *Lenin and Philosophy*. New York: Monthly Review Press.

Anderson, B. 1983. *Imagined communities: Reflections on the origin and spread of nationalism*. New York: Verso.

Appadurai, A. 1990. Disjuncture and difference in the global cultural economy. In *Global culture: Nationalism, globalization and modernity*, ed. M. Featherstone, 295–310. London: Sage.

Aries, P. 1962. *Centuries of childhood*. New York: Random House.

Atkinson, M. 2003a. The civilizing of resistance: Straightedge tattooing. *Deviant Behavior* 24: 197–220.

– 2003b. *Tattooed: The sociogenesis of a body art*. Toronto: University of Toronto Press.

Atkinson, M. and B. Wilson. 2002. Subcultures, bodies and sport. In *Theory, sport and society*, ed. J. Maguire and K. Young, 375–95. Amsterdam, The Netherlands: Elsevier Science.

Baron, S. 1989a. Resistance and its consequences: The street culture of punks. *Youth and Society* 21 (2): 207–37.

– 1989b. The Canadian west coast punk subculture: A field study. *Canadian Journal of Sociology* 14 (3): 289–316.

– 1997. Canadian male street skinheads: Street gang or street terrorists? *Canadian Review of Sociology and Anthropology* 34 (2): 125–54.

Barthes, R. 1973. *Mythologies*. London: Paladin.

Baudrillard, J. 1983a. *Simulations*. New York: Semiotext(e).

– 1983b. *In the shadow of silent majorities*. New York: Semiotext(e).

– 1987. *Forget Foucault*. New York: Semiotext(e).

– 1988. *Selected writings,* ed. M. Poster. Cambridge: Polity Press.

Bauman, Z. 2001. *Community: Seeking safety in an insecure world*. Malden, MA: Blackwell.

Beal, B. 1995. Disqualifying the official: An exploration of social resistance through the subculture of skateboarding. *Sociology of Sport Journal* 12 (3): 252–67.

Becker, H. 1963. *Outsiders*. New York: Free Press.

Bellett, G. 1998, September 17. Richmond turns down the volume on raves: Complaints from Vancouver residents led councillors to draft tough new regulations. *Vancouver Sun*, B4.

Bennett, A. 1999. Subcultures or neo-tribes? Rethinking the relationship between youth, style and musical taste. *Sociology* 33 (3): 599–617.

– 2000. *Popular music and youth culture: Music, identity and place*. New York: St. Martin's Press.

– 2001. *Cultures of popular music*. Philadelphia: Open University Press.

Bennett, A. and K. Khan-Harris, eds. 2003. *After subculture: Critical studies of subcultural theory*. New York: Palgrave.

Berger, B. 1995. *An essay on culture: Symbolic structure and social structure*. Berkeley: University of California Press.

Berger, P. and T. Luckmann. 1971. *The social construction of reality*. New York: Doubleday.

Berman, M. 1988. Reprint. *All that is solid melts into air: The experience of modernity*. New York: Penguin Books, 1982.

Bernard, T. 1992. *The cycle of juvenile justice*. New York: Oxford University Press.

Best, J. 1989. *Images of issues: Typifying contemporary social problems*. New York: Aldine de Gruyter.

Best, J. and D. Luckenbill. 1994. *Organizing deviance*. Englewood Cliffs, NJ: Prentice Hall.

Bey, H. 1991. *T.A.Z.: The temporary autonomous zone, ontological anarchy, poetic terrorism*. Brooklyn, NY: Autonomedia.

Bibby, R. 2001. *Canada's teens: Today, yesterday, and tomorrow*. Toronto: Stoddard.

Bibby, R. and D. Posterski. 1992. *Teen trends: A nation in motion*. Toronto: Stoddard.

Blanchfield, M. 1996, September 28. Police seize potentially fatal drug: Versions of Ecstasy found in Ottawa. *Ottawa Citizen*, C1.

Blumer, H. 1969. *Symbolic interactionism: Perspective and method*. Englewood Cliffs, NJ: Prentice Hall.

– 1971. Social Problems as Collective Behavior. *Social Problems* 18: 298–306.

Bourdieu, P. 1984. *Distinction: A social critique of the judgment of taste*. London: Routledge and Kegan Paul.

Bradley, B. 1994, July 18. Raves all the rage. *Winnipeg Free Press*, 5.

Brake, M. 1980. *The sociology of youth culture and youth subcultures*. Boston: Routledge and Kegan Paul.

– 1985. *Comparative youth cultures*. London: Routledge and Kegan Paul.

Brook, J. and I. Boal, eds. 1995. *Resisting the virtual life: The culture and politics of information*. San Francisco: City Lights.

Brown, A. 1997. Let's all have a disco: Football, popular music and democratization. In *The clubcultures reader: Readings in popular cultural studies*, ed. S. Redhead, D. Wynne, and J. O'Connor, 79–101. Malden, MA: Blackwell.

Brymer, R. 1991. The emergence and maintenance of a deviant subculture: The case of hunting/poaching subculture. *Anthropologica* 33: 177–94.

Buechler, S. 2000. *Social movements in advanced capitalism: The political economy and cultural construction of social activism*. New York: Oxford University Press.

Carrigan, D. 1998. *Juvenile delinquency in Canada: A history*. Concord, ON: Irwin Publishing.

Carrington, B. and B. Wilson. 2002. Global clubcultures: Cultural flows and "late modern" dance music culture. In *Young people in risk society: The restructuring of youth identities and transitions in late modernity*, M. Ceislik and G. Pollock, 74–99. Aldershot, Hampshire, UK: Ashgate Publishing.

– 2004. Dance Nation: Rethinking Youth Subcultural Theory. In *After Subculture: Critical Studies of Subcultural Theory*, ed. A. Bennett and K. Khan-Harris, 67–77. New York: Palgrave.

Carrington, P. 1999. Trends in youth crime in Canada, 1977-1996. *Canadian Journal of Criminology* 41 (1) 1–32.

Castells, M. 2002. *The power of identity*. Oxford: Blackwell.

Champion, S., ed. 1998. *Disco 2000: Nineteen new stories from the last hours of 1999*. London: Sceptre.

– ed. 1999. *Disco biscuits*. London: Hodder and Stoughton. Chatterton, P. and R. Hollands. 2003. *Urban nightscapes: Youth culture, pleasure spaces and corporate power*. London: Routledge.

Chen, K. 1991. Post-Marxism: Between/beyond critical postmodernism and cultural studies. *Media, Culture and Society* 13: 35–51.

Cieslik, M. and G. Pollock. 2002. *Young people in risk society: The restructuring of youth identities and transitions in late modernity*. Burlington, VT: Ashgate.

Clarke, J. 1976. Style. In *Resistance through rituals: Youth sub-cultures in post-war Britain*, ed. S. Hall and T. Jefferson, 175–91. London: Hutchison.

Clifford, J. 1988. *The predicament of culture: Twentieth century ethnography, literature, and art*. Cambridge: Harvard University Press.

Clifford, J. and E. Marcus, eds. 1986. *Writing culture: The poetics and politics of ethnography*. Berkeley: University of California Press.

Cloud, J. 2000, June 5. The lure of ecstasy. *Time* (Can. ed.), 34–40.

Cloward, R. and L. Ohlin. 1960. *Delinquency and opportunity: A theory of delinquent gangs*. New York: Free Press.

Cohen, A. 1955. *Delinquent boys*. Glencoe, IL: The Free Press of Glencoe.

– 1997. General theories of subcultures. In *The subcultures reader*, ed. K. Gelder and S. Thornton, 44–54. New York: Routledge.

Cohen, P. 1972. Subcultural conflict and working-class community. *Working papers in cultural studies* 2 (Spring): 5–52.

– 1999. *Rethinking the youth question: Education, labour and cultural studies*. Durham, NC: Duke University Press.

Cohen, R. 1998. *The love drug: Marching to the beat of ecstasy*. Binghamton, NY: The Haworth Medical Press.

Coleman, J. 1992. The nature of adolescence. In *Youth policy in the 1990s: The way forward*, ed. J. Coleman and C. Warren-Adamson, 8–27. New York: Routledge.

Collin, M. 1997. *Altered state: The story of ecstasy culture and acid house*. London: Serpent's Tail.

Cooley, C. 1967. *Social organization*. New York: Schocken.

Corbin, J. and A. Strauss. 1990. Grounded theory research: Procedures, canons, and evaluative criteria. *Qualitative Sociology* 13 (1): 3–21.

Corrigan, P. 1979. *Schooling the smash street kids*. London : Macmillan.

Côté, J. and A. Allahar. 1994. *Generation on hold: Coming of age in the late twentieth century*. Toronto: Stoddard Publishing.

Coupland, D. 1991. *Generation X: Tales for an accelerated culture*. New York: St. Martin's Press.

Cowie, E. 1977. Women, representation and the image. *Screen Education* 2–3: 15–23.

Cudmore, J. 1999, March 9. Rave drug GHB doesn't mix well: T.O. club goers increasingly end up in hospital. *National Post*, B4.

Culbert, L. 1998, June 2. UBC calls an end to all-night rave parties: A party on the weekend ended with four overdoses and a home invasion. *Vancouver Sun*, B3.

Currie, D. 1999. *Girl talk: Adolescent magazines and their readers*. Toronto: University of Toronto Press.

Damon, W. 1997. *The youth charter: How communities can work together to raise standards for all our children*. Toronto: The Free Press.

Davies, S. 1994. In search of resistance and rebellion among high school drop-outs. *Canadian Journal of Sociology* 19 (3): 331–50.

De Certeau, M. 1984. *The practice of everyday life*. Berkeley: University of California Press.

De Saussure, F. 1966. *Course in general linguistics*. New York: McGraw-Hill.

Deleuze, G. and F. Guattari. 1987. *A thousand plateaus: Capitalism and schizophrenia*. Minneapolis: University of Minnesota Press.

Denzin, N. 1970. Strategies of multiple triangulation. In *The research act: A theoretical introduction to sociological methods*, ed. N. Denzin, 298–313. Chicago: Aldine Publishing.

– 1989. *Interpretive interactionism*. Newbury Park, CA: Sage.

– 1990. The spaces of postmodernism: Reading Plummer on Blumer. *Symbolic Interaction* 13 (2): 145–54.

– 1992. *Symbolic interactionism and cultural studies: The politics of interpretation*. Cambridge, MA: Blackwell.

Dickens, D. and A. Fontana. 1994. *Postmodernism and social inquiry*. New York: The Guilford Press.

Ditchbum, J. 1996. Drug called ecstasy remains pillar of "rave" dance scene. *The Record* (Kitchener, ON), D4.

Donnelly, P. 1985. Sport subcultures. In *Exercise and sport sciences review*, vol. 13, ed. R. Terjung, 539–78. New York: MacMillan.

– 2000. Interpretive approaches to the sociology of sport. In *Handbook of sport and society*, ed. J. Coakley and E. Dunning, 77–91. London: Sage.

Downing, J. 2001. *Radical media: Rebellious communication and social movements*. Thousand Oaks, CA: Sage.

Dubey, A. 2000. Ecstatic about ecstasy – but at what cost? *The Journal of Addiction and Mental Health* 3 (5): 4.

– 1996. Tainted ecstasy surfaces at raves. *The Journal* (of the Addiction Research Foundation) 25 (2). www.arf.org/Ecstacsy.html

Duffy, A., J. Hall, and B. DeMara. 1992, May 5. Metro police, mob clash on Yonge St. *Toronto Star*, A1.

Duncan, M. 1990. Sports photographs and sexual difference: Images of women and men in the 1984 and 1988 Olympic games. *Sociology of Sport Journal* 7 (1): 22–43.

Duncombe, S. 1997. *Zines: Notes from the underground and the politics of alternative culture*. New York: Verso.

Eagleton, T. 1991. *Ideology: An introduction*. London: Verso.

– 1996. *The illusions of postmodernism*. Cambridge, MA: Blackwell.

Edwards, S. 1998, November 2. Study says ravers risk memory loss and other brain damage if they take Ecstasy. *National Post*, D3.

Eisner, B. 1994. *Ecstasy: The MDMA story*. Berkeley, CA: Ronin Publishing.

Epstein, J. 1998. *Youth culture: Identity in a postmodern world*. Malden, MA: Blackwell.

Erlandson, D., E. Harris, B. Skipper, and S. Allen. 1993. *Doing naturalistic inquiry: A guide to methods*. Newbury Park, CA: Sage.

Eyerman, R. and A. Jamison. 1998. *Music and social movements: Mobilizing traditions in the twentieth century*. Cambridge: Cambridge University Press.

Fine, G. and S. Kleinman. 1983. Network and meaning: An interactionist approach to structure. *Symbolic Interaction* 6: 97–110.

Fiske, J. 1987. *Television culture*. London: Methuen.

Foley, D. 1990. The great American football ritual: Reproducing race, class, and gender inequality. *Sociology of Sport Journal* 7: 111–35.

– 1992. Making the strange familiar: Writing critical sports narratives. *Sociology of Sport Journal* 9: 36–47.

Forsey, R. 1998, October 27. MPP aims to put youth crime out of commission: Brown dismisses report that teen crime is dropping. *Toronto Star*, F3.

Frieson, B. 1990. Powerlessness in adolescence: Exploiting heavy metal listeners. In *Marginal convention: Popular culture, mass media and social deviance*, ed. C. Sanders, 65–77. Bowling Green, Ohio: Bowling Green State University Popular Press.

Frith, S. 1987. Toward an aesthetic of popular music. In *Music and society: The politics of composition, performance and reception*, ed. R. Leppert and S. McClary, 133–49. Cambridge: Cambridge University Press.

Fritz, J. 1999. *Rave culture: An insider's overview*. Canada: Smallfry Press.

Furlong, A. and F. Cartmel. 1997. *Young people and social change: Individualization and risk in late modernity*. Buckingham, UK: Open University Press.

Galloway, B. and J. Hudson, eds. 1996. *Youth in transition: Perspectives on research and policy*. Toronto: Thompson.

Garfinkal, H. 1967. *Studies in ethnomethodology*. Englewood Cliffs, NJ: Prentice Hall.

Garratt, S. 1998. *Adventures in wonderland: A decade of club culture*. London: Headline Book Publishers.

Geertz, C. 1973. *Interpretations of culture*. New York: Basic books.

– 1988. *Works and lives: The anthropologist as author*. Stanford: Stanford University Press.

Giddens, A. 1984. *The constitution of society: Outline of the theory of structuration*. Cambridge, UK: Polity.

Gilbert, J. and E. Pearson. 1999. *Discographies: Dance music, culture and the politics of sound*. New York: Routledge.

Gillis, J. 1974. *Youth and history*. New York: Academic Press.

Glaser, B. and A. Strauss. 1967. *The discovery of grounded theory: Strategies for qualitative research*. Chicago: Aldine.

Glenday, D. 1996. Mean streets and hard times: Youth unemployment and crime in Canada. In *Not a kid anymore: Canadian youth, crime, and subcultures*, ed. G. O'Bireck, 147–74. Toronto: Nelson Canada.

Goffman, E. 1959. *The presentation of self in everyday life*. Garden City, NY: Doubleday.

Goldman, A. 1978. *Disco*. New York: Hawthorne Books.

Gordon, R. 1995. Street gangs in Vancouver. In *Canadian Delinquency*, ed. R. Silverman and J. Creechan, 311–21. Scarborough, ON: Prentice Hall.

Gore, G. 1997. The beat goes on: Trance, dance and tribalism in rave culture. In *Dance in the city*, ed. H. Thomas, 50–67. New York: St. Martin's Press.

Gramsci, A. 1971. *Selections from the prison notebooks*. New York: International Publishers.

Gruneau, R. 1988. Introduction: Notes on popular culture and political practice. In *Popular cultures and political practices*, ed. R. Gruneau, 11–32. Toronto: Garamound Press.

Guattari, F. 1996. *Soft subversions*. New York: Semiotext(e).

Haas, J. and W. Shaffir. 1991. *Becoming doctors: The adoption of a cloak of competence*. Greenwich, CT: JAI Press.

Haden-Guest, A. 1997. *The last party: Studio 54, disco, and the culture of the night*. New York: William Morrow and Company.

Hagan, J. and B. McCarthy. 1992. Street life and delinquency. *British Journal of Sociology* 43 (4): 533–61.

Hall, A. 1996. *Feminism and sporting bodies: Essays on theory and practice*. Champaign, IL: Human Kinetics.

Hall, S. 1980. Encoding/decoding. In *Culture, media, language: Working papers in cultural studies, 1972-79*, ed. S. Hall, D. Hobson, A. Lowe and P. Willis, 128–38. London: Hutchison.

– 1985. Signification, representation, ideology: Althusser and post-structuralist debates. *Critical Studies in Mass Communication* 2 (2): 91–114.

– 1986. On postmodernism and articulation: An interview with Stuart Hall. *Journal of Communication Inquiry* 10 (2): 78–98.

Hall, S., C. Critcher, T. Jefferson, J. Clarke, and B. Roberts. 1978. *Policing the crisis: Mugging, the state and law and order*. London: MacMillan.

Hall, S. and T. Jefferson, eds. 1976. *Resistance through rituals: Youth sub-cultures in post-war Britain*. London: Hutchison.

Hammersley, M. 1992. *What's wrong with ethnography?* New York: Routledge.

Harrison, M., ed. 1998. *High society: The real voices of club cultures*. London: Piatkus.

Harvey, D. 1989. *The condition of postmodernity: An inquiry into the origin of culture and change*. Oxford: Blackwell.

Hebdige, D. 1979. *Subculture: The meaning of style*. London: Methuen.

– 1987. *Cut 'n' mix*. London: Comedia.

– 1988. *Hiding in the light*. London: Routledge.

Hewitt, J. 1994. *Self and society: A symbolic interactionist social psychology*. Toronto: Allyn and Bacon.

Hier, S. 2002. Raves, risk and the ecstasy panic: A case study in the subversive nature of moral regulation. *Canadian Journal of Sociology* 27 (1): 33–57.

Ingham, A., J. Howell, and T. Shilperoot. 1987. Professional sports and community: A review and exegesis. *Exercise and Sport Sciences Review* 15: 427–65.

Ingham, A. and M. McDonald. 2003. Sport and community/communitas. In *Sporting dystopias: The making and meanings of urban sport cultures*, ed. R. Wilcox, D. Andrews, R. Pitter, and R. Irwin, 17–33. Albany: State University of New York Press.

Jaffe, P. and L. Baker. 1999. Why changing the YOA does not impact youth crime: Developing effective prevention programs for children and adolescents. *Canadian Psychology* 40 (1): 22–9.

James, M. 1997. *State of bass – jungle: The story so far*. Chatham, Kent: Boxtree.

Jameson, F. 1984. *Post-Modernism or, the cultural logic of late capitalism*. Durham, NC: Duke University Press.

Joll, J. 1977. *Gramsci*. London: Fontana.

Kedzie, C. 1997. A brave new world or new world order? In *Culture of the Internet*, ed. S. Kiesler, 209–32. Mahwah, NJ: Lawrence Erlbaum.

Kellner, D. 1995. *Media culture: Cultural studies, identity and politics between the modern and the postmodern*. New York: Routledge.

Kelly, J. 1998. *Under the gaze: Learning to be Black in a White society*. Halifax: Fernwood.

Kempster, C., ed. 1996. *History of house*. Kent: Staples of Rochester.

Kinga, M. [1995?]. Rave scene. *Club Scene Magazine*, 14.

Knight, G. 1998. Hegemony, the media, and new right politics: Ontario in the late 1990s. *Critical Sociology* 24 (1–2): 105–29.

Laclau, E. and C. Mouffe. 1985. *Hegemony and socialist strategy: Towards a radical democratic politics*. London: Verso.

Landale, E. 1998, July 14. Raves all the rage to connect. *Toronto Star*, F1.

Lasn, K. 1999. The new activism 03: We're not academic. *Adbusters, Journal of the Mental Environment* 26 (July/August): 36–7.

Lehmann-Haupt, R. 1995. Sacred raves. *Yoga Journal* (May/June): 77–81.

Lewis, J. 1991. *The ideological octopus.* New York: Routledge.

Lewis, L. and M. Ross. 1996. *A select body: The gay dance party subculture and the Hiv-AIDS pandemic.* New York: Cassell Academic.

Lincoln, Y. and E. Guba. 1985. *Naturalistic inquiry.* Beverly Hills, CA: Sage.

Lipsitz, G. 1997. *Dangerous crossroads: Popular music, postmodernism and the poetics of place.* New York: Verso.

Lofland, J. 1976. *Doing social life: The qualitative study of human interaction in natural settings.* New York: John Wiley and Sons.

Luciano, G. 1999. Quality of "love" drugs at raves is declining – and so is rave culture. *The Journal of Addiction and Mental Health* 2 (6): 3.

Lull, J. 1985. The naturalistic study of media and youth culture. In *Media gratifications research: Current perspectives,* ed. K. Rosengren, L. Wenner, and P. Palmgreen, 209–24. Beverly Hills, CA: Sage.

– 1995. *Media, communication, culture: A global approach.* New York: Columbia University Press.

Maffesoli, M. 1991. The ethics of aesthetics. *Theory, Culture and Society* 8: 7–21.

– 1995. *The time of the tribes: The decline of individualism in mass society.* London: Sage.

Maguire, J. 1994. Sport, identity politics, and globalization: Diminishing contrasts and increasing varieties. *Sociology of Sport Journal* 11: 398–427.

Maines, D. 1982. In search of mesostructure. Studies in the negotiated order. *Urban Life* 11: 267–79.

– 1996. On postmodernism, pragmatism, and plasterers: Some interactionist thoughts and queries. *Symbolic Interaction* 19: 325–42.

Malbon, B. 1998. Clubbing: Consumption, identity and the spatial practices of every-night life. In *Cool places: Geographies of youth cultures,* ed. T. Skelton and G. Valentine, 266–86. New York: Routledge.

– 1999. *Clubbing: Dancing, ecstasy and vitality.* New York: Routledge.

Marcus, G. and M. Fisher. 1986. *Anthropology as cultural critique: An experimental moment in human sciences.* Chicago: University of Chicago Press.

Marx, G., and D. McAdam. 1994. *Collective behavior and social movements: Process and structure.* Englewood Cliffs, NJ: Prentice Hall.

Marx, K. 1963 (first published in 1852 as first issue of the journal *Die Revolution,* New York). *The eighteenth brumaire of Louis Bonaparte.* New York: International Publishers.

Mathews, F. 1993. *Youth gangs on youth gangs*. Ottawa: Solicitor General Canada.

Matza, D. 1964. *Delinquency and drift*. New York: John Wiley and Sons.

McAdam, D. 1982. *The political process and the development of Black insurgency*. Chicago: University of Chicago Press.

McCall, G. and J. Simmons. 1969. *Issues in participant observation*. Reading, MA: Addison-Wesley.

McCall, T. 2001. *This is not a rave: In the shadow of subculture*. New York: Thunder's Mouth Press.

McGuigan, J. 1992. *Cultural populism*. New York: Routledge.

McKay, J. 1995. "Just do it": Corporate sports slogans and the political economy of enlightened racism. *Discourse: Studies in the Cultural Politics of Education* 16 (2): 191–201.

McLaren, L. 1998, June 6. Rave culture: And the beat goes on, and on, and on. *Globe and Mail*, D1.

McRobbie, A. 1977. *Working-class girls and the culture of femininity*. Unpublished MA thesis, Centre for Contemporary Cultural Studies, University of Birmingham, UK.

– 1991. *Feminism and Youth Culture*. Boston: Unwin Hyman.

– 1993. Shut up and dance: Youth culture and changing modes of femininity. *Cultural Studies* 7 (3): 406–26.

– 1994. *Postmodernism and popular culture*. London: Routledge.

McRobbie, A and S. Thornton. 1995. Rethinking "moral panic" for multi-mediated social worlds. *British Journal of Sociology* 46 (4): 559–74.

Melucci, A. 1996. *Challenging codes: Collective action in the age of information*. New York: Cambridge University Press.

Merton, R. 1957. *Social theory and social structure*. Glencoe, IL: The Free Press of Glencoe.

Muggleton, D. 1997. The post-subculturalist. In *The clubcultures reader: Readings in popular cultural studies*, ed. S. Redhead, D. Wynne, and J. O'Connor, 186–203. Malden, MA: Blackwell.

– 2000. *Inside subculture: The postmodern meaning of style*. New York: Berg.

Musgrove, F. 1964. *Youth and social order*. London: Routledge and Kegan Paul.

Nauright, J., and P. White. 1996. Nostalgia, community and nation: Professional hockey and football in Canada. *Avante* 2 (3): 24–41.

Neitzche, F. 1968. *The will to power* New York: Vintage Books.

– 1986. *Human, all too human*. Cambridge: Cambridge University Press.

O'Bireck, G., ed. 1996. *Not a kid anymore: Canadian youth, crime, and subcultures*. Toronto: Nelson Canada.

Oh, S. 2000. Rave fever: Raves are all the rage, but drugs are casting a pall over their sunny peace-and-love ethos. *Maclean's* (April 24): 39–43.

O'Neill, K. 2002. Web sites of resistance: Internetworking and civil society. In *Citizenship and participation in the information age*, ed. M. Pendakur and R. Harris, 322–36. Aurora, ON: Garamond Press.

Onstad, K. 1997. What are we afraid of?: The myth of youth crime. *Saturday Night* (March): 46–58.

Pierson, R. 1986. *"They're still women after all": The second world war and Canadian womanhood*. Toronto: McClelland and Stewart.

Pini, M. 1997. Women and the early British rave scene. In *Back to reality: Social experience and cultural studies*, ed. A. McRobbie, 152–69. Manchester: Manchester University Press.

– 2001. *Clubcultures and female subjectivity: The move from home to house*, New York: Palgrave.

Plummer, K. 1990. Staying in the empirical world: Symbolic interactionism and postmodernism, A response to Denzin. *Symbolic Interaction* 13 (2): 155–60.

Prus, R. 1987. Generic social processes: Maximizing conceptual development in ethnographic research. *Journal of Contemporary Ethnography* 16: 250–93.

– 1994. Generic social processes: Intersubjectivity and transcontextuality in social science. In *Doing everyday life*, ed. M. Dietz, R. Prus, and W. Shaffir, 393–412. Mississauga, ON: Copp Clark Longman.

– 1995. *Envisioning power as intersubjective accomplishment: Acknowledging the human enterprise entailed in tactician-target interchanges*. Paper presented at Society for the Study of Symbolic Interaction, Washington, DC, August 20–21.

– 1996a. *Symbolic interaction and ethnographic research: Intersubjectivity and the study of human lived experience*. Albany: State University of New York.

– 1996b. Adolescent life-worlds and deviant involvement. In *Not a kid anymore: Canadian youth, crime, and subcultures*, ed. G. O'Bireck, 7–70. Toronto: Nelson Canada.

– 1999. *Beyond the power mystique: Power as intersubjective accomplishment*. Albany: State University of New York Press.

Prus, R. and C. Sharper. 1977. *Road hustler: The career contingencies of professional card and dice hustlers.* Lexington, MA: Lexington Books.

Rail, G. 1998. *Sport and postmodern times.* Albany: State University of New York Press.

Raphael, M. 1998, December, 29. Drug chic hits the mall: The buzz at Eatons – Ravers and marijuana aficionados are reading a lot of nudge, nudge, wink, wink into the latest advertising campaigns such as Eaton's, Roots, and the Body Shop. The companies say it's a non-issue. Whatever. *National Post,* B5.

Redhead, S. 1990. *End of the century party: Youth and pop towards 2000.* New York: St. Martin's Press.

– 1997. *Subcultures to clubcultures: An introduction to popular cultural studies.* Malden, MA: Blackwell.

Redhead, S., D. Wynne, and J. O'Connor, eds. 1997. *The clubcultures reader: Readings in popular cultural studies.* Malden, MA: Blackwell.

Reynolds, S. 1994. Generation E. *Artforum* (February): 54–7.

– 1997. Rave culture: Living dream or living death. In *The clubcultures reader: Readings in popular cultural studies,* ed. S. Redhead, D. Wynne, and J. O'Connor, 102–11. Malden, MA: Blackwell.

– 1998. *Generation ecstasy: Into the world of techno and rave culture.* Toronto: Little, Brown and Company.

Richardson, L. 1998. Writing: A method of inquiry. In *Collecting and interpreting qualitative materials,* ed. N. Denzin and Y. Lincoln, 345–71. Thousand Oaks, CA: Sage.

– 2000. New writing practices in qualitative research. *Sociology of Sport Journal* 17 (1): 5–20.

Rietveld, H. 1998. *This is our house: House music, cultural spaces and technologies.* Brookfield, VT: Ashgate Publishing.

Robinson, L. 1998. *Crossing the line: Violence and sexual assault in Canada's national sport.* Toronto: McClelland and Stewart.

Rose, D. 1990. *Living the ethnographic life.* Newbury Park, CA: Sage.

Rushkoff, D. 1996. *Playing the future: How kids' culture can teach us to thrive in an age of chaos.* New York: HarperCollins.

– 1997. *Ecstasy club.* San Franciso: HarperEdge.

Saunders, N. 1996. *Ecstasy: Dance, trance and transformation.* Oakland: Quick American Archives.

Schissel, B. 1993. *Social dimensions of Canadian youth justice.* Toronto: Oxford University Press.

– 1997. *Blaming children: Youth crime, moral panics and the politics of hate.* Halifax: Fernwood Press.

Schouten, J. and J. McAlexander. 1995. Subcultures of consumption: An ethnography of the new bikers. *Journal of Consumer Research* 22: 43–61.

Shaffir, W., and R. Stebbins. 1991. *Experiencing fieldwork: An inside view of qualitative research*. Newbury Park, CA: Sage.

Silcott, M. 1999. *Rave America: New school dancescapes*. Toronto: ECW Press.

Sinker, M. 1996. Electro kinetic. In *History of house*, ed. C. Kempster, 93–102. Kent: Staples of Rochester.

Skelton, T., and G. Valentine. 1998. *Cool places: Geographies of youth cultures*. New York: Routledge.

Smith, J. 1997. *Hanging out and the mall: The production of an adolescent social space*. Unpublished masters thesis, McMaster University, Hamilton.

Smith, M. 1979. *The city and social theory*. New York: St. Martins Press.

Smith, R. and T. Maughan. 1998. Youth culture and the making of the post-Fordist economy: Dance music in contemporary Britain. *Journal of Youth Studies* 1 (2): 211–28.

Solomon, P. 1992. *Black resistance in high school: Forging a separatist culture*. Albany: State University of New York Press.

Sprott, J. 1996. Understanding public views of youth crime and the youth justice system. *Canadian Journal of Criminology* 38 (3): 271–90.

Stallybrass, P. and A. White. 1986. *The politics and poetics of transgression*. London: Methuen.

Stanley, C. 1997. Not drowning but waving: Urban narratives of dissent in the wild zone. In *The clubcultures reader*, ed. S. Redhead, D. Wynne, and J. O'Connor, 36–54. Malden, MA: Blackwell.

Straw, W. 1991. Systems of articulation, logics of change: Scenes and communities in popular music. *Cultural Studies* 5 (3): 361–75.

– 1997. Scenes and communities in popular music. In *The subcultures reader*, ed. K. Gelder and S. Thornton, 494–505. London: Routledge.

Strauss, A., L. Schatzman, R. Bucher, D. Ehrlich, and M. Sabshin. 1963. The hospital and its negotiated order. In *The hospital in modern society*, ed. E. Freidson, 147–69. New York: Free press.

Strongman, J. 1999. Rave: The culture that isn't. *Discord* 10, www.discord.co.uk/rave.html

Surratt, C. 1998. *Netlife: Internet citizens and their communities*. Commack: Nova Science Publishers.

Sutherland, E. 1937. *The professional thief.* Chicago: University of
Chicago Press.

Tagg, P. 1994. From refrain to rave: The decline of figure and the rise
of ground. *Popular Music* 13 (2): 209–22.

Takahashi, M. and T. Olaveson. 2003. Music, dance and raving bodies:
Raving as spirituality in the central Canadian rave scene. *Journal of
Ritual Studies* 17 (2): 72–96.

Tanner, J. 1978. Youth culture in a Canadian high school: An empirical
analysis. *Canadian Journal of Sociology* 3: 89–102.

– 1996. *Teenage troubles: Youth and deviance in Canada.* Toronto:
Nelson Canada.

Tapscott, D. 1997. *The digital economy: Promise and peril in the age
of networked intelligence.* Toronto: McGraw-Hill.

– 1998. *Growing up digital: The rise of the net generation.* Toronto:
McGraw-Hill.

Taylor, S. and R. Bogdan. 1984. *Introduction to qualitative research
methods: The search for meaning.* New York: John Wiley.

Tedlock, B. 2000. Ethnography and ethnographic representation.
In *Handbook of qualitative research* (2d ed.), ed. N. Denzin and
Y. Lincoln, 455–86. Thousand Oaks, CA: Sage.

Telander, R. 1990. Senseless. *Sports Illustrated* (May 14): 36–8, 43–4,
46, 49.

Teshler, E. 1998, June 17. Teen's actions prove power of young people.
Toronto Star, A2.

Thomas, W. 1923. *The unadjusted girl.* Boston: Little, Brown.

Thornton, S. 1994. Moral panic, the media and British rave culture. In
Microphone fiends: Youth music, youth culture, ed. A. Ross and T.
Rose, 176–92. New York: Routledge.

– 1995. *Club cultures: Music, media and subcultural capital.* Hanover:
Wesleyan University Press.

Tomlinson, L. 1998. "This ain't no disco?" ... or is it: Youth culture and
the rave phenomenon. In *Youth culture: Identity in a postmodern
world,* ed. J. Epstein, 195–211. Malden, MA: Blackwell.

Tonnies, F. 1957. *Gemieinschaft and gesellschaft.* East Lansing, MI:
Michigan State University Press.

Trask, S. 1996. Future shock. In *History of house,* ed. C. Kempster, 41–8.
London: Sanctuary Publishing.

Turner, V. 1969. *The rituul process: Structure and anti-structure.*
Chicago, IL: Aldine.

Tyler, S. 1986. Post-modern ethnography: From document of the occult to occult document. In *Writing culture: The poetics and politics of ethnograph*, ed. J. Clifford and G. Marcus, 122–40. Berkeley: University of California Press.

Tyyskä, V. 2001. *Long and winding road: Adolescents and youth in Canada today*. Toronto: Canadian Scholars' Press.

Van Roosmalen, E. and H. Krahn. 1996. Boundaries of youth. *Youth and Society* 28 (1): 36–45.

Vaughan, C. 1992, June 8. Everything old seems new again, to teens. *Globe and Mail*, A13.

Visano, L. 1996. What do "they" know? Delinquency as mediated texts. In *Not a kid anymore: Canadian youth, crime, and subcultures*, ed. G. O'Bireck, 71–106. Toronto: Nelson Canada.

Vobejda, B., and L. Perstain. 1998, June 18. Girls will be ... boys – and it's not a pretty sight. *Toronto Star*, A1.

Webb, E., D. Campbell, R. Schwartz, S. Richard, L. Sechrest, and J. Grove. 1981. *Nonreactive measures in the social sciences*. Boston: Houghton, Mifflin.

Weber, M. 1978. *Economy and Society*. Berkeley: University of California Press.

Weber, T. 1999a, February 18. *A snapshot of raving in Toronto*. Presentation given at the forum "Raving in Toronto," put on by the Toronto Drug Awareness Coalition, North York (Toronto), ON.

– 1999b. Raving in Toronto: Peace, love, unity and respect in transition. *Journal of Youth Studies* 2 (3): 317–36.

Welsh, I. 1997a. *The Irvine Welsh omnibus: Trainspotting, The acid house, Marabou stork nightmares*. London: Jonathon Cape/Secker and Warburg.

– 1997b. *Ecstasy: Three tales of chemical romance*. London: Vintage.

West, R., and S. Hager. 1992. Rave new world. *Best of High Times* 17: 8–11.

Westhues, K. 1972. Hippiedom 1970: Some Tentative Hypotheses. *Sociological Quarterly*, 81–9.

Wheaton, B. and A. Tomlinson. 1998. The changing gender order in sport?: The case of windsurfing subcultures. *Journal of Sport and Social Issues* 22 (3): 252–74.

Williams, R. 1977. *Marxism and literature*. London: Oxford University Press.

Willis, P. 1977. *Learning to labour: How working class kids get working class jobs*. New York: Columbia University Press.

– 1978. *Profane culture*. London: Routledge.

– 1990. *Common culture*. San Francisco: Westview.

– 1997. Reprint. Theoretical confessions and reflexive method. In *The subcultures reader*, ed. K. Gelder and S. Thornton, 246–53. New York: Routledge. Originally published in 1980as "Notes on method," in *Culture, media and language*, ed. S. Hall, D. Hobson, A. Lowe, and P. Willis, 88–95 (London: Hutchinson).

Wilson, B. Forthcoming. Ethnography, the Internet and youth culture: Strategies for examing social resistance and "online-offline" relationships. *Canadian Journal of Education*.

– 2002. The "anti-jock" movement: Reconsidering youth resistance, masculinity and sport culture in the age of the Internet. *Sociology of Sport Journal* 19 (2): 207–34.

Wilson, B. and M. Atkinson. 2005. Rave and straightedge, the virtual and the real: Exploring on-line and off-line experiences in Canadian youth subcultures. *Youth and Society* 36 (3): 276-311.

Wilson, B. and R. Sparks. 1996. "It's gotta be the shoes": Youth, race and sneaker commercials. *Sociology of Sport Journal* 13 (4): 398–427.

– 1999. Impacts of black athlete media portrayals on Canadian youth. *Canadian Journal of Communication* 24 (4): 589–627.

Wilson, B. and P. White. 2001. Tolerance rules: Identity, resistance, and negotiation in an inner city recreation/drop in center. *Journal of Sport and Social Issues* 25 (1): 73–103.

Wilson, B., P. White, and K. Fisher. 2001. Multiple identities in a marginalized culture: Female youth in an "inner city" recreation/drop-in center. *Journal of Sport and Social Issues* 25 (3): 302–24.

Witheford, N., and R. Gruneau. 1993. Between the politics of production and the politics of the sign: Post-marxism, postmodernism and "new times." *Current Perspectives in Social Theory* 13: 69–91.

Wood, R. 2001. *Straightedge youth: Subculture genesis, permutation, and identity formation*. Unpublished doctoral dissertation, University of Alberta, Edmonton, Alberta.

Woolgar, S. 1988. Reflexivity is the ethnographer of the text. In *Knowledge and reflexivity: New frontiers in the sociology of knowledge*, ed. S. Woolgar, 14–34. London: Sage.

Young, I. 1995. *The Stonewall experiment*. London: Cassell.

Young, K. 1988. Performance, control, and public image of behavior in a deviant subculture: The case of rugby. *Deviant Behavior* 9 (3): 275–93.

Young, K. and L. Craig. 1997. Beyond white pride: Contradiction in the Canadian skinhead subculture. *Canadian Review of Sociology and Anthropology* 34 (2): 175–206.

Index